Becoming Queer and Religious in Malaysia and Singapore

Bloomsbury Studies in Religion, Gender, and Sexuality

Series Editors: Dawn Llewellyn, Sîan Hawthorne and Sonya Sharma

This interdisciplinary series explores the intersections of religions, genders, and sexualities. It promotes the dynamic connections between gender and sexuality across a diverse range of religious and spiritual lives, cultures, histories, and geographical locations, as well as contemporary discourses around secularism and non-religion. The series publishes cutting-edge research that considers religious experiences, communities, institutions, and discourses in global and transnational contexts, and examines the fluid and intersecting features of identity and social positioning.

Using theoretical and methodological approaches from inter/transdisciplinary perspectives, *Bloomsbury Studies in Religion, Gender, and Sexuality* addresses the neglect of religious studies perspectives in gender, queer, and feminist studies, and offers a space in which gender-critical approaches to religions engage with questions of intersectionality, particularly with respect to critical race, disability, post-colonial and decolonial theories.

Forthcoming titles:

Beyond Religion in India and Pakistan, Navtej K. Purewal and Virinder S. Kalra
Narrative, Identity and Ethics in Postcolonial Kenya,
Eleanor Tiplady Higgs (forthcoming)
Knitting, Modernity and the Sacred, Anna Fisk (forthcoming)

Becoming Queer and Religious in Malaysia and Singapore

Sharon A. Bong

BLOOMSBURY ACADEMIC
LONDON • NEW YORK • OXFORD • NEW DELHI • SYDNEY

BLOOMSBURY ACADEMIC
Bloomsbury Publishing Plc
50 Bedford Square, London, WC1B 3DP, UK
1385 Broadway, New York, NY 10018, USA
29 Earlsfort Terrace, Dublin 2, Ireland

BLOOMSBURY, BLOOMSBURY ACADEMIC and the Diana
logo are trademarks of Bloomsbury Publishing Plc

First published in Great Britain 2020
This paperback edition published in 2021

A catalogue record for this book is available from the British Library.

A catalog record for this book is available from the Library of Congress.

ISBN: HB: 978-1-3501-3273-3
       PB: 978-1-3502-6687-2
     ePDF: 978-1-3501-3274-0
    eBook: 978-1-3501-3275-7

Series: Bloomsbury Studies in Religion, Gender, and Sexuality

Typeset by Integra Software Services Pvt. Ltd.

To find out more about our authors and books visit www.bloomsbury.com
and sign up for our newsletters.

To B. and S.

Contents

Acknowledgements

Adam, Alexis, Andy, AY, CK, Dave, J, Jagadiswari, Janic, Jimmy, Joe, Juuk, Kun, Ling Jackie, Peter and Stephanie – I am deeply indebted to you for courageously coming forward in response to my call for interviews and generously sharing intimate lived experiences with me, a stranger then to most of you.

The heartwarming response to the project is due also to individual gatekeepers who had played a key role in nudging friends to participate in the project.

I am also grateful to Professor Graham Oppy and Associate Professor Gil-Soo Han who initiated the award of the New Appointees Research Grant Plan of Monash University (project number ARTS-1-1-07) that facilitated this research. My thanks go also to Professor Joern Dosch for his sound advice on publishing this manuscript and, in particular, Professors Mikito Toda and Etsuko Matsuoka of Nara Women's University, Japan, for the kind hospitality extended that afforded me the much-needed space to think and write.

My PhD supervisees deserve special mention here too for their forgiving hearts in allowing me to sometimes privilege the completion of this manuscript above my responsibilities as their main supervisor: Ng Siow San, Laura E. Wong and Joseph N. Goh whose work I am proud to cite in this book. The enthusiasm of my undergraduate students in engaging with gender studies inspires me to continue delving into highly sensitive topics – genders, sexualities and religions in Southeast Asian contexts.

To my family, especially my mum, for their unwavering support of this endeavour that began in 2007, and my husband, Lan Boon Leong, for always watching over my back, in more ways than one.

And not the least, to the publisher, chief and acquisition editors, board of editors and anonymous peer reviewers in bringing to fruition this vision of making visible narratives often silenced or misrepresented, which are not only mine but that of sixteen others who chose to remain with the project – a heartfelt *ribuan terima kasih* (thousand thank yous).

1

Introduction: The journey into the interior

What does it mean to become religiously or spiritually sexual and sexually religious or spiritual in one's everyday practice as a gay, lesbian, bisexual, transgender, intersex, queer or questioning (GLBTIQ) person living in Malaysia and Singapore? How does one make sense of these everyday practices at individual, familial, interpersonal and institutional levels? What kinds of strategies are afforded by these practices? To what extent are these strategies transformative of mindsets and ways of becoming beginning with GLBTIQ persons' own? The book offers important insights to these research questions based on in-depth interviews conducted with sixteen GLBTIQ persons: twelve in Malaysia and four in Singapore.

I use GLBTIQ in cognizance that sexuality studies scholars find it problematic, notwithstanding the intent to be inclusive, as it seemingly orders hierarchically gay, lesbian, bisexual, transgender, intersex and queer identities in descending order with 'T', 'I' and 'Q' perhaps accorded with diminishing value. This is preferred to the term 'non-heterosexual' which simultaneously invests GLBTIQ persons as 'dissident [identities]' yet hardens the binary of heterosexual/non-heterosexual and in doing so, '[reinforces] heteronormativity' (Yip 2005: 61–2). Through the textual analysis of narratives of GLBTIQ persons interviewed in this study, I would contend that heterosexuality and non-heterosexuality are mutually constitutive not mutually exclusive categories. In this study, in line with problematizing narratives of the closet (Sedgwick 1990) and deconstructing the binary of coming out/closeted, I remain sceptical of privileging or overvaluing dissidence or resistance over plural strategies which at times, for certain individuals, in certain contexts, is practised as not coming out.

I begin with a mapping of how these everyday practices are framed. In the context of Malaysia and Singapore as postcolonial Southeast Asian nation-states, the body of their citizenry is marked by diverse ethnicities, religious affiliations, class, genders and sexualities. The postcolonial time and space are notable in this study as it calls to question how the liberated-from-colonization states (as former colonies of the British Empire) are managing not only ethnic and religious diversity but also gender and sexual diversity of the populace. The 'post' in postcolonialism, in signifying the progress of a nation, is contested by the lack of legitimacy accorded not only to ethnic and religious minorities but also to gender and sexual minorities in these nation-states. I borrow from Peletz to contend that there is ethnic, religious, sexual and gender diversity but not ethnic, religious, sexual and gender pluralism as pluralism is contingent on legitimacy (Peletz 2007: 44). So the prefix 'post' is prematurely celebratory (Ahmed 2000: 10) for gender and sexual minorities as quasi citizens where equality and equity as full citizens is, at best, a work-in-progress and, at worst, a nonissue or foregone conclusion. This is because 'colonizing' discourses, in the state of 'post'-coloniality, prevail in visible and invisible ways in which bodies and sexualities are produced by nation-building rhetoric and practices that are not only heteronormative (in normalizing and legitimizing heterosexuality for the majority of the populace) but also heterosexist (in discriminating against sexualities in all its plurality). In short, all is not well for gender and sexual minorities in these 'post'-colonial nation-states beset by internal neocolonialism where some are not only born more equal but made more equal than others.

These hegemonic discourses of a nation in which the individual and the family are its organic principles construct the citizenry as a heterosexual thus stable subject. A heterosexualized person and family that are made natural are consonant with the drive towards modernization that Michel Foucault, in his seminal text *The History of Sexuality, vol. 1* (1978), had exposed. According to Foucault, in the section 'Right of death and power over life' (1978: paragraph 139), a sovereign's power over death of its subordinates has since modernity evolved (or morphed) to the state's power over life of its citizenry; this 'biopower' is two-pronged:

> One of these poles – the first to be formed, it seems – centered on the body as a machine: its disciplining, the optimization of its capabilities, the extortion of its forces, the parallel increase of its usefulness and its docility, its integration into systems of efficient and economic controls, all this was ensured by the procedures of power that characterized the *disciplines: an anatomo-politics of the human body*. The second, formed somewhat later, focused on the species body, the body imbued with the mechanics of life and serving as the basis of the biological processes: propagation, births and mortality, the level of health, life expectancy and longevity, with all the conditions that can cause these to vary. Their supervision was effected through an entire series of interventions and *regulatory controls: a biopolitics of the population*.

The '*biopolitics of the population*' find expression in state rhetoric and practice that effect the reproduction of sexuality (rather than the repression of sex) through legal, political, medical, literary, psychoanalytical and religious discourses, that constitutes normal as opposed to deviant, even perverse bodies and sexualities. The discipline of bodies and sexualities – '*an anatomo-politics of the human body*' – which includes the management of desire, in turn, effects the production of labour for the propagation of the human species, advancement of economic stability of a nation, even the hardening of boundaries between man/woman, privileged/underprivileged and young/old. In applying his thesis on the history of sexuality of Europe to the Malaysian and Singaporean contexts, notwithstanding the time-space compression, what is resonant are the competing demands exacted by competing discourses that are 'directed toward the performances of the body, with attention to the processes of life … to invest life through and through' (Foucault 1978: paragraph 139). These investments include religions (particularly the fundamentalist variant), the culture of 'Asian values' (Stivens 2006: 356), that among other value systems, privilege Communitarian good above individual rights, deeply rooted conservatism and globalizing sexuality rights (to be elaborated in the next section), and the naturalization of the heterosexual family and procreative sexuality between heterosexuals.

In the interest of mapping the terrain, a cursory survey of media texts as popular discourse provides a quick-take on how bodies and sexualities of gender and sexual minorities in particular (as the discipline of sexuality is firstly extended to heterosexuals as they can and should procreate)[1] become sites of contestation for these competing discourses. The ontological 'perversion' of GLBTIQ persons is entrenched in Malaysia (then Malaya) and Singapore's shared British legacy, the sodomy law, Section 377 of the Penal Code that criminalizes 'carnal intercourse against the order of nature', and more ambiguously, 'any act of gross indecency' (Shah 2009). Local and global news commentators point to the notoriety of the sodomy law as an antiquated legislation in violating sexuality rights of GLBTIQ persons in particular and as a contemporised 'tool of political repression' when Anwar Ibrahim, the then Deputy Prime Minister of Malaysia, now political leader, was twice prosecuted for sodomy (Amnesty International 2012).

Two groundbreaking episodes punctuate this ontological 'perversion' of GBTIQ persons. In 2007, Singapore 'struck colonial-era penal code Section 377 from its books' (Mosbergen 2015). In 2001, Malaysia amended Article 8(2) of the Federal Constitution by adding 'gender' as grounds for non-discrimination: 'there shall be no discrimination against citizens on the ground only of religion, race, descent, place of birth or gender' (Commissioner of Law Revision,

Malaysia 2010: 23). However, the limits of legislative breakthroughs remain. In Singapore, there is no explicit law that protects the GLBTIQ community 'against discrimination on the grounds of gender expression or sexual orientation' (Mosbergen 2015). Marriage equality, e.g. gay marriage, remains illegal in Singapore, as it is in Malaysia. In Malaysia whilst amending Article 8(2) is lauded as a 'step forward', the Bar Council of Malaysia counsels that the amendment needs to be extended to 'other existing laws, policies and appointments in the future' as a 'laudable and bold attempt to empower each gender to achieve their full potential generally' (Mah 2001). Essentially Malaysia – and Singapore by extension – 'has yet to introduce legislation on gender equality' that is aligned with UN instruments such as CEDAW, the Convention on the Elimination of All Forms of Discrimination against Women (Aziz 2008).

So on the one hand, the marginalization of gender and sexual minorities is apparent as this is largely state driven. The Malaysian government openly endorses gay conversion therapy as its Islamic Development Department produced a video likening 'sexual orientation to horse riding' and exhorted homosexuals to repent by fulfilling their desires 'through marriage' or suppressing 'their appetite' through fasting (Roberts 2017). Its Ministry of Health (MOH) organized a video competition with a category on 'gender identity disorder' aimed at preventing homosexuality and transgenderism where submitted entries need to show the '"consequences" of being LGBT, as well as 'how to "prevent, control and seek help" for them' (Shurentheran 2017b). The Malaysian citizenry, deemed a heterosexual stable subject, is further constructed in positioning the GLBTIQ community as other; 'not suited to our culture and customs' and therefore ineligible to join the country's armed forces, states Deputy Prime Minister Datuk Seri Ahmad Zahid Hamidi during a Transformasi Nasional 2050 forum which is a national initiative to plan for the future of Malaysia, from 2020 to 2050 (Anand 2017).

The triple marginalization of economically disadvantaged GLBTIQ persons compounds their stigmatization and discrimination. In AFP (2011), it is noted that transsexuals and transgender people 'face daily discrimination and harassment in Malaysia and many of them are forced to earn their living as sex workers because they cannot get any other job'. Sayoni, an LGBT-rights group in Singapore, documents how, among trans women and 'gay women' in particular, 'the poor and the under-educated are particularly vulnerable to abuse', e.g. a trans woman sex worker who was gang-raped and afraid to report the crime to the police (Mosbergen 2015).

This triple marginalization exacerbates the vulnerability of high-risk groups where HIV and AIDS awareness, treatment and prevention are concerned.

The Malaysian AIDS Council (MAC) challenged the MOH's singling out this segment of Malaysian society, as doing so not only 'violates the core principles of equality, tolerance and compassions upon which the AIDS response was founded' but also risks jeopardizing the 'high-impact prevention strategies' (e.g. community-based testing within a non-judgemental environment) in realizing the national goal of achieving '90 per cent reduction in new HIV infections – or ending AIDS – by 2030' (MAC 2017). Action for AIDS Singapore maintains that it is only reaching '10 percent of the community' where more than 50 per cent of the 6000 people diagnosed with HIV in Singapore are gay men because of media laws that prohibit 'LGBT-specific campaigns' (e.g. condom advertisements), as Singapore's Media Development Authority's (MDA) guidelines caution against the promotion, justification or glamorization of aberrant 'lifestyles', e.g. homosexuality, transsexualism, incest (Mosbergen 2015).

Maintaining the fiction of a heterosexual stable subject thus requires indefatigable effort by multilevel institutions. This is evidenced by examples in Malaysia that follow the extraordinary outcome of the fourteenth General Elections in May 2018 – the toppling of National Front, *Barisan National* (in power since independence from the British in 1957), by the then Opposition Front, *Pakatan Harapan* – where hopes for greater respect of gender diversity and inclusion were unmet. These include the caning of two Malay-Muslim lesbian women aimed at educating rather than hurting them, for allegedly attempting to have sex in a public parking lot in Terengganu, a highly conservative eastern state in West Malaysia (Palansamy 2018); the reaction of the nonagenarian Prime Minister Mahathir Mohamad whose initial concern was that the caning 'gave a bad impression of Islam and did not reflect the religion's quality of justice' (Sreenevasan and Ding 2018) and later maintained that Malaysia will not recognize LGBT culture or same-sex marriage as these are 'Western values' (The Star Online 2018a); the removal of two portraits of LGBT activists, Pang Khee Teik and Nisha Ayub, from the state-sponsored photography exhibition celebrating the heritage of Georgetown, Penang, because it is 'against [Malaysian] values' (Nambiar 2018); and transphobia that remains unabated with the killing of trans women (The Star Online 2018b).

Other examples include the court's rejection of Mohd Ashraf's application to change her gender and name to Aleesha Farhana Abdul Aziz that moved the nation as she, a post-operative male-to-female transgender person, subsequently passed on (Zolkepli and Ramli 2011); the naturalization of effeminate boys through rehabilitation at an 'anti-gay camp' organized by government and education officials of the conservative state of Terengganu (BBC 2011); the *fatwa* (religious edict) issued by the National Fatwa Council to ban *pengkid* or tomboyism (Kala 2008); guidelines listing 'symptoms of gays' and 'symptoms of lesbians' for parents to facilitate early detection of homosexuality in their children which the Education Ministry had subsequently denied endorsing (Mosbergen 2012); and the banning of *Seksualiti Merdeka*, a sexuality rights festival comprising fairs, forums and performances (Ar 2013), by the police in 2011 and upheld by the court (following a failed appeal for judicial review), with a member of parliament interjecting that 'it involves wild relationships that will damage the country and nation. It is planting the seeds for the emergence of wilder relationships' (MT Webmaster 2011).

The fiction of a heterosexual stable subject is maintained by the majority of Singaporeans, as a study by the Institute of Policy Studies shows that '78.2 percent of Singaporeans felt sexual relations between two adults of the same sex was always or almost always wrong, and 72.9 percent of them were against gay marriage' (Shen 2014). This collective sentiment finds expression in the MDA's media guidelines that result in skewered characterization of the LGBT community, where they 'have to be sad, troubled, or suicidal [and in] Chinese dramas, the gay character is often a serial killer or a comical sidekick' (Mosbergen 2015); restriction to the right to assemble following a change in the Public Order Act which allows only Singaporean citizens and permanent residents to participate in the annual Pink Dot LGBT rights rally thereby excluding foreigners who comprise 30 per cent of the city-state's population (BBC 2017); and the genesis of the WearWhite movement as a protest against the Pink Dot movement in particular and the 'growing normalizations of the LGBT' community in general that was launched by an *ustaz* (Muslim teacher) and joined by sympathetic Faith Community Baptist Church and the LoveSingapore network of churches (Shen 2014).

On the other hand, the heterosexual stable subject is inadvertently destabilized by the insistent bracketing off of these plural sexualities. It not only makes visible but also exposes what Foucault terms as the 'biopower' (1978: paragraph 139): the work invested in legitimizing the heterosexual subject and heterosexual union with the potential for and realization of procreation for the sake of the nation's sustainability and progress. In these nation-states where sexuality remains a taboo subject, media attention inadvertently gives rise to the visibility of GLBTIQ persons and the support and, in some cases, societal outrage at the violation of their rights. These episodes in Singapore encompass the landmark High Court ruling that allowed a Singaporean Chinese gay couple who have lived together since 2005 to adopt their five-year-old son conceived through a surrogate mother in the United States on the premise of single-parent adoption and in the interest of the child's well-being (Kok 2018); the ongoing debate to repeal Section 377A that states that 'any two consenting men who commit "gross indecency" shall be punished with imprisonment for up to two years' despite the circular stalemate and the government's assurance that it will not be enforced (Aw 2012); the exhortation for the cessation of the 'culture war' between liberals (pro-LGBT) and conservatives (pro-family) by Pritam Singh, the party chief of the Workers' Party, to focus instead on widening the definition of family as an 'enlightened and inclusive one' to support those who come out and 'might face prejudice and depression' (Au-Yong 2019); the first Pink Dot LGBT rights rally held in 2009 with the organizers' assurance that it did not touch on taboo 'topics of race or religion' and it 'was not a protest or a political rally' (Leyl 2009); the government's 'quietly' lifting the ban to hire homosexuals for the sake of the economy (i.e. in a bid to not repel foreign gay talent) tempered by the admission of the then Prime Minister Goh Chok Tong who, in the early 1990s, stated, 'We are born this way and they are born that way but they are like you and me' (Arnold 2003); and twenty years later, a similar cautionary advice given to GLBTIQ persons to employ 'pragmatic resistance' that is 'non-confrontational' which complements the social-political conservatism of the state (Gjorgievska 2012); the founding of the Inter-University LGBT Network which supports LGBT students across campuses such as the National University of Singapore and Nanyang Technological Society by millennial activist Daryl Yang who is also canvassing for political literacy among youth (Zhuo 2019).

In Malaysia, these episodic disruptions to the stability of a heterosexual subject include the much publicized wedding reception of an openly gay pastor Ou Yang Wen Feng that provoked the reaction by the then Minister in the Prime Minister's Department, Datuk Seri Jamil Khir Baharom, that 'Malaysians of all races should protest en masse the practice of same-sex marriages as it will erode the family institution' (Leach 2012); the union of a lesbian couple signified by the tea ceremony which is regarded to be a quintessential Chinese wedding tradition (Tay 2011); a landmark ruling by the Court of Appeal which 'struck down a Negri Sembilan state law forbidding Muslim men from dressing up as women as being unconstitutional' following the appeal made by four Muslim transsexuals who challenged Section 66 of the Syariah Criminal (Negri Sembilan) Enactment 1992 but lost the case in 2012 (New Straits Times 2014). Within the transgender community, these episodic disruptions include netizens grieving over the brutal murder of Shameera Krishnan and appealing for the end of 'hate crimes against the transgender community' (Shurentheran 2017a);

the ordination of a new leader for a local Indian transgender community that spans seven generations, Thirunangai Association of Malaysia and Singapore (Muthiah 2012); the 'colourful send-off' for her iconic predecessor, M. Asha Devi, *Asha Amma* (Mother Asha), 'the oldest transgender woman in Malaysia' who is reverently remembered as helping many transgender persons 'acquire new identification cards as women and counselled many who wanted to undergo sex change operations' (Lim 2012); and Nisha Ayub as recipient of the 2016 US Secretary of State's International Women of Courage Award, a trans woman herself who is recognized for her contribution in co-founding two transgender-affirming organizations, the SEED Foundation and Justice for Sisters (Azizan 2016).

In queering public and private spaces amid hegemonic rhetoric and practices that sideline gender and sexual minorities, GLBTIQ-friendly and affirming networks are incrementally fostering webs of connection. In Singapore, there are the performing arts, annual public rallies and events that are held to sensitize the public such as Pink Dot (News Editor 2012a); IndigNation, in its 2012 and eight-year run of 'LGBT pride season' that aims to document 'gay history … [through] the process of remembering' (News Editor 2012b); Gay Health Singapore (formerly People Like Us) which focuses on public education and advocacy of GLBTIQ issues with supporting networks that include, among others, Action for AIDS in Singapore, TheBearProject for bears (hairier, larger gay-identifying or bisexual men), bears-in-training and bear admirers, The G Spot comprising students from Yale NUS College who support inclusivity and diversity; Safe Singapore that aims to provide 'information and resources to help friends, parents, and family members of LGBTQ persons understand their loved ones better'; Red Queen, Singapore's oldest email discussion group for queer women; Oogachaga, a gay counselling service; SG Rainbow and Young Out Here who reach out to GLBTIQ youth; SgButterfly, Singapore's first transgender community portal; and Singapore Queer-Straight Alliance which seeks to 'bridge gaps between queer and straight people, thereby contributing to the creation of a harmonious, compassionate Singaporean society where there is substantive equality, regardless of individual differences such as gender identity and sexual orientation'.

And on the legal front, there is firstly the Facebook community of Repeal 377A for those who support the repeal of Section 377A from Singapore's Penal Code as a piece of legislation which explicitly criminalizes sex between mutually consenting men. Secondly, Singapore LGBT Law, a team comprising lawyers and activists, produced *Same But Different* (Rajeswari 2017), an invaluable legal e-book for LGBT couples and families in Singapore, covering topics such as marriage, divorce and cohabitation contracts, children, property and finance, wills and inheritance for both Muslims and non-Muslims, supplemented by medical, legal and community resources.

In Malaysia, GLBTIQ-friendly and affirming networks include the PT Foundation (formerly Pink Triangle), the largest community-based non-governmental organization (NGO) whose outreach programmes on HIV and AIDS (counselling, anonymous HIV screening) are directed to the most marginalized and at-risk communities, e.g. drug users, sex workers, transgender persons, men-who-have-sex-with-men (MSM); Seksualiti Merdeka's Facebook site, the LGBT rights festival and Queer Lapis (Pang 2019), Malaysia's LGBTIQ+ Online Community and Resource Hub; Diversity which is a Malaysian-based LGBT rights NGO; PurpleLab Network (currently under construction), a 'virtual network of womyn-kind';[2] and Justice for Sisters' blog aimed at sensitizing the public about gender-based violence and persecution of the *mak nyah* (trans women) community in Malaysia.

There are today networks that are inclusively faith-based and these are significant when juxtaposed against the extremities of the drive towards Islamization in Malaysia and the insistence of secularism in Singapore as these forces impinge on the bodies and sexualities of GLBTIQ persons (to be elaborated in the next section). These faith-based networks are also notable in light of the ethos of the overarching research aim that seeks to show how becoming spiritually sexual and sexually spiritual (and religious) are mutually constitutive and not a contradiction in terms. They are, in Singapore: the Free Community Church that 'affirms that all individuals, including lesbian, gay, bisexual and transgender persons, are individuals of sacred worth created in God's image' that hosts the Pelangi Pride Centre (where *pelangi*, meaning rainbow in Malay, signifies the diversity and inclusivity of GLBTIQ persons) and has ministries that include Safehaven, FCC Wo-men's Ministry and the FCC Women's LUSH (Lesbians United for Self-Help) which are Christian cell group communities that provide a safe environment for GLBTIQ Christians who are seeking to reconcile their sexuality with their faith;[3] Heartland, the gay Buddhist fellowship; and As-Salam Singapore which is dedicated towards helping GLBTIQ Muslims living in Singapore to reconcile their sexuality with their faith through a safe and peaceful (or *as-salam*) platform.

In Malaysia, its openly gay pastor Reverend Ou Yang Wen Feng's vision of 'establishing the nation's first gay church ... [that] met with a torrent of outrage and criticism' two years ago (Al Arabiya News 2010) has materialized today as the Good Samaritan Metropolitan Community Church. Its visions include the following, among others: 'To provide a safe space for the lost and broken-hearted, who have difficulty accepting their sexual orientation … To build a spiritual home … [and] … To build a "Kindom"[4] of God through Love and Justice amongst the LGBTQ community'. For Muslims, there is the Facebook site of Komuniti Muslim Universal Malaysia that supports discourses based on human rights and progressive religious values. And for LGBTiQA Buddhists (lesbian, gay, bisexual, transgender, intersex, queer or questioning and asexual), there is the Queer Buddhist Malaysia's Facebook site.

Having surveyed the time-space of gender and sexual minorities in Malaysia and Singapore through the prism of popular discourses, I next dwell on a discussion of key ideas that have emerged through the trope of becoming that provides an insight to the ethos and rationale of the book, the fieldwork given the prominence of narrativization through interpretation of the interview data and finally a chapter outline that prefaces the journey into the interior.

Narratives of becoming

What are the coming-of-age narratives of the nation-states of Malaysia and Singapore? More pertinently, what are the coming-of-age narratives of the nation-states of Malaysia and Singapore from the standpoint of gender and sexual minorities? And in what ways would these narratives resonate with the narratives of becoming of GLBTIQ persons interviewed for this study? At the heart of these narratives lie the challenges of managing pluralism equitably and inclusively. A complementary commitment lies in seeking a rite and route of reconciliation among competing discourses that stake their various claims on bodies and sexualities, as intimated in the opening paragraphs above. The narratives of becoming of GLBTIQ persons interviewed show how transformative rhetoric and practices are not only glimpsed but more importantly lived out and embodied in their everyday realities. Four coming-of-age narratives will be explored: becoming Asian, becoming postcolonial, becoming religiously or spiritually sexual and sexually religious or spiritual, and becoming persons in the next sections.

Becoming Asian

The coming-of-age narratives of the nation-states of Malaysia and Singapore when considered from the standpoint of gender and sexual minorities are marked by ambivalences in their quest to embrace the pluralism of identities, bodies and sexualities. It is a need, at its most basic, and a right to be counted as full citizens. These narratives show that the trajectory from colonization to postcolonialism is not a linear one. Whilst GLBTIQ persons have remained systemically disenfranchized, they have remained resilient with episodic successes at destabilizing the heterosexualized stable subject as shown in the preliminary analyses of media texts above.

Key scholarship in the field points to distinctive Asian sexualities. Essentially, what is 'Asian' about 'Asian homosexualities' (Altman 1996 cited in Peletz 2007: 54)? 'Becoming' as Tom Boellstorff (2005a: 575) opines with regard to Indonesian *gay* (which he italicizes to differentiate it from the 'Western' gay label) and *lesbi* 'refers to self-awareness' and this is distinguished from 'opening oneself to oneself' in the sense of 'coming out to oneself' and incrementally to the world as Western gay men and lesbians tend to do. *Lesbi* which includes *tombois* and their lovers in Indonesia (Blackwood 1998, 2005, 2007a, b, 2008), not unlike masculine-identified women (*toms*) and their normatively feminine girlfriends (*dees*) in Thailand (Sinnott 2004, 2008), are practised as same-sex but different gender (hence heterogender) relationships which are differentiated from a 'Western' lesbian subjectivity which is oftentimes premised on same-sex and same-gender (hence homogender) relationships.

To compound the multiplicities of these subject positions, a *lesbi* is not synonymous with a *tomboi* as the latter term 'refers to gender behaviour [and] does not necessarily connote sexuality' (Blackwood 2008: 490). A *tom*'s 'untouchability' is part of how she performs hegemonic masculinity: she initiates and gives but does not, in return, receive sexual pleasure (Sinnott 2004: 147). For Indonesian *gay* and *lesbi* (Blackwood 2007b; Boellstorff 2005a), it is deemed natural to marry heterosexually and procreate in line with state-sponsored family and nation-building discourses. And *toms* who 'relinquish' their girlfriends, for that same purpose, deem it a meritorious act in line with the Buddhist tenet of non-attachment where desires, as extensions of worldly attachment, lead one to suffer (Sinnott 2004: 94). *Toms*, like *kathoeys*, who are transgender males, are embroiled in a 'discourse of suffering' with *dees* notably falling outside it, as they share ontologically 'an inability to achieve true maleness or femaleness' (Sinnott 2004: 94).

The encounter between hegemonic global (i.e. Western) and local (not merely localized) discourses and practices of sexualities therefore finds expression in 'Asian homosexualities' where the 'Asian' is reinstated (Altman 1996 cited in Peletz 2007: 54); *lesbi* world ('*dunia lesbi*') that resists being 'interpellated' by 'homogenous national or international lesbian identities' (Blackwood 2007b: 195–6). 'Asian homosexualities' is also expressed as a 'bricolage [encompassing] a mix of local, national, and transnational identities' (Blackwood 1998: 511). It is thirdly 'archipelagic' as *gay* and *lesbi* Indonesians 'imagine a new kind of national belonging where difference stands no longer as raw "diversity" to be ground into national "unity," but glittering islands of possibility in an archipelago of tolerance and justice' (Boellstorff 2005b: 229).

The plurality of becoming Asian narratives is similarly highlighted by the eminent scholar Michael G. Peletz (2011) who traces Muslim Southeast Asia since early modern times, fifteenth to eighteenth centuries. He notes how (especially in the first half of this period) 'traditions of pluralism with respect to gender and sexuality' are deeply entrenched in cultural-political terms (Peletz 2011: 662). These are evidenced through the 'bilateralism' of kinship systems that valorizes relations through both the father and the mother rather than a 'unilineal' (either the father's or mother's line of descent) and often 'patrilineal' (favouring the father's line of descent) one. Religious traditions were 'profoundly dualistic' where male and female elements of deities were given prominence (Reid 1993 cited in Peletz 2011: 662). And there was 'considerable fluidity and permeability in gender roles (e.g. women's autonomy in trade and commerce leading to more egalitarian male-female relationship), and by relative tolerance and indulgence with respect to many things sexual, at least for the commoner majority (i.e. extra-marital sexual relations)' (Peletz 2011: 663). He attributes the grounding of these patterns in the 'Austronesian (that predated Indic and Islamic influences in the region) and Hindu-Buddhist (especially Tantric and Saivite) sensibilities that informed early Southeast Asia Islam' that, in the thirteenth century, was in turn grounded in the '"sex-positive" religion' of Sufism, a 'mystically oriented variant of Sunni Islam' (Peletz 2011: 663–4).

The paradigmatic figure of 'gender (and sexual) pluralism' is arguably the "transgender" who is defined as 'individuals involved in customary behaviors that transcend or transgress majoritarian gender practices' (Peletz 2011: 661). Peletz rightly contends that 'the vicissitudes of transgenderism index' the vicissitudes of 'gender pluralism' (Peletz 2011: 662). The shifts become apparent in the second half of the early modern period, seventeenth and eighteenth centuries in Muslim Southeast Asia, impacted by Dutch and British colonialism, Protestant missionary activity and the muscularization of states that effect increasing centralization and bureaucratization of governance and control. As Peletz states:

> There is little space in such schemes of institutional and cultural rationalization for the valorization of locally distinctive ritual or esoteric knowledge ... architects of rationalization ... are notoriously unfriendly to all phenomena deemed to be ambiguous or liminal with respect to gender, sexuality ... political and religious elites cast as guardians of these religions are deeply suspicious of ethical pluralism and the value diversity that it logically entails. (2011: 668)

Where transgender ritual specialists, the *Bissu* among the Bugis of Sulawesi, were once revered, they incrementally lost their legitimacy. The erosion of 'gender pluralism' in this instance parallels the systematic delegitimization of cultural and religious pluralism in the form of syncretism: ritualistic and shamanic practices of the *Bissu* that are richly rooted in Austronesian-Hindu-Buddhist-Sufism traditions (Peletz 2011: 668). However, the resilience of the "transgender" or 'gender transgressors' is manifest. It is embodied by 'transvestite performers' of a dance-drama of Thai origin known as *mak yong* who dwelled in 'specialised homosexual villages' under the patronage of the *sultan* (monarch), now existing mainly in the Malaysian eastern state of Kelantan (Peletz 2011: 673).[5] The ambivalent treatment of transgender persons is evident in the contemporary lived realities and subject positions of androgynous *bissu* shamans, *calalai* ('false man'), *calabai* ('false women') (Davies 2010), and Malaysian male-to-female transsexuals or *mak nyahs* (approximating 5 per cent of *mak nyahs* living in Malaysia), that are marked by institutional stigmatization, chiefly by the police, religious officials, medical practitioners, the workplace, even the public at large (Teh 2002).

Becoming postcolonial

In this second half of the early modern period, during British colonialism, the curtailment of 'gender pluralism' and 'sexual pluralism', which Peletz defines as gender and sexual diversity that is accorded legitimacy (Peletz 2007: 44–5), continues. The era of Western colonialism began with the Portuguese conquest of an already Islamized Melaka in 1511, a thriving port then in the Malay Archipelago. This was followed by the Dutch in 1641 and finally the British Empire from 1786 to 1957 where Malaya, which Singapore was a part of, was a Straits Settlement (along with Melaka and Penang). Malaya finally gained her independence as a colonial colony towards a postcolonial nation leading to the formation of Malaysia in 1963. And Singapore, which had been a part of this federation of states, finally broke away in 1965 (Andaya and Andaya 2001). The source of the overt curtailment of 'gender pluralism' and 'sexual pluralism' lies in the much-cited piece of legislation, Section 377, which is the 'colonial version of the Offences Against the Person Act of 1861'. As a nineteenth-century British sodomy law introduced in all colonies of the British Empire, it sought to 'prohibit "buggery," or anal sex' and penalize other '"unnatural" sexual acts' such as bestiality, even fellatio (Faucette 2010: 413, 415), as opposed to 'natural' sexual acts that lead to procreation. Characteristic of the systemization of the British rule, the 'language of Section 377, as found in the Indian Penal Code of 1860 [is] replicated throughout the colonies' which reads as follows:

> Whoever voluntarily has carnal intercourse against the order of nature with any man, woman or animal shall be punished with imprisonment for life, or with imprisonment of either description for a term which may extend to ten years, and shall be liable to fine.
>
> Explanation – Penetration is sufficient to constitute the carnal intercourse necessary to the offence described in this section. (Faucette 2010: 416)[6]

In 1885, Britain also passed a law that included a 'provision on "gross indecency"' that included 'sexual acts between men beyond penetrative sex' and which appeared under 'various names as a supplement to Section 377 in colonies' (Faucette 2010: 416). The sodomy law was subsequently repealed in the UK (beginning with England and Wales in 1967). In postcolonial times, former colonies such as Canada (1969), New Zealand (1986) and Australia (1972–1997) likewise repealed the sodomy law (Faucette 2010: 415–16). In Asia, the Supreme Court of India repealed Section 377 of the Indian Penal Code effectively decriminalizing consensual gay sex (TOI-Online 2018). In 2007, Singapore repealed Section 377 but retained Section 377A,[7] the 'gross indecency' provision to 'convict MSM' (Faucette 2010: 419–20). Section 377 and its supplement remain as colonial legacies in India (with a notable amendment wherein it does not apply to consensual private acts as ruled by the Delhi High Court in 2009) and Malaysia (Faucette 2010: 419).

As postcolonial nation-states, what can be inferred when Malaysia retains Section 377 (and all amended supplements), and Singapore, Section 377A? On the one hand, Section 377 is regarded as a 'medieval sexual ethos' (Chua 2003: 215) or 'colonial relic', given that the UK itself has not only repealed but also 'legalised sodomy' (Lee 2008: 391). On the other hand, Section 377 is not antiquated on grounds alone that it is a colonial legacy as it is imbibed with contemporary political and social-cultural valence that has become intrinsic to the postcolonial construction of national identity through the regulation of the bodies and sexualities of its citizenry. The public and publicized debates (e.g. in media forums, parliament, academia and the 'Singapore: Repeal 377A Now!' movement) on repealing 377A in Singapore are therefore revelatory in breaking the taboo on plural sexualities through the open (albeit not open-ended) negotiation of tensions between the competing Communitarian and Liberal discourses. The former, which is state driven, opposes the repeal and the latter advocates for it. These are positioned as mutually exclusive standpoints but in a sense, they quite inadvertently add up to inclusiveness as both (from the standpoint of their proponents) provide legitimate and compelling grounds for opposition and proposition (Chua 2003; Lee 2008).

The Liberal arguments for repealing 377A are based on, firstly, the principle of liberty that foregrounds the primacy of individual autonomy, personal liberty and privacy rights. The GLBTIQ community has asked that they be treated equally as heterosexuals (equality as sameness in this sense) given the repeal of 377 which decriminalizes private, consensual anal sex among heterosexuals (Lee 2008: 348) and fellatio as foreplay culminating in penile-vaginal intercourse that could potentially lead to procreation (Chua 2003: 219). The *heterosexual standard*[8] is clearly evident as GLBTIQ persons have to settle for less, given the Singapore government's as-good-as-it-gets stance that it would continue to be non-proactive in enforcing 377A in relation to private and consensual sex (Lee 2008: 348). In this way, 'homosexuals would be accommodated and have space to lead quiet lives' (Lee 2008: 349). Liberalism also posits that the harm onto society is absent when sexual acts are performed in private by consenting adults, both heterosexual and homosexual alike.

Secondly, the principle of equality deems 377A to be in violation of Article 12(1) of the Constitution, the supreme law, which guarantees equality[9] and, by extension, 'sexual orientation' as a prohibited ground of discrimination under Article 12(2)[10] and global human rights instruments such as the International Convention of Political and Civil Rights (ICCPR) which the Singapore government has not ratified.[11] Thirdly, the principle of 'special protection' beyond 'equal protection of the law' should be accorded to GLBTIQ persons as they constitute 'sexual minorities' (Lee 2008: 351–69). And the final principle is that of 'state neutrality' that does not seek to 'endorse by legislation what visions of the "good life" are acceptable or unacceptable in a diverse society' (Chua 2003: 229–30). This upholds the sovereignty of the individual's right to self-determination on matters related to his or her body and sexuality, in this instance[12] as opposed to regulatory mechanisms (Foucault 1977) deployed by a paternalistic state that is also 'heterosexist' (Offord 2003: 135).

In contrast, the Communitarian counterarguments for supporting 377A are based on, firstly, the principle of the 'common good' which upholds the primacy of the community as the individual is not an atomistic but relational being, 'with bonds to family, associations and community' (Lee 2008: 372). The common good of the community must be jealously guarded against the adverse domino effects of repealing 377A that would invariably trigger a series of reforms in criminal and civil law. This is because the 'homosexualism agenda', in drawing from foreign experience (the 'decadent' West) which provides a cautionary tale, precipitates the following social ills. These include the 'repeal of the blanket criminalisation of adult same-sex activity', 'equalisation of age of consent to heterosexual and homosexual sexual activity', 'prohibition of discrimination based on sexual orientation' and 'provision of equal access for same-sex couples to rights and obligations attached to marriage' (Lee 2008: 370–1). This would threaten the heterosexualized 'natural family' propounded by the state in opening up its traditional definition of 'a man and woman bound in a lifelong covenant of marriage' for the purposes of, among others, the 'continuation of the human species, the rearing of children [and] the regulation of sexuality' (Stivens 2006: 361). According legitimacy to the pluralism of *doing family*, i.e. gay, lesbian, bisexual and transgender parenting, beyond the narrow boundaries of a 'natural family', is thus foreclosed.

Secondly is the much-touted principle of 'Asian values' which undergirds Communitarianism which, in turn, is the bedrock of the 'public philosophy of the Singapore government' (Lee 2008: 373). As enshrined in its 1991 *Shared Values White Paper* which operationalizes 'Asian values', Singapore, as an Asian society, has 'always weighted group interests more heavily than individual ones' (Lee 2008: 373). As a 'postcolonial project' that was promulgated by the then Prime Ministers of Malaysia and Singapore, Mahathir Mohamad (who is back in power following the fourteenth General Elections in 2018) and the late Lee Kuan Yew, respectively, 'Asian values' privilege

> societal interests over the narrow, individual self-interest, order and harmony over personal freedom; it also values respect for authority and strong leadership, strong attachment to family, conventional authority patterns and loyalty within the family, 'traditional' [*sic*] gender relations, strong filial piety, discipline, hard work and thrift. (Stivens 2006: 356)

The third principle, 'public morality as a social good' (Lee 2008: 378), deems gender and sexual minorities as undeserving of 'special protection'. In evaluating the 'social value of 377', a 'thicker conception of community' dictates that the repeal of 377A is likely to jeopardize public health as the 'homosexual anal sex ... is inherently unhealthy, indicating its unnatural, harmful nature' and worse health risks associated with gay promiscuity, e.g. 'bug-chasers (alluding to the gay fantasy of passing on HIV)' (Lee 2008: 374–5). A further assertion is that 'private' (immoral) acts can have 'public' consequences given that 'harm is not a self-evident concept'. And it rejects sexuality rights as the harbinger of the 'ideology of hedonism' which repealing 377 would evidently entail (Lee 2008: 379–80). Finally, it is the complementary principles of 'state paternalism' and 'majority preference' (Chua 2003: 248, 254) and not the unregulated sexualities of GLBTIQ persons that are the more accountable custodians of communal good (the individual as a subset) through the exercise of the 'rule of good law' and order (Lee 2008: 373). The Communitarian argument prevailed.

These postcolonial narratives of becoming Asian and postcolonial are narratives of managing pluralism. This is evident in the shifts between legitimacy to tolerance to disgust accorded to or directed at diversity in terms of sexualities in ethnicity, culture, religion from early modernity to the twenty-first century. And it includes different and competing 'visions of the "good life" including sex' in the context of the Communalism/Liberalism debate (Chua 2003: 252). According to Lee (2008: 391), to assert that 377A is merely a 'colonial relic Singapore inherited from Britain' is 'itself a form of neo-colonial (im)moral imperialism' in, as inferred, taking on 'decadent' Western values[13] (with unbridled liberty leading to libertarianism) rather than the Confucian-inspired[14] bulwark of Asian values. In contrast, Chua maintains that whilst 'the births of 377 and 377A may be forgivable (as a rushed piece of legislation that "[slipped] through with nineteenth century prostitution laws" to the colonies),[15] but their conscious retention is a different matter' (2003: 253–4). The lack of pluralism occurs when differences become intolerable and eventually mutually exclusive. This is even more apparent when sexualities in religions and spirituality are considered. But postcolonial narratives of becoming resiliently maintain that this is not the only way of managing pluralism. And the narratives of GLBTIQ persons interviewed in this study embody the vicissitudes of negotiating such tensions.

Becoming sexually religious or spiritual and religiously or spiritually sexual

How then does one bridge the seemingly insurmountable gap between the self-identifying declaration of 'I am gay and religious' with the equally weighted pronouncement that 'being gay and religious is a contradiction in terms'? The more pertinent point is why some choose to do so and how they find the common ground between seemingly irreconcilable differences. It is precisely because cultures and religions still matter as 'Asian values' among others that, in turn, is not static but evolving, that makes this not only a worthwhile endeavour but also an imperative in opening up not foreclosing private and public spaces of belonging. And it calls to question the hierarchization of heterosexual/non-heterosexual identities and practices and sexual majority/sexual minorities.

A quick detour on demographics of Malaysia and Singapore shows not only the diversity in ethnicities, cultures and religions but also high percentage of religious affiliation among Malaysians (98 per cent) and Singaporeans (83 per cent). Based on the decennial 2010 Population and Housing Census of Malaysia (or Census 2010) – another legacy of the British Empire – of the total population of 28.3 million, with Malaysians consisting of 91.8 per cent, adherents to Islam comprise 61.3 per cent; Buddhism 19.8 per cent; Christianity 9.2 per cent; Hinduism 6.3 per cent; and Confucianism, Taoism and tribal/folk/other traditional Chinese religion 1.3 per cent; other religion 0.4 per cent; no religion 0.7 per cent and unknown 1.0 per cent. In terms of ethnic composition, Malaysian citizens comprise *Bumiputera* (Malay-Muslim, *Orang Asli* or original peoples of West Malaysia and Indigenous peoples of East Malaysia) 67.4 per cent, Chinese 24.6 per cent, Indians 7.3 per cent and others 0.7 per cent (Department of Statistics Malaysia 2011). Based on the Census of Population 2010 released by the Singapore Department of Statistics, Singapore's total population was 5.08 million as at end-June 2010, with an ethnic composition of Chinese, Malays and Indians comprising 74 per cent, 13 per cent and 9.2 per cent, respectively (2011: 3, 5). In terms of religious affiliation, adherents number: Buddhism 33.3 per cent, Islam 14.7 per cent, Christianity 11.3 per cent, Taoism 10.9 per cent, Catholicism 7.1 per cent, Hinduism 5.1 per cent, other religions 0.7 per cent, none 16.9 per cent.

It is also fitting at this juncture to offer working definitions for 'sexuality' and, by extension, 'sexual health', 'sexual rights', 'gender identity', 'sexual orientation', 'religion' and 'spirituality' that inform the discourses of sexuality and religiosity and spirituality in this book. The World Health Organisation (WHO) defines sexuality as

a central aspect of being human throughout life [that] encompasses sex, gender identities and roles, sexual orientation, eroticism, pleasure, intimacy and reproduction. Sexuality is experienced and expressed in thoughts, fantasies, desires, beliefs, attitudes, values, behaviours, practices, roles and relationships. While sexuality can include all of these dimensions, not all of them are always experienced or expressed. Sexuality is influenced by the interaction of biological, psychological, social, economic, political, cultural, legal, historical, religious and spiritual factors. (WHO 2019)

Sexuality is encompassing and constitutes an integral component of one's personhood. Related concepts such as 'sexual health' (holistic well-being in relation to sexuality) and 'sexual rights' (the right to gender equality and equity regardless of a person's sex, gender and desire) are premised on the integrity accorded to a person's sexuality. According to the Yogyakarta Principles (YP) (International Commission of Jurists 2007: 6), the most incisive document that outlines sexuality rights as human rights is: 'Principles on the application of International human rights law in relation to sexual orientation and gender identity':

> Gender identity is understood to refer to each person's deeply felt internal and individual experience of gender, which may or may not correspond with the sex assigned at birth, including the personal sense of the body (which may involve, if freely chosen, modification of bodily appearance or function by medical, surgical or other means) and other expressions of gender, including dress, speech and mannerisms.

And

> Sexual orientation is understood to refer to each person's capacity for profound emotional, affectional and sexual attraction to, and intimate and sexual relations with, individuals of a different gender or the same gender or more than one gender.

The adoption of the Yogyakarta Principles plus 10 (following a ten-year review of the YP), which consists of additional principles (30–8) and 111 state obligations related to areas such as torture, asylum, privacy, health and the protection of human rights defenders, complements the Yogyakarta Principles on the application of international human right law in relation to sexual orientation, gender identity, gender expression and sex characteristics (SOGIESC). The YP+10 defines the latter (and later) two concepts as follows:

> Gender expression [is understood] as each person's presentation of the person's gender through physical appearance – including dress, hairstyles, accessories, cosmetics – and mannerisms, speech, behavioural patterns, names and personal

references, and noting further that gender expression may or may not conform to a person's gender identity.

And 'sex characteristics' is defined as

> each person's physical features relating to sex, including genitalia and other sexual and reproductive anatomy, chromosomes, hormones, and secondary physical features emerging from puberty... [and is] an explicit ground for protection from violations of human rights. (YP+10 2017)

The pluralism of sexual orientation, gender identity, gender expression and sex characteristic is as apparent as the pluralism of ethnicities, cultures and religions. The point of contention lies in how this pluralism is managed: at one level, through state privileging of heterosexuality and de-privileging of other sexualities; and at another level, state privileging of one ethnicity and concomitant culture and religion above others (Abraham 2004; Cheah 2002; Clammer 2002; Goh 2002; Ho 2003; Kessler 2008; Mandal 2004; Mohamad 2002; Shamsul 1996, 1997, 1998; and Zawawi 1998). Becoming sexually religious or spiritual and religiously or spiritually sexual considers how bodies and sexualities are regulated, held under surveillance and produced – in the Foucauldian sense of 'bio-power' – within these multiple and complex levels of dominance/marginalization.[16] In Malaysia, being Malay and being Muslim is synonymous by constitutional definition. The postcolonial construct of the *Bumiputera*, literally, 'sons of the soil', accords greater legitimacy to Malays, the ethnic majority with attendant life-long health, business, financial and social and political benefits. Although *Bumiputera* constitutionally encompasses the first peoples or indigenous peoples of Malaysia (*Orang Asli* in West or Peninsula Malaysia; natives, e.g. *Dayak* or *Orang Ulu* in Sarawak, and *Anak Negeri* in Sabah, East Malaysia), in reality, they have differentiated access to the privileges above and continue to face state-driven discrimination and violation of their rights, particularly with regard to land rights.[17]

Malaysia, like Singapore, is a secular democracy as the supreme law in these lands is the Constitution, a shared colonial legacy of the British Empire. In Malaysia unlike Singapore, the official religion is Islam with two implications: firstly, the existence of a dual legal system, Islamic and secular; and secondly, the constitutionally protected freedom of religious practice granted to adherents of other religions and spiritualities, excepting Muslims as they are subjected to provisions in state Islamic law (Ahmad 2005). This freedom is, however, a contested reality given the documented discriminatory practices levelled at ethnic, cultural and religious minorities in Malaysia. The Human Rights

Overview Report on Malaysia 2018 in the year following the fourteenth General Elections holds the former opposition, now government, *Pakatan Harapan*, accountable for reneging on its pledge (pre-electoral manifesto) to ratify the International Convention on the Eradication of Racial Discrimination (ICERD) following protests from Malay-dominated political parties, e.g. UMNO, PAS and 'Malay supremacist groups' (SUARAM 2018). The right to a fair trial, custodial deaths, freedom of expression and assembly, independence of the judiciary, discrimination against GLBTIQ groups remain challenges to be addressed.

In Singapore, the ethnic majority is the Chinese with the 'managed elitism' (between English-speaking and university-educated 'cosmopolitans' and Chinese-speaking 'heartlanders') and Chineseness of Singapore, often touted as the homogenizing driving force behind the nation-state's stability (in turn, premised on the docility of its citizenry), progress and prosperity (Kuah 2018; Tan 2002; Trocki 2006: 148). The former Prime Minister and late Senior Minister Lee Kuan Yew institutionalized the 'Asian model' in eschewing the Western model and 'Asian values' – 'the belief in thrift, hard work, filial piety, and loyalty in the extended family, and, most of all, the respect for scholarship and learning' (Zakaria and Lee 1994: 114) – premised on Confucian values in modelling Singapore, as homeland to diasporic Chinese, on the economic successes of East Asia. Singapore, the most developed Southeast Asian nation-state today, is globally dubbed the 'nanny state' as 'the strong arm of the state' is pervasive in all areas of 'the life of its citizenry' (e.g. from housing to marriage to national harmony to heritage conservation policies) through systemic 'social cultural engineering' by its main political party, the Chinese-dominated People's Action Party, that has been in governance since 1965 (Kuah 2018: 1). In doing so, it exemplifies Foucauldian 'biopower' in exercising power over the life of its citizenry and produces an efficient albeit docile 'species body'.

Within the framework of political economies of Malaysia and Singapore as outlined above, integrating sexuality with 'religious and spiritual factors', as intimated in WHO's expansive definition of sexuality, given the binaries of majority/minorities that frame ethnic, cultural and religious relationships as delineated, entails cautionary zeal. In terms of working definitions, 'religion' is often distinguished from 'spirituality' in the following ways. Religion is 'an institutional phenomenon' as it is marked by formalized boundaries that differentiate one religion from another, through particularized beliefs, conditions, sustenance and mobilization of membership within the faith community. Religion is also regarded as 'a social phenomenon' as inherent spiritual concerns are often interwoven with 'nonspiritual concerns', e.g. cultural, economic, political and social. Spirituality is deemed as an individual phenomenon that is often not observable by others (meditational practices or works of charity as exceptions) and 'relational' through one's intimate and highly personalized relationship with a sacred or transcendent being (Miller and Thoresen 2003: 27).

However, aligning religiosity with material, tangible and observable reality and spirituality with the inverse, i.e. immaterial, intangible and non-observable reality, can be limiting rather than revelatory. In essence, religiosity as used in this study refers to an interviewee's stated adherence to institutionalized and officially sanctioned beliefs and structures whilst spirituality refers to his or her individuated beliefs and practices whilst still self-identifying as Christian, Muslim, Tibetan Buddhist and Hindu.

The integration of sexuality with 'religious and spiritual factors' is the very impetus for this project that aligns itself with, yet differentiates itself from, other such initiatives that seek to break through the impasse of competing discourses and, in doing so, offers new insights. In foregrounding studies or commentaries on sexuality and religion or spirituality in the context of Southeast Asia, that are richly informed by scholarship beyond Southeast Asia, the following standpoints emerge. Foremost is the worldview of 'incommensurability': that being religious and gay, lesbian, bisexual, transgender, intersex and questioning or queer (GLBTIQ) is ontologically 'ungrammatical' or 'unintelligible', as noted by Tom Boellstorff (2005a) in his long-term study on being Muslim and gay in Indonesia, a secular state which hosts the world's largest Muslim population. At its most insidious, maintaining such discursive strategies erases or negates GLBTIQ sexualities through according legitimacy only to heteronomative sexuality (Peletz 2007: 44). 'Male homosexuality', as Boellstorff opines, 'does not bifurcate into the meritorious and sinful: It is incomprehensible as a form of sexual selfhood' (Boellstorff 2005a: 575). Discursively, it does not and cannot exist. The principle of 'incommensurability' resonates with Judith Butler's 'cultural matrix' (elsewhere 'heterosexual matrix') that frames which bodies and sexualities have 'become intelligible' and how these are produced: 'it requires that certain kinds of "identities" cannot "exist" – that is, those in which gender does not follow from sex and those in which the practices of desire do not "follow" from either sex or gender' (Butler 1990: 17). In being born male, it 'follows' that one ought to be gendered masculine and desire the opposite sex hence being Muslim and gay in Indonesia is 'unintelligible' – it 'cannot "exist"'.

Yet the 'persistence and proliferation' of such bodies and sexualities beyond the sex/gender/desire economy of the 'cultural matrix' embodied by GLBTIQ persons 'provide critical opportunities to expose the limits and regulatory aims of that domain of intelligibility' (Butler 1990: 17). That such bodies and sexualities *must not exist* belies a purposeful and systemic management of pluralism that finds belligerent expression most commonly in discourses that condemn, demonize, criminalize and marginalize GLBTIQ sexualities morally, theologically, legally and ontologically. GLBTIQ sexualities are constructed as aberrant, abnormal, wanton and sinful. Therefore, an adjunct of 'incommensurability' is the standpoint of incompatibility between the discourses of sexuality rights and certain religious discourses that are often used to regulate sexuality. On the one hand, sexuality rights encompass the right to participate in sexual activity, the right to pleasure, the right to sexual (and reproductive) self-determination, the right to self-definition, the right to self-expression, the right to self-realization, the right of consent to sexual practice in personal relationships, the right to freely choose our sexual partners and the right to publicly recognize sexual relationships (Richardson 2000). On the other hand, religious orthodoxy, transmitted through mainstream and traditional exegesis of proscriptive Qur'anic and Biblical verses on homosexuality, for instance, curtails the enjoyment of the full breadth of sexuality rights as it regulates and heterosexualizes desire for procreative ends in compliance not only with natural law but principally God's law (Hamzić 2011; Kugle 2003; National Council of Churches of Singapore 2004; Shah 2018; Yip 2005).

So how GLBTIQ and heterosexual persons live out their sexualities in religiosity or spirituality, as members in families, faith communities and the nation-state, is differentiated. This is an effect of discourses of nation-building that are (a) emblematic of 'normative masculinity' with male homosexuality in particular, perceived as a threat to the nation and homophobic violence deemed a proportionate and 'proper masculine response' (Boellstorff 2004: 465) and the 'Confucian gentleman' as the ideal Singaporean citizen (Kuah 2018: 17); (b) premised on the 'natural family [which] is a man and woman bound in a lifelong covenant of marriage for the purposes of: the continuation of the human species ... [and] the regulation of sexuality' (Stivens 2006: 361); and (c) bolstered by secular heterosexism as 'the nation [is] a protectorate of family values' (Offord 2003: 153) and religious heterosexism and would invariably impinge on sexuality rights as human rights. The centrality of state-sponsored sexuality that is heterosexuality (think tax incentives for married heterosexual spouses and their families) becomes, as Lisa Duggan (cited in Jakobsen and

Pellegrini 2004: 122) quips, 'the law of the land' and its sanctity, as divinely ordained, a 'religion of heteronormativity'. It thus 'follows' in Butlerian terms that GLBTIQ bodies and sexualities that 'cannot "exist"' 'cannot [then] occupy the symbolic "heart"' of their nations that is reserved for and inhabited by those whose sex/gender/desire are intelligible (Jakobsen and Pellegrini 2004: 86).

This incompatibility is exacerbated by the competing claims of ascendency between the universalism of sexuality rights as secular 'law' (where it is binding for States Parties who have ratified or acceded to particular conventions) and sacrality of religious truths as divine 'law' (for believers). The introduction to the Yogyakarta Principles states: 'All human rights are universal, interdependent, indivisible and interrelated. Sexual orientation and gender identity are integral to every person's dignity and humanity and must not be the basis for discrimination or abuse' (ICJ 2007: 6).[18] Sexuality rights as the last bastion of human rights, accorded to every person, are 'interdependent, indivisible and interrelated' in eschewing the historical prioritization given to the 'first generation' of civil and political liberties, over 'second generation' of economic, social and cultural rights and 'third generation' or 'collective rights' of indigenous peoples to self-determination. Rights as 'interdependent, indivisible and interrelated' are enshrined in the various human rights instruments, notably, the 1948 Universal Declaration of Human Rights, complemented by the 1966 International Covenant on Civil and Political Rights and the 1966 International Covenant on Economic, Social and Cultural Rights (Tergel 1998: 63–4).

Whilst the principles of sexuality rights as indivisible and inalienable are not problematic, the universality of rights potentially is. It is the principle of universality of sexuality rights, as applicable to all, across time and space, and *equally* applicable to all – enabled by its being positioned as secular – that runs counter to the cultural relativism (moral validity) of cultures and religions, particularly, religious orthodoxy. Rights as universal is often held to be synonymous with rights as secular as gleaned from Principle 21 of the Yogyakarta Principles on 'The rights to freedom of thought, conscience and religion' that directs states to ensure that the 'expression, practice and promotion of different opinions, convictions and beliefs with regard to issues of sexual orientation or gender identity is not undertaken in a manner incompatible with human rights' (ICJ 2007: 26). The 'vertigo of secularization' that is exacerbated by the fear and terror of 9/11 where societies globally 'seek to find political orders with legitimate grounding as separated from the sphere of religion' (Lara 2003: 184) finds resonance here. Given the insistence on secularization, competing claims of ascendency becomes apparent: 'different opinions, convictions and beliefs' as effects of cultures (e.g. 'Asian values') and religions cannot be 'undertaken in a manner incompatible with human rights'. Where there is incompatibility, as inferred, human rights take precedence.

And there are certainly incompatibilities. Culturally, 'Asian values', as envisaged by its chief proponent, the then and now prime minister of Malaysia (1981–2003, 2018–), Tun Dr Mahathir Mohamad, disqualify as family, 'two men living together' (Barr 2002: 43). The Minister for Islamic Affairs in the prime minister's department of the Malaysian government, in reacting to the marriage of Malaysian gay pastor Reverend Ou Yang Wen Feng, says, 'Malaysians should protest "en masse the practice of same-sex marriages as it will erode the family institution"' (Leach 2012). Singapore's former PM Goh Chok Tong's announcement that the Singapore Civil Service would openly hire gay people even at high security clearance levels elicited degrees of conservatism from various stakeholders, among whom imagined 'the heterosexual family … to be a key Asian value' (Tan 2008: 420).

Religiously, the Mufti office emphasized 'Islam's total opposition to homosexuality' as it is a 'sinful act' that is 'inconsistent with Singapore's official vision of the family'. The Singapore Buddhist Federation noted that although 'there is nothing on the matter under the five Buddhist precepts' which interestingly includes sexual misconduct, homosexuality remains not 'right' and calls for compassion towards homosexuals. And the Christian communities both Roman Catholic and Protestant, with the 'most developed anti-gay arguments and strategies', distinguished between (a) being gay and doing gay where the former is deserving of compassion (if celibate) and the latter, condemnation (in 'practising gay sex'); and (b) the church as (unapologetically) heteronormative in devaluing 'non-procreative sexuality' but not homophobic through its exhortation to 'love the sinner but hate the sin' (Tan 2008: 421–6). The 'unintelligible' bodies and sexualities of GLBTIQ persons become intelligible (obvious) sites of contestation between universality/relativism and secularism/religiosity: the '"*fundamentalism*" of human right [*sic*]' that is inherently secular hence universal (Piechowiak 1999: 11) is pit against religious fundamentalism that is 'secularisation-resistant' hence transcendent (Gellner 1992: 6).[19] An impasse ensues in the face of such absolutism with practitioners of sexuality rights *and* religions, as GLBTIQ persons, left with the choice of becoming either sexual or religious. Can segmentation of one's personhood constitute a choice, freely undertaken rather than coerced? And is this as good as it gets? Thankfully, not! And the next narratives of becoming explain why.

Becoming persons

Oppositional standpoints corresponding to incommensurability, incompatibility and ascendency claims make fuzzy rather than harden boundaries between sexuality rights and religious discourses. These standpoints include commensurability (of a Muslim gay man) in 'loving the sin' (Jakobsen and Pellegrini 2004), compatibility between sexuality and religious discourses (Cheng 2010; Falk 2007; Goh 2012a, b, 2018; Ngeo 2013; and Vanitha 2004, 2005) and eschewing ascending claims through revisioning the mutuality of universalism and particularism (Bong 2006; Matsuoka 2007). These queer (strange and unsettling) strategies, already evident from scholarship in the field, and significantly narratives of the sixteen GLBTIQ persons interviewed in this study show why, to many, both (sexuality) rights and religions matter and how they find the common ground between these where others insist are irreconcilable differences. These bodies of knowledge arising from the lived realities of GLBTIQ persons are not only subjugated (previously marginalized) but also oppositional (potentially subversive) knowledge. This knowledge is founded on the fluidity and plurality of ways of knowing and doing, essentially, ways of becoming persons.

Firstly, to 'love the sin' (Jakobsen and Pellegrini 2004), not only the sinner radicalizes how being sexual and being religious are commensurable within the same body, not only those belonging to GLBTIQ persons but also those who are heterosexual, asexual, celibate and do not embody or embrace procreative sexuality. To 'love the sin' also exposes the limits of unconditional love (itself a contradiction in terms) which is tolerance as practised by most churches who 'love the sinner but hate the sin' (National Council of Churches of Singapore 2004; Tan 2008: 424). The book *Love the Sin: Sexual Regulation and the Limits of Religious Tolerance*, although set in the context of the United States, is highly instructive in this regard. Its authors Janet R. Jakobsen and Ann Pellegrini propose 'to make religion the ground of sexual freedom, rather than the *justification* for sexual regulation' by concurrently arguing for not only sexual freedom but also religious freedom (beyond Christianity as the de facto state religion), in order to imagine future democratic possibilities and moral alternatives that are more inclusive and socially just for its plural society (2004: 16–17).

By extension, the contiguity of sexuality rights and religion finds expression in the shared affirmation of the inherent worth of a human person. 'All human beings are born free and equal in dignity and rights' underscores the Yogyakarta

Principles (ICJ 2007: 10), as sexuality rights as human rights are inalienable or inseparable from our humanness. And 'The Statement on Homosexuality' issued by the National Council of Churches of Singapore acknowledges that as 'every person is loved by God ... Homosexuals should be regarded and treated no less as persons of worth and dignity' (2004: 128). Between the interstices of 'all human beings are born free and equal in dignity and rights' but some are more 'free and equal' and homosexuals as 'persons of worth and dignity' but 'homosexual practices as sin' (National Council of Churches of Singapore 2004: 117) is the truth claim that all bodies and sexualities are thus created to exist and have the right to exist.

Complementing the rights and religious dimensions on commensurability is an ontological one where Butler's most quotable thesis on 'gender performativity' deconstructs the 'heterosexual matrix' (Butler 1990: 151) and opens up previously unimagined possibilities of becoming:

> That gender reality is created through sustained social performances means that the very notions of an essential sex and a true or abiding masculinity or femininity are also constituted as part of the strategy that conceals gender's performative character and the performative possibilities for proliferating gender configurations outside the restricting frames of masculinist domination and compulsory heterosexuality. (1990: 141)

Narratives of becoming of GLBTIQ persons occupy the heart of this study and show the ways in which bodies and sexualities that do not always comply with 'masculinist domination and compulsory heterosexuality' remain intelligible and can and do exist. That sex/gender/desire is 'performative' holds true not only for GLBTIQ persons but anyone who, on an everyday reality, is 'doing gender' (Lorber 1994), in learning and unlearning within particularized contexts, how it often follows that if one is born male, one is gendered masculine and ought to desire women or if one is born female, one is gendered feminine and ought to desire men. These 'social performances' are not natural but made to be natural.

Similarly, Butler reframes 'sex' not as 'essential' but a 'gendered category' (Butler 1990: 7). In so doing, she radically destabilizes the immutability or fixity of sex as pre-discursive. Sex like gender becomes a construct. Neither is there 'a true or abiding masculinity or femininity' with the former aligned only with being an authentic or 'real' man and the latter, a 'real' woman. In making visible the 'strategy that conceals' the authentication of a masculine man and feminine woman and heterosexualizing desire between them, Butler opens up grounds for according legitimacy to other ways of becoming. This, in turn, resonates with

Peletz's (2007: 44) 'gender pluralism' which is the effect of legitimacy accorded to bodies and sexualities that are diverse in the context of Asia. Therein lies the more subversive effects of 'gender performativity' which are 'proliferating gender configurations outside [these] restricting frames' so that it also follows that if one is born male (not only conventionally understood as biologically determined but also gendered following Butler), one can be gendered masculine or feminine or both or neither and one could desire women or men or both or neither.

'Gender performativity' is thus embodied in the existence, intelligibility and commensurability of a Buddhist then Muslim trans man, Christian lesbian mentor, Tibetan Buddhist bisexual mother, gay Catholic father, Hindu intersex-lesbian mystic among the sixteen interviewees of this study. The foundational principle of commensurability leads to the second oppositional standpoint of compatibility between the secularity of rights discourse and sacrality of religious and spiritual discourses. This is evidenced through the validation of plural bodies and sexualities that comes from diverse sources that are here positioned as complementary rather than competing: firstly, the secular framework of sexuality rights in the Yogyakarta Principles (ICJ 2007),[20] and secondly, religious and spiritual frameworks. With regard to the latter, the spiritualism of Buddhism upholds 'a mode of being that is genderless' in reaching Buddhahood or enlightenment, where sexual differentiation manifests our fallen human condition and is made irrelevant (Falk 2007: 49–50). And the core teachings of the Buddha affirm 'soteriological inclusiveness' with all accorded equal access to enlightenment notwithstanding social and cultural practices that sustain gender inequality and inequity, e.g. 'ascetic misogyny' (the subordination of women as polluting agents) or 'institutional androcentrism' (the dominance of male and masculine knowledge) (Falk 2007: 44). Hinduism, as Ruth Vanita, the Hindu lesbian scholar notes, shares with Christianity and Islam the understanding of gender as simultaneously 'very powerful and as irrelevant' (Vanita 2005: 71). The paradox or tension between spiritual inclusiveness (genderless as transcendent) and societal discrimination that is rooted in gender and sexual differences, across time and space within these faith traditions, is teased out. Where Judeo-Christian-Islamic traditions posit that 'God is neither male nor female' in subtle contrast, Hinduism 'allows God to be visualized and worshipped as male, female and androgynous' and quite significantly, Hindu deities have fluid genders and sexualities (Vanita 2005: 78) which GLBTIQ persons can find hope in.

Within Judeo-Christian traditions, the political, moral and ontological dimensions also coalesce and find full expression in queer theologizing that starts theology from the sacredness of the GLBTIQ person, both the doer and deed, in loving the sinner and the sin. Illustrative of queer theologizing is Asian-American Patrick Cheng's (2010) four-point 'Christological model' (based on the redemptive figure of Christ who was crucified for all) that stands in contrast to the 'traditional legal model' (based on the Biblical 'texts of terror' that proscribe homosexuality) in rethinking sin and God's grace for GLBTIQ persons[21] and Malaysian Joseph N. Goh's 'queer body-sacramentality' of *mak nyahs*, male-to-female transsexuals in Malaysia (2012a) and 'Incarnational Theology' for 'queer Malaysians' (2012b).[22] These queer bodies constitute 'sacred sites' as Goh postulates, as these Muslim *mak nyahs*, in making sense of the stigmatization, harassment and violence which is their lived reality, '[manifest] divine activity in and through their bodies' (2012a: 519). The materiality of their experiences and human agency evinced through reflection and action among these *mak nyahs* which include spiritualizing Islam for themselves become transcendent hence divine. This coheres with the Christian understanding of 'sacramentality' which 'refers to what *God is doing for God's people* throughout their lives and the polyvalent ways in which people consequently *respond* to these divine actions' (Goh 2012a: 514). The intersections of human-divine, material-immaterial, serve also as the basis for Goh's 'Incarnational Theology' (2012b). The fluidity of immanence-transcendence is embodied in the figure of Christ who is 'the Word of God who "became flesh"' and lived among humankind. The incarnation of Christ, that evidences for humanity that 'God is *always* and *continuously* corporeally manifested on earth', affirms the inherent dignity and worth of all human persons, as they are created in God's image (*imago dei*) (2012b: 150).

And with regard to gender and sexuality in Islam, the scholarship of Scott Siraj al-Haqq Kugle is instructive. In *Progressive Muslims*, he starts with the overall faith position that Islam is 'sex-positive' (2003: 192), unlike Christianity and Buddhism which are to some degree sex-negative, in part due to their ascetic traditions (e.g. Catholicism) and valuing of procreative sexuality for lay communities. The sensuous depiction of heavenly bliss, sexual activity made analogous with 'worshipful pleasure', and the embrace of non-procreative sexual acts challenge erotophobia – the fear and disgust of the erotic – that has characterized much of religious thought and practice in effecting the dualism (oppositional and hierarchical differences) of spirit/body aligned with maleness/femaleness. The thesis of 'diversity in creation' (2003: 194) – and by extrapolation, gender and sexual diversity – is especially salient in paving the way for a 'sexuality-sensitive interpretation' of the Qur'an which he duly credits with feminist hermeneutic roots (2003: 194, 203). He fleshes out 'productive ambiguities' (2003: 194) inherent in the Qur'an; e.g. there is no term for either 'gender' or 'sexuality' to enable a more rigorous and just reading of the problematic Lut story (comparable to the Lot story in the Bible) that is often held up by most Islamic jurists as the definitive verse (*surah*) that condemns homosexuality (anal sex) between (presumed homosexual) men.

He advocates for plural '"ways" of reading' notwithstanding the heterosexual norm of the Qur'an and attendant 'masculine prerogative, privilege and patriarchal power' (2003: 202). He critiques the reductionist strategy of 'definition' and 'substitution' used by classical commentators in their interpretation of the Lut story in conflating 'sexual acts of a specific nature with sexual desire of a particular orientation' (2003: 205). Instead, he argues for firstly a 'semantic analysis' of the Qur'an that more faithfully recognizes the 'web of relationships' (e.g. there is a range of meaning for every term that is repeated in different contexts) that are embedded in the 'Speech of Allah' in eschewing a literal and narrow interpretation. Secondly, he calls for a 'thematic analysis' which seeks to identify a single theme and traces its multiple appearance throughout the Qur'an to arrive at a composite meaning or 'inner unity of the Qur'an' (2003: 207–8). He thus arrives at this interpretation of the Lut story: the people of Lut displayed inhumanity – they chased rather than hosted strangers, they robbed rather than fed travellers and they raped rather than cared for the needy – fundamentally because they were profoundly alienated from God (2003: 212). The transgressions of infidelity and inhospitality (ethics of care) rather than sex acts per se account for the narrative tension in the Lut story. As such, the alignment of 'anal sex between two men' as a '*hadd* crime' as the 'legal equivalent of *zina* (adultery between a man and a woman who are not married to each other)' that requires capital punishment (i.e. stoning to death) is acting in bad faith as the Qur'an explicitly lists five *hadd* crimes of which consensual anal sex is not one of them (2003: 216).

In these ways, religion and spirituality become 'the ground of sexual freedom rather than the *justification* for sexual regulation' (Jakobsen and Pellegrini 2004: 16). When religion and spirituality become 'the ground of sexual freedom' it becomes 'compatible with human rights' (ICJ 2007: 26) and 'sexual freedom' and the right to freedom of thought, conscience and religion become mutually constitutive. As such, buying into ascendency claims between secular and sacred discourses becomes counterintuitive. This third and final oppositional standpoint rests on mediating between the absolutism of sexuality rights as universal and the cultural relativism of religious and spiritual discourses. Cultural relativism recognizes the moral validity of all cultures and religions: that there is inherently 'no distinction between a good culture and a bad culture' (Matsuoka 2007: 57) and by extension of logic, no 'good' religion and 'bad' religion or spirituality. Cultural relativism is, however, often positioned as antithetical to the universality of rights in relation to the particularized and varied 'expression, practice and promotion of different opinions, convictions and beliefs with regard to issues of sexual orientation or gender identity' (ICJ 2007: 26). Ensuing reactions range from hating the sinner and the sin to loving the sinner but hating the sin. Sexuality rights as human rights that in turn are positioned as secular, thus universal, are intolerant of 'expression, practice and promotion of different opinions, convictions and beliefs with regard to issues of sexual orientation or gender identity [that is] undertaken in a manner incompatible with human rights' (ICJ 2007: 26).

In order to move beyond the impasse of ascendency claims, it is a breakthrough to revision and practise the hyphenated strategies of universalism–cultural relativism or *critical relativism* (Bong 2006) rather than falling prey to an either/or absolutist hence reductionist stance. 'Critical relativism' offers a reimagining of cultural relativism through critically engaging universalism with particularism, secularism with sacredness and rights with religions. Critical relativism potentially advances rather than impedes the realization of rights as it considers the integrity and mutuality embedded in universalism–particularism, secularism–sacredness and rights–religions discourses and practices. The wisdom in neither valuing universalism without regard for particularity (as it can lead to 'moral imperialism') nor valuing particularity without regard for universalism (as it can lead to 'moral relativism') is similarly practised by Etsuko Matsuoka (2007: 55). Matsuoka's insights stem from her fieldwork experience in procuring informed consent from women in maternity wards in localities as diverse as the UK, Japan, Java and China. Where informed consent is positioned as a universal value in the field of (American) bioethics, as a cultural anthropologist who looks to cultural relativism as foundational to the discipline, the differentiated processes of getting informed consent lead her to reimagine pragmatic ways in eschewing the ascendency claims of universalism and cultural relativism. Cultural relativism, as Matsuoka states, 'does not intend to stop people from pursuing the universal, rather, it is a way of thinking that motivates people to reach a common ground from where different cultures [and religions or spiritualities] can be seen equally within the perspective' (Matsuoka 2007: 62).

Being 'seen equally' is a moral and political imperative to realizing sexuality rights in dialogue with religions or spiritualities as 'the [grounds] of sexual freedom'. The iterative movement from the universal to particularities (in not only tolerating but also according legitimacy to differentiated practices of doing sexuality rights in religions and spiritualities) is in concert with the 'move from particularities to universalities' (Matsuoka 2007: 62). This latter move is compelled by the global ethics of sexuality rights and the universal bodily integrity of GLBTIQ persons as enshrined in both secular and sacred texts. This mediated strategy and radical ethos does not provide easy or quick-fix solutions given the varied understandings and applications of sexuality rights but they are valued as a 'common ground' in moving forward. This 'common ground' is already inhabited by the rights-*and*-faith-based networks for GLBTIQ persons (as discussed in the first section of this chapter). And the extent to which this 'common ground' is and can be inhabited is a continuous negotiation among the sixteen GLBTIQ interviewees in their processes of becoming persons which is the heart of this study.

Fieldwork

The genesis of the research project was the outcome of a response to a call for papers for a 2007 conference themed, 'Re-imagining women, marriage and family life in Asia: A twenty-first century theological challenge' organized by the Ecclesia of Women in Asia, a forum for Catholic feminist women doing theology in the context of Asia which I am a member of. Due to the unexpected generosity of GLBTIQ persons who so readily came forward in response to the call for interviewees particularly in Malaysia that had been posted on GLBTIQ-friendly websites and the kind assistance of friends and gatekeepers such as the Free Community Church (as responses were initially less forthcoming from Singapore), this has metamorphosed into a larger study given the rich qualitative data generated. The interviews commenced in 2007 and 2008 following approval from the Monash University Human Research Ethics Committee (MUHREC).[23]

Over the intervening years since the first interviews were conducted with a sample size of thirty persons in same-sex partnerships (twenty-two from Malaysia and eight from Singapore), sixteen narratives (twelve from Malaysia and four from Singapore) have been accorded epistemic privilege and feature in this book for the following reasons. Firstly, these sixteen voluntarily desire to remain a part of the protracted book project. Two interviewees have sadly since passed away and several withdrew or eschewed contact for fear of being identified ironically with the reality of the publication of their narratives. Secondly, the ethics in sustaining rapport and trustworthiness among the sixteen (mainly through social media platforms, e.g. Facebook, Instagram, email) invests their narratives of becoming with an integrity and authenticity that lie beyond a one-off formal interview in embedding the everyday realities of what it means to live out one's sexuality and religiosity or spirituality. Formal follow-up interviews were conducted in 2019 with those whose material realities had radically shifted, notably, with a Singapore-based Hindu lesbian–intersex–mystic who has become a priest and a Malaysian trans man; once a Buddhist, now a Muslim; once a lesbian woman, now a married man who has fully transitioned.

The mutual privilege – with everyone, interviewer and interviewees alike, being a decade older – of witnessing joys, sorrows and ambivalences of the messy business of living and living abundantly is profoundly cherished. These include but are not limited to the death of loved ones, infirmities leading to loss of mobility, the still closeted relationships to families, the intimate partnerships sustained through the years, the breakups (where partners were co-interviewed for this study), the growing up of offspring from children to teens and young adults, the flourishing of home businesses, personal developments (e.g. completion or starting of postgraduate degrees, job promotions), the prevailing disenchantment with the state, the lessening of faith as well as deepening of old and new faiths.

The messy business of living resonates with the above discussion on the parallelism between managing (or rather regulating) gender and sexual diversity, and ethnic and religious diversity in Malaysia and Singapore, that in turn renders researching on GLBTIQ persons, particularly those in same-sex partnerships and religion as highly 'sensitive topics'. A 'sensitive topic' is defined as '*one that potentially poses for those involved a substantial threat, the emergence of which renders problematic for the researcher and/or researched the collection, holding, and/or dissemination of research data [sic]*' (Renzetti and Lee 1993: 5). It encompasses research which intrudes into the private sphere or delves into some deeply personal experience, where the study concerns deviance and control, where it is likely to impinge on the vested interests of the powerful or evoke the exercise of coercion (which does not preclude bodily harm), and where it deals with 'things sacred to those being studied that they do not wish profaned' (Renzetti and Lee 1993: 6).

Research data was obtained by in-depth, semi-structured and audio-recorded interviews with persons identifying as GLBTIQ based in Malaysia and Singapore. Interviews in Malaysia were conducted from February to May 2007 and those in Singapore in February 2008. Snowball sampling commenced in January 2007 with calls for interviewees posted in e-networks for gay, lesbian, bisexual, transsexual and transgender persons and thirty GLBTIQ persons responded; twenty-two from Malaysia and eight from Singapore. Although the initial criteria for sampling and selection of interviewees were that they should be in same-sex partnerships, I also interviewed persons who came forward but were then single. And interviewees who were involved at the time of the interview were subsequently single. The criteria for exclusion were those who identify as heterosexual and below twenty-one years of age who were either non-Asian or not residing in Malaysia and Singapore were excluded because the sociopolitical milieu of these postcolonial nation-states, as shown, presents unique challenges to negotiating what it means on an everyday reality to fully live out one's sexuality and religiosity or spirituality in public and private spaces.

The understanding of identities and partnerships in this study are pivotal to the processes of becoming: becoming Asian, becoming postcolonial and becoming sexually religious or spiritual and religiously or spiritually sexual which culminate in becoming queer persons in the Butlerian sense of 'gender performativity' (Butler 1990). 'Queer', as Jagose (1996: 131) notes, 'is always an identity under construction: a site of permanent becoming.' In queering the field (Rooke 2010; Schippert 2011), this study attempts to tease out the tensions between the valence and limits of identity politics (i.e. self-identifying as "G" or "L" or "B" or "T" or "I" or "Q" is a prerequisite to belonging). The study also seeks to investigate the resonance of queer theory for the study of GLBTIQ persons who continue to negotiate what it means to become sexually religious or spiritual and religiously or spiritually sexual in an Asian context. The fluidity of becoming is contingent on how identities are 'multiple, contradictory, fragmented, incoherent, disciplinary, disunified, unstable, fluid' (Gamson 2000: 356). Their bodies, sexualities and lived realities are sites of contestation where the tensions between their sexualities and religions or spiritualities intersect and are played out in negotiating ways to inhabit the 'common ground' as Matsuoka (2007) puts it.

As such, the definition of partnership or union in this study is fluid, as it is left to the interpretation of interviewees themselves. It is not based on the number of years together, not on whether the union has been solemnized or legalized, or if the partners have any intention to marry or have children. It is a partnership if the partners themselves deem it to be one. Being previously or currently involved in opposite-sex relationships did not disqualify an interviewee who self-identifies as a GLBTIQ person. This in part constitutes ethics in researching as interviewees participate in meaning-making as stakeholders in their respective partnerships.

Ethics in researching also involved member checking where interviewees were given the opportunity to vet the interviews which I had personally transcribed in the interest of confidentiality and use of pseudonyms which were conceived by interviewees themselves.

The final sample of sixteen interviewees today bears some heterogeneity in terms of the diversity of ethnicity and religiosity or spirituality that is however not reflective of the demographics of Malaysia (as Malays are notably absent having withdrawn from the book project). They consist of eleven Chinese Christians comprising six gay-identifying men (AY, CK, Jimmy, Peter from Malaysia and Dave and Joe from Singapore) and five lesbian women (Alexis, Andy, Janic who also identifies as a Tibetan Buddhist, and Ling Jackie from Malaysia and J from Singapore); two Chinese Buddhists comprising one gay man (Kun) and one bisexual woman (Stephanie, whose partner is Janic); one Chinese nonbeliever comprising a lesbian woman (Juuk); one Chinese Buddhist then, now Muslim female-to-male transgender person or trans man (Adam); and one Indian–Hindu mystic now a priest who is an intersex lesbian (Jagadiswari). Among the sixteen individuals are two parents (Peter and Stephanie with children from previous heterosexual marriages). Ages of interviewees today range from late thirties to fifty-something-year-old persons within a largely lower- to middle-income bracket.

In relation to the dimension of religion or spirituality, GLBTIQ persons were asked: (a) how do you experience your partnership in relation to your religiosity or spirituality and (b) how do you experience your religiosity or spirituality in relation to your relationship. The data comprising interview transcripts was analysed, essentially, coded, through ATLAS.ti (version 4.2) which is a Computer-assisted Qualitative Data Analysis Software (CAQDAS), with reference to the 'hypothesis', a provisional relationship between two or three categories, in this instance, religion or spirituality and sexuality. I used a Constructivist Grounded Theory Methodology (Charmaz 2000, 2006),[24] essentially, an inductive methodology, to yield fecund interpretive insights that are grounded in and emerge from the materiality of lived experiences that are offered in this book.

Outline of the book

The interior or heart of the book comprises the next eight chapters which are intended to reflect the broad spectrum of queer strategies emerging from participants' narratives of becoming. These narratives encompass becoming Asian, becoming postcolonial, becoming sexually religious or spiritual and religiously or spiritually sexual, and becoming persons. The layout of these chapters is intended neither to be linear nor to privilege any queer strategy above the other. These queer strategies become responses to the incommensurability or incompatibility of what it means to be a GLBTIQ person who identifies as Muslim, Christian, Buddhist, Hindu, even atheist; the ambivalence of becoming that is an everyday lived reality of facing condemnation, taboo or dealing with guilt, shame and pain; and the commensurability and compatibility of loving the 'sinner' and the 'sin' as healing and transformative praxis in finding reconciliation, affirmation and peace.

As such, Chapter 2, 'Managing Incompatibility and Exclusivity', framed by the worldview of 'incommensurability', presents and discusses narratives of GLBTIQs as self-identified Muslims, Christians, Hindu, Buddhists who remain conflicted or whose sexuality is not affirmed by their selves, families and/or faith communities. Managing the tension inherent in one's relational ties with one's self and others is manifest in the following ways: believing that sexuality and spirituality are incompatible and mutually exclusive (locked in an either/or binary) with queer strategies that include compartmentalizing sexuality and spirituality and putting aside either sexuality or spirituality.

Chapter 3, 'Adopting Celibacy', challenges the assumption that doing celibacy either divests one of agency or invests one with agency. The narratives discussed in this section flesh out the ambivalence inherent in one's adoption of or attempt to adopt celibacy. Celibacy as understood and practised by interviewees in this study is equated with the most extreme form of suppressing sexual desire; is equated with abstinence from sexual pleasure due to religious observances; adheres to, yet redefines, sexual orientation; and unsettles the religious injunction to love the sinner but not the sin.

In Chapter 4, 'Facing Condemnation and Taboo', narratives of GLBTIQ persons show how feeling conflicted, depressed, guilty and pain leads some to bargaining (with God), denying their selves, being intolerant of, condemning and demonizing their sexuality, or, at best, pre-empting coming outs as sexualities remains a taboo subject. These queer strategies are a response to the hardening of boundaries between genders and sexualities that matter and those that deserve condemnation. GLBTIQ persons through these queer strategies show how mutable and contestable these boundaries are.

The narratives discussed in Chapter 5, 'Dealing with Guilt, Shame and Pain', show how the experience of guilt is multifaceted, arising from 'sex guilt', religious guilt, relational and familial guilt. In relation to the binary of heterosexuality/ homosexuality where the former is made normal and good whilst the latter is made deviant and sinful, guilt becomes an effect of acquiescing with this binary. Guilt also becomes an effect of resisting this binary. The strategy of doing guilt thus serves as both acts of acquiescence and resistance.

In Chapter 6, 'Negotiating Ambivalence', narratives of in-betweenness that exemplify ambivalence are discussed: denying the self and not denying the self, lying to the self and not lying the self, accepting what is and is not sexual misconduct, desiring and not desiring to serve one's faith community fully, and desiring and not desiring one's partner to be Christian. *Strategic ambivalence* becomes a queer strategy in managing the tension between one's private moral codes that are not often in sync with public moral codes. In doing so, GLBTIQ persons show how the boundary between the heterosexual self and non-heterosexual other is a porous one.

Chapter 7, 'Queering Time', is an exposition on how processes of becoming, as an everyday lived reality of GLBTIQ persons, are not only framed within a linearity of time but also one that is iterative and, for some, cyclical. The complexity and circularity of this process inadvertently reconfigure the spatiality of the 'closet'. So coming in-out of the 'closet' is performed not only as a singular, one-off and distinctive act but one that is often repetitive, multiple and ambivalent. Queer temporality is embodied through their recognizing this process as a journey, coming to terms with their differences from the mainstream, educating others and being educated, seeking psychiatric and/ or spiritual counselling and making sense of one's sexuality in religion or spirituality and experiencing peace.

In Chapter 8, 'Managing Compatibility and Inclusivity', within the oppositional standpoints of commensurability and inclusivity, the narratives of GLBTIQ persons who have in some way reconciled their sexuality and religion or spirituality are discussed. Such narratives of commensurability and inclusivity between becoming GLBTIQ and religious or spiritual find expression in the various queer strategies which include committing their relationships or sexuality to God or faith, believing that they are created by God or a deity and therefore no longer feel guilty in being gay, demystifying sexuality myths, having a mindset change, realizing that sexuality and spirituality are mutually constitutive, questioning and challenging religious interpretation, and essentially, reconciling sexuality and spirituality.

Chapter 9, 'Finding Reconciliation and Affirmation', is framed by oppositional standpoints of commensurability and inclusivity. Commensurate with such standpoints is the notion of 'gender performativity' (Butler 1990) that non-heteronormative genders and sexualities can and do exist, as embodied in the narratives of GLBTIQ persons from the Free Community Church in Singapore wherein the political, moral and ontological dimensions coalesce and find fuller expression in queer theologizing that starts theology from the sacredness of the GLBTIQ person, both the doer and deed, in loving the sinner and the sin.

The concluding chapter, 'Conclusion: Becoming and Belonging', reviews the main insights of previous chapters within the larger framework of becoming, belonging and inclusivity for GLBTIQ persons as citizens within narratives of becoming Asian, postcolonial, religiously sexual and sexually religious, and becoming persons.

2

Managing incompatibility and exclusivity

Can the impasse of competing discourses be overcome? Can one become queer *and* religious? The narratives highlighted in this chapter resonate with Boellstorff's concept of 'incommensurability': that being religious and GLBTIQ is ontologically 'ungrammatical' or 'unintelligible' (2005a: 575). State rhetoric and practices that maintain such discursive strategies erase or negate GLBTIQ sexualities through according legitimacy only to heteronomative sexuality as this is procreative in populating and building the postcolonial nation-states of Malaysia and Singapore. The non-heteronormative person consequently is not the subject of the production of the 'species body' in Foucauldian terms as these bodies and sexualities, discursively, do not and cannot exist. They cannot be regulated as they lie outside the 'heterosexual matrix' – that 'grid of cultural intelligibility through which bodies, genders and desires are naturalized' (Butler 1990: 151). This matrix premised in part through technologies of the self, such as the 'heterosexual contract' and 'compulsory heterosexuality' (e.g. Section 377 in Malaysia and 377a in Singapore) render these bodies as incoherent, unstable and unintelligible. To illustrate, Malaysia's Tourism Minister at a recent trade fair in Berlin, Germany, caused a stir when he remarked that 'I don't think we have anything like that (referring to "gays") in our country' and proceeded to evade the question on whether or not Malaysia is a safe destination for 'homosexuals and Jews' (The Straits Times 2019).

The narrative tension afforded here shows how interviewees struggle to overcome the impasse of sexuality rights as adopted in the Yogyakarta Principles and YP+10 in realizing their sexual orientation, gender identity, gender expression and sex characteristics (SOGIESC) – without the full commitment of states' obligations honouring these principles – and religious orthodoxy, transmitted through mainstream and traditional exegesis of proscriptive Qur'anic and Biblical verses on non-heteronormative sexualities. The narratives of GLBTIQ persons, as self-identified Muslims, Christians, Hindu, Buddhists who remain conflicted or whose sexuality is not affirmed by their selves, families and/or faith communities, are presented and discussed. Managing the tension inherent in one's relational ties with one's self and others is manifest in the following ways: believing that sexuality and spirituality are incompatible and mutually exclusive (locked in an either/or binary) with coping mechanisms that include compartmentalizing sexuality and spirituality and putting aside either sexuality or spirituality. The coping strategies of others in the attempt to reconcile their sexualities and spiritualities compel them to confess, repent, change and essentially unlearn or surrender their sexuality.

Believing that sexuality and spirituality are incompatible

In this section, the narratives of Juuk, CK and Joe are highlighted. Juuk is 49, a company director, lectures business degree courses part-time, is a doctoral candidate and is in a committed relationship. She is also founder of a website that is GLBTIQ-friendly, whose eclectic spirituality includes dealing in tarot cards as a former means of making a living. She says:

> I think personally I find that homosexuality in the religious view is very much like, um, a Methodist marrying a Buddhist. It was a no-no or a Chinese marrying a Malay or Indian in that sense. So the non-acceptance from family members and your mutual friends whom you grew up with, they will look at you like wow, you're a Methodist now you're going to marry a what, Catholic? Because Catholics, non-Catholic, they even have different views on Christianity so, because I went to this church who thinks that Catholics are bad [laughs]. So that's why I begin to question the fact that, um, if God is good, religion is good…there shouldn't even be thoughts of comparing one denomination to another. [9:12 (124:137)][1]

Within the plural society of Malaysia that is multiethnic (comprising Malays, Chinese, Indians, mixed, indigenous, and so on), multicultural and multireligious (comprising Muslims, Christians, Buddhists, Hindus, indigenous, and so on), Juuk rehearses societal biases which are founded on differences, for instance, the 'different views on Christianity' that Catholics and non-Catholics have. She had perceived this from her exposure to Christianity when she was in high school as she mentions elsewhere in the interview. She points out the 'non-acceptance from family members and your mutual friends whom you grew up with', that is a reaction to interethnic, intercultural and inter-religious unions such as 'a Methodist marrying a Buddhist' or 'a Chinese marrying a Malay or Indian' which is discouraged, 'a no-no'. And she interestingly aligns this with the intolerance of 'homosexuality in the religious view'. Where Catholics 'are bad', it is inferred through the parallelism drawn by Juuk that homosexuals are likewise condemned as 'bad' because they are essentially 'different'. Homosexuality thus becomes incompatible with 'the religious view'.

Where Juuk's '[beginning] to question' (further explored in Chapter 9) starts to challenge the ethnic, cultural and religious divisions intimated above and, by extension, the incompatibility of 'homosexuality in the religious view', 41-year-old CK, who is an Operation Program Manager for a semiconductor firm, questions what it means to be Christian and gay. He says:

> I think in a way, it's true that when you are in your relationship, it's hard to witness to others about God when first of all, your walk with God is not right you know. And in terms of like sharing my faith with other non-Christians, maybe in front you can share to them you're a caring person, you're a loving person. And maybe you can bring them to church or what. But somehow, someday when they know that you're gay, I don't know what they will think about me as a Christian … am I hypocrite because I try to share God you know, everything about God. But behind I'm a gay that [is] living with, I mean having a relationship with another man. So [it] is like what I preach and what I practise is not right. So it's hard to share God, to share my faith with others. [17:72 (802:812)]

CK remains tormented by his yearning to 'witness to others about God' and his compromised integrity as a Christian, as he is 'having a relationship with another man'. That '[his] walk with God is not right' attests to his taught belief – that 'it's true' – one's queer sexuality is incompatible with one's religiosity or spirituality. The duplicity of being a 'caring person', 'a loving person' but gay and the fear of being exposed 'somehow, someday' by 'non-Christians' whom he is proselytizing to, renders him to label himself a 'hypocrite because I try to share … everything about God. But *behind* I'm a gay' (emphasis mine). The disjunction between '[preaching]' and '[practising]' accentuates the hypocrisy that torments CK. And the reiteration of 'not right' with regard to his sexuality and spirituality as Christian and gay marks the disjunction between his sexuality and spirituality. He subsequently adds that he has '[stopped] serving in church' as he does not think that he is 'suitable' [17:73 (813:823)]. CK's desire to serve the church fully as 'a leader for the youth' as he was invited to do so is similarly constrained by his being 'a gay man having a relationship with a gay'. The realization of his personhood as 'a loving person' is thwarted as loving God, in desiring to make right his 'walk with God', and loving men are in his view incompatible. CK cannot love God fully and freely as he is 'a gay' and he cannot love men fully and freely as he is Christian.

CK's conflict is echoed by Joe, who is in his early forties, in marketing and single. He recounts coming out to 'two pastors [whom he] was closest to' and 'then I just stepped down from ministry because I couldn't reconcile it at all' [27:4 (46:53)]. For Joe, like CK, the incompatibility of being Christian and gay, despite efforts to 'reconcile it', is apparent. He adds: 'So even after I stopped attending church in a formal way … in my heart I still felt that I was, um, Christian as in I was God's child but I just had problems. I just had questions that I couldn't reconcile at that point in time. So I stopped attending, yeah' [27:6 (61:67)]. Joe's withdrawal is two-fold: he had 'stepped down from ministry' and 'stopped attending church in a formal way'. The ambivalence of knowing and not knowing is marked. On the one hand, 'in [his] heart', Joe self-identifies as a 'Christian' as he is created in God's image, as 'God's child' (this becomes the basis of reconciling one's sexuality and spirituality as discussed in Chapter 9). On the other hand, he pre-empts the disavowal of his self by his faith community by withdrawing from them, as he questions how it is possible to be 'God's child … [with] problems (in being gay)'. The religious basis for self-censure coheres with a secular base where one could equally ask, how is it possible to be Singapore's son given the circular debate of repealing or not Section 377a that even unenforced carries the accusatory note of homosexuals as lesser men in engaging in sexual practices that are non-procreative?

As he adds with certainty elsewhere: 'I thought it (homosexuality) was wrong … I'm not living a life that's compatible with someone that is in ministry' [27:27 (299:306)]. That he had internalized the naturalization of heterosexuality and concomitantly, the de-naturalization of homosexuality (Dyer 1997), as accentuated by Christian teachings (imbibed through his theological training), is evident when he says that 'even the attraction, even if I didn't act on it, I felt it was already such a part of me that … it wouldn't be possible for me to serve effectively' [27:28 (307:315)]. Joe forecloses the pastoral care extended to GLBTIQ persons where the church is exhorted to love the sinner but not the sin. In believing that his personhood, as 'God's child', is essentially yet problematically flawed on account of his 'attraction (to men as a man) even if [he] didn't act on it', he believes that he has already sinned. The suppression of his personhood is two-fold: he cannot serve God fully as he is gay and he cannot love men freely as he is Christian albeit one who has not only withdrawn from ministry but also his (former mainstream) church.

Joe is a member of the Free Community Church in Singapore which is a GLBTIQ-friendly church and co-leads Living Water, an outreach programme of the FCC which aims to facilitate a reconciliation of one's sexuality and spirituality. These avenues are examples of sexual and gender minorities-affirming (SGM) religious denominations along with 'SGM-affirming religious [youth] leaders' such as Joe (Newman et al. 2018: 541) that are the antithesis of religiously based sexual prejudice that excuses by endorsing homophobic bullying evident in other denominations that will be explored in Chapter 4 in relation to sexual reorientation or conversion therapy. Although his sexuality-spirituality journey of reconciliation is one of the key narratives that are highlighted in Chapter 9, here, Joe recounts his early conflicts. As he says:

> So I just had problems, I'm reconciling it with an idea that I had inside that it's possible to actually love someone, be in a relationship that could edify both people [*clears throat*]. And more importantly, that … in your relationship you could worship and you could glorify God. And you could please the heart of God. And you could, by your relationship, also edify the church which means the full integration with faith. And I couldn't quite understand it. I mean it took me a long time to even be able to, um, verbalize all these, yeah. So that was what I couldn't reconcile with. [27:9 (94:102)]

Joe's not being able to 'reconcile' his homosexuality and Christian faith is a recurrent refrain in his journey of becoming Christian *and* gay. Knowing 'in [his] heart' that such a reconciliation is possible – to firstly 'be in a relationship that could edify both people … [secondly] glorify God … [and thirdly] edify the church' – sustained Joe's insistent aspiration and struggle towards 'full integration (of his sexuality) with (his) faith'. The abundant life[2] echoes through his envisioning the (im)possibility of '[loving] someone (a man as a man)' and '[pleasing] the heart of God'. That 'it took [him] a long time to even be able to, um, verbalize all these' – the compatibility of queer sexualities and spirituality – and 'understand it' marks his personal journey of denaturalizing heterosexuality and naturalizing homosexuality as a self-identified and committed Christian whose yearning to serve God and church finds full expression with the FCC years later.

For Juuk who now embraces an eclectic spirituality, the incompatibility of 'homosexuality in the religious view' is overcome by her core belief that 'if God is good, religion is good … there shouldn't even be thoughts of comparing one denomination to another'. In doing so, she challenges the parallelism drawn between the 'non-acceptance' of homosexuality 'in the religious view' and the ethnic, cultural and religious divisions that is an effect of managing pluralism in Malaysia. CK and Joe, gay men in their early forties, wrestle with the incompatibility of their sexuality and Christian faith and manage the existential anguish of 'am I hypocrite' by withdrawing from their faith communities and church ministries despite their deep yearning to more fully serve God and community. One either loves God or men, not both God and men.

Believing that sexuality and spirituality are mutually exclusive

The narratives in this section are an extension of believing that sexuality and spirituality are incompatible and therefore mutually exclusive, locked in an either/or binary. Adherence to the 'heterosexual matrix' of 'sex/gender/desire' as conceptualized by the feminist-postmodernist theorist, Judith Butler (1990), and compounded by the 'religious view' as Juuk puts it in the previous section, dictates that one born a man ought to be gendered masculine and desirous of a woman or one born a woman, ought to be gendered feminine and desirous of a man. So queer sexualities embodied in being born a man, gendered masculine or feminine and desirous of a man or being born a woman, gendered masculine or feminine and desirous of a woman, become 'aberrations' from heteronormativity (heterosexuality as the sanctioned norm). These queer sexualities destabilize 'sex/gender/desire' contained within the 'heterosexual matrix' as they proliferate ways of being and becoming. The containment of such possibilities and fluidity of being and becoming is contained in these narratives to follow: Andy, Janic, Jimmy, CK, J and Jagadiswari.

Andy, who is almost fifty, an educator and attached, similarly debunks the equation of homosexuality with being 'un-Christian-like' [2:31 (365:373)]. She says: 'So if people ask me, how can you be both? Well, I'm very baffled by that question because to me it's like, should it be a question you know [*laughs*].' It's just like in those days, people ask you, '"You're black. How can you go to church?" [*both laugh*] You know, it's as ridiculous as that.' The recurrent refrain of 'how can you be both' levelled at Andy who is invested in varying degrees in her church ministry, is revelatory of societal compulsion to adhere to the 'heterosexual matrix' in order for 'bodies to make sense' (Butler 1990: 151). The incongruity of '[being] both' Christian and gay or Christian and 'black' as Andy illustrates is not at all 'ridiculous' to many as these bodies '[do not] make sense': they fall out of the ordering of sex/gender/desire.

Andy's parallelism drawn between being a gay Christian and black Christian interestingly resonates with how 'race' is understood not only as a construct, as gender is, but also and more insidiously how 'race' is heterosexualized (Dyer 1997). She thus infers that the hyphenated identities of a black-gay-Christian would be doubly marginalized on account of his/her 'race' and sexuality, as a polluting body within heteronormativity. Andy's 'baffled' retort of 'should it be a question' destabilizes the binaries of white/black, normal/deviant and straight/gay, as she calls to question the privileging of the first terms over the second terms. Through embodying such a 'polluting' body that does not make heteronormative sense, she subverts heterosexism (the discrimination of those who do not comply with heteronormativity) in firmly identifying as Christian and gay, as she adds that 'if people ask me what faith I'm in, I don't think twice, I'll just tell them'.

Where Andy encounters those who espouse the 'how can you be both' mindset – believing that gay sexuality and religiosity or spirituality are mutually exclusive – Jagadiswari, a 45-year-old Hindu priest, today marks out the incongruity of not only sexuality and spirituality but also sexuality and culture as a minority-within-a-minority – queer and Indian in Chinese-dominated and heterosexualized Singapore. As she says: 'I'm a bit of an oddity because most Indian chicks give up their faith ... So it's a case of whether you want to live with the faithness [*sic*] of it all or you want to leave your Indian-ness and a lot of them leave their Indian-ness' [25:15 (97:105)]. As an 'Indian [chick]' whose sexuality is not easily contained by labels such as 'lesbian' even 'bisexual', her personhood is empowered by her not opting for either her 'faithness' or her 'Indian-ness'. In fact, like Andy who challenges heteronormativity by self-identifying as Christian and lesbian, Jagadiswari says: 'And I irritate them because I stay there and I go ... "There's a lot more here [*coughs*] that we can work with you know"'. Jagadiswari sees alternatives to being and becoming – that 'There's a lot more here [*coughs*] that we can work with' – that many resist. As she adds, 'So, it's really sad' how many are compelled to choose either their sexuality and/or their spiritual and/or cultural identities.

That 'it's really sad' how many impose the mutual exclusivity of a gay sexuality and spirituality on GLBTIQ persons is vehemently pointed out by Janic, J, Jimmy and CK. Those 'conflicting years' of believing that one has to choose between one's sexuality and spirituality have also been experienced by Janic, J, Jimmy and CK. According to Janic who is a 46-year-old and single (as her partner passed on), who moved back to her hometown and is currently rebuilding her life and career, she did not 'despise' Christianity, as she says that 'when I was going through that period of time thinking the more I study, the more I understand, the more faith I have in God, the more willingness I have in God to be who I am supposed to be, the other part of me will become lesser and lesser' [7:106 (1385:1395)]. The 'the other part of [her]' that she refers to, a woman attracted to women, which, in being suppressed by 'who [she is] supposed to be', a woman attracted to men, is intended to diminish or become 'lesser and lesser'. The mutual exclusivity of her sexuality and spirituality is apparent: as Janic delved deeper into studying Christianity, she '[shelved] that part of [her]' [7:105 (1369:1384)], as she says elsewhere. Although she did not 'despise' Christianity but submitting her sexuality to God in suppressing it 'can be quite painful', she admits.

In contrast, J chose to deny God, as she says:

> And then after that, going to a Methodist college in Junior college (JC) and all that, so it was very real to me the issue of how my sexuality conflicted with my relationship with God. And there were many times when it affected my relationship with my girlfriends. So because, I couldn't, um, like we broke and patch and broke and patch because I was always trying to be straight because the guilt was just terrible. And so, it was either I drift away from God, so that it's easier or I just don't be with women. But I tried being with a guy before, for like a month in JC, because of peer pressure and because I wanted to be straight in terms of you know, for religion. But it didn't work out. And I knew then that never, never will I be able to be with a guy. So, um, what happened was, I decided that OK, the only way was to just not be close to God. And I drifted away for quite a number of years, like I did go to church but that was about it. You can just go to church without feeling anything. [23:16 (207:221)]

J, a 36-year-old, single banker in Singapore who likes to travel, articulates an experience of 'guilt [that] was just terrible' that led her to adopting various coping strategies. From 'always trying to be straight' with the disruptive effect of 'broke and patch and broke and patch' in her relationships with her girlfriends, she 'tried being with a guy' for a month, in part, 'because of peer pressure' but largely, because she 'wanted to be straight … for religion'. Dating that guy is not only an effect of passing as straight but also makes visible the gender work involved in becoming straight. In that regard, the repetitive acts of 'always trying to be straight' – as 'sustained social performances' – cohere with Butler's concept of 'gender performativity':

> That gender reality is created through sustained social performances means that the very notions of an essential sex and a true or abiding masculinity or femininity are also constituted as part of the strategy that conceals gender's performative character and the performative possibilities for proliferating gender configurations outside the restricting frames of masculinist domination and compulsory heterosexuality. (1990: 141)

Although J is wrecked by the 'guilt [that] was just terrible' she inadvertently disrupts the naturalization of categories of sex/gender/desire in 'proliferating gender configurations outside...compulsory heterosexuality' in not desiring men but rather desiring women as a woman. The self-imposed exorcism (a conversion therapy of sorts) of that 'unnatural' desire through 'always trying to be straight' as an everyday reality reveals 'gender's performative character' – there is nothing natural about becoming heterosexual. The glimpse of subversive potential in un-concealing how heteronormativity becomes normative leads to J's emphatic refusal to 'be straight', articulated in her reiteration of 'never' in 'And I knew then that never, never will I be able to be with a guy' and led to her deciding that 'the only way was to just not be close to God'. She thereby manifests a de-ritualization of becoming straight, for God.

Locked in the either 'be close to God' or 'be close to [women]' binary, J chose the latter, with the painful effect of '[drifting] away' from God and in '[going] to church without feeling anything', essentially, numbing herself in '[her] relationship with God'. J manages the 'guilt' in being both Christian and lesbian by choosing one over the other: 'It was either I drift away from God, so that it's easier or I just don't be with women.' That 'it's [not] easier' is evident in the pain and 'guilt' that persists in choosing to 'be with women' rather than to 'be with [God]'. Years later upon discovering LUSH (Lesbians United for Self Help) and consequently facilitating its therapeutic sessions, J's healing begins as within that 'very secure kind of environment where you can share', she discovers that 'there are a lot of people out there who have the same idea that you have; that you know, being gay and being Christian is wrong' [23:25 (257:269)]. In doing so, she begins to unlearn that 'being gay and being Christian is [not] wrong'. Like Joe, J finds self-affirmation through 'SGM-affirming religious denominations' like the FCC and is herself a 'SGM-affirming religious [youth] leader' (Newman et al. 2018: 541). The 'religious social ecology' consisting of not only the FCC but also LUSH and Living Water contributes to religious-based intervention strategies of affirming sexual and gender minority youths at individual and microsystem levels. But a complementary reorientation is lacking at the levels of exosystem (involving communities, media) and macrosystem (e.g. other religious denominations, government of Singapore) to better effect change.

Jimmy, who is in his forties and formerly a landscape architect, like J, desires to 'change' but unlike J desires to become straight 'not because of religion' but 'because [of his] family' [15:27 (360:375)]. He says that 'I don't want to disappoint them. They didn't know. And then, they always want me to get married'. On the one hand, there is the option of being accountable to his family as a filial son where he has kept them in the dark about his sexuality, hence their assumption of his heterosexuality and concomitant desire for him 'to get married' to a woman. On the other hand, there is the conflicting option of being accountable to himself as a Christian gay man. He concedes that 'even one time, ah, I thought of getting married' with the combination of 'religion, family, pressure'. For Jimmy, his gay sexuality and Christian faith are mutually incompatible as he deliberated then on whether to 'totally give up [his] homosexuality [or] ... turn straight [*laughs*]'. And his unhappy choices are to either 'to disappoint them (his family)' or 'to disappoint [himself]' in realizing the desires of one and not the other as they are deemed to be incompatible. Jimmy's filial piety to his parents in dealing with the marriage imperative resonates not only with 'Asian values' but also 'coming home', a counter-discourse and practice to the Westernized model of 'coming out'. Traditionally, sons and daughters who have moved to urban spaces make the journey home for festive occasions. For queer sons and daughters, 'coming home' has the added burden of 'reining in and concealing queer desires' and in doing so, they engage in a 'poetics of reticence' (hidden, multilayered meanings) for the sake of family harmony (Huang and Brouwer 2018: 104).

The reiteration of 'change' in J's articulation of 'I wanted to change. Change not because of religion I want to change. I wanted to change also because of my family' [15:27 (360:375)] resonates with CK's conflict. CK attests that 'the only thing that I'm not able to do right now is to carry the cross and deny myself' [17:31 (379:388)]. He lays out his options which are to either 'stay away from this homosexual relationship ... stay away from all this thing' or have 'a right relationship with God'. He admits that 'but right now, I can't (carry the cross) because I can't deny ... the thing that I enjoy, the um, the lust that I'm having'. Where to 'carry the cross' is to 'deny' his sexuality and 'the lust' that he 'enjoy[s]' shows the mutual exclusivity of his sexuality and Christian faith. Conflicted then, he implores God, 'What am I supposed to do?' CK's coping strategy is essentially keeping in abeyance, '[putting] it aside' the decision to opt for either his sexuality or his spirituality, as he says elsewhere: 'I think I put it aside ... I'll go to church, I'll tell God, that, "I need forgiveness and that I'm gay"'. 'And then somehow, I have not made the decision or the choice that either to be with God, fully with God or be with another man' [17:39 (466:473)]. The choice to 'either [be] with God ... or be with another man' is not really a viable and sustainable choice for one who self-identifies as both Christian and gay albeit with misgivings as he feels he is in 'need [of] forgiveness [as he is] gay'.

For Andy, when confronted by those who question 'how can you be both' Christian and lesbian, she has responded by questioning heteronormativity, by drawing a parallelism between heterosexism and racism. In claiming her gay sexuality as a Christian woman, she challenges the binaries of straight/gay, Christian/un-Christian, saved/condemned (or sinful), normal/deviant, and white/black. In the like manner, Jagadiswari's response to the positioning of gay sexuality and spirituality as mutually exclusive is to offer diverse ways of being and becoming rather than to choose between one's sexuality and/or spirituality and/or cultural identity.

For Janic, J, Jimmy and CK, they have internalized the heterosexist imperative of 'how can you be both'. Their lived realities as such bear the living out of those 'conflicting years' in believing that one has to choose between one's sexuality and spirituality as Christians. Their early coping strategies include either loving women as a woman or loving men as a man or loving God as 'it's (seemingly) easier' than the pain and guilt of having to reconcile one's sexuality and spirituality. So for J, it lies in blaming religion and subsequently '[dropping] religion' and '[drifting] away from God'; for Janic, J and Jimmy, it lies in suppressing one's sexuality in adopting celibacy, becoming straight by dating a guy or contemplating marriage 'for religion' and the family, respectively. For CK, it lies in keeping in abeyance the either/or decision by '[putting] it (carrying the cross and denying one's sexuality) aside'. That choosing either/or is not 'easier' is evident from the pain of fragmenting their selves; their personhood is unrealized as one's sexuality and spirituality are incongruent rather than deeply integrated.

The next two sections offer further discussion of narratives based on related strategies to positioning sexuality and spirituality as incompatible and mutually exclusive as discussed, that include putting it aside and compartmentalizing sexuality and spirituality.

Putting it aside or being in limbo

The narrative of CK is foregrounded here. In continuing from CK's narrative highlighted above, it is apparent that the recurrent refrain in his narratives is: 'I put it aside. I put it aside' [17:41 (483:487)]. As he adds in the following exchange:

CK: So seems like right now, I just put God aside you know … I do not want to go through the struggling or the pain by denying myself and follow God like what is … being taught in Bible, what He wants you know and just put away everything and just be with Him.

SAB: Yeah.
 CK: That would be very hard but if I want to do it, I know that God will be
     able to put me through. But seems that I think, I want to stay in my own
     comfort zone. Sorry.
SAB: It's OK. OK. [17:40 (474:483)]

By his own admission, he '[puts] it aside'. Here, he refers neither to the
deferment of choosing between his sexuality nor to spirituality (which is more
apparent in the previous section) but more specifically, the Christian albeit
heterosexist imperative of 'denying [himself] and [following] God like what
is ... being taught in Bible'. His reluctance even refusal to budge from '[his] own
comfort zone' stems from the pleasure derived from '[not] denying [himself]'
in loving men as a man although he is cognizant that this displeases God whom
he believes requires of him to 'just put away everything (deny himself) and just
be with Him'. By stating that 'I do not want to go through the struggling or the
pain by denying myself and follow God', CK infers that it is a greater '[struggle]'
and 'pain' to deny himself. His resistance to the perceived ultimatum imposed
on him – the absolutism of either '[following] God' or following his heart – is
apparent from his choosing not to 'want to do it' although he knows that 'God
will be able to put [him] through' if he chose to deny himself, his sexuality. Hence
his repentant articulation of 'I want to stay in my own comfort zone. Sorry' in
wilfully following his will and not God's will.

He adds:

So as for me right now, I'm still struggling with my faith as a Christian [*pauses*].
So it's painful to be gay and Christian, just that I just try to ignore that feeling.
Putting that aside. And I don't know how long I can, I mean putting all this
aside just cover it ... And until maybe one day it will you know, just talk to me or
confront me, I do not know. [17:70 (788:798)]

As an extension of positioning sexuality and spirituality as incompatible and
therefore mutually exclusive, CK deploys the coping strategy of '[putting] it
aside' which entails both the deferment of and resistance to denying himself
or repressing his sexuality as prescribed by God. CK's keeping in abeyance the
realization of his personhood resonates with others who are 'in limbo' as his
gay sexuality is made invisible through his passing as straight and not proving
false the assumption of heterosexuality by his family and good friends in the
absence of finding support from people like him. CK, in fact, is ironically
'denying [himself]' in deferring and resisting the reconciliation of his sexuality
and spirituality.

Compartmentalizing sexuality and spirituality

In the like manner that '[putting] it aside' is a practice that stems from the belief that a queer sexuality is incompatible with one's religiosity, compartmentalizing sexuality and spirituality affords a further coping mechanism for those who resist or defer making that choice for themselves.

The aspiration towards self-actualization resonates in Janic's embarkation of 'a path to search' for a way to 'bring it together … [where] it didn't jive': her sexuality and spirituality as a Christian missionary then. She says:

> So if you were to say that this is also wrong and you tell me there is a God, then OK, I have to bring these two topics together now. If not, it is totally separate for me. So if you're saying that … God don't create you this way, OK, if I were to bring it together, then it didn't jive. It didn't jive for years and years and years. But yet, these two existed. It's real to me at the same time. So I went on a path to search you know, if there is, to prove one first by not focusing on the other. So if God is real, that's number one first you know. So that's why I threw myself into the study of Christianity and to see the works and the miracles of Christianity. Then I don't have any doubt in those areas. [7:85 (1100:1115)]

Janic's anguish lies in the incompatibility of her sexuality and religiosity, as impressed on her by others who 'say' it is so. As she rationalizes, firstly, if her sexuality 'is also wrong', then how it is possible that 'God [created me] this way'; and secondly, the incompatibility would not arise if she did not believe that 'there is a God'. So being a lesbian and Christian compels her to 'bring these two topics together now' where if she were one and not the other, it is a nonissue; 'it is totally separate for me' and compartmentalizing them would, as inferred, 'jive'. But as a lesbian and Christian, her torment in '[bringing] it together' is apparent: 'It didn't jive for years and years and years'. Her embodiment of a 'wrong' sexuality and her belief that 'God [created her] this way' lead her to acknowledge that 'these two existed. It's real to me'. As such, compartmentalizing both is unsustainable for Janic.

This agonizing reality precipitated her going 'on a path to search', becoming celibate that is a function of compartmentalizing her sexuality and spirituality (discussed in depth in the next chapter), in a bid 'to prove one first by not focusing on the other'. Her '[throwing herself] into the study of Christianity' resonates with others who bury themselves in God. What ensues is a seven-year vow of celibacy [7:82 (1061:1072)] and another 'four … years before I totally felt at peace, totally at peace' [7:92 (1186:1200)] in emerging from celibacy which is emblematic of her compartmentalizing her sexuality and spirituality: '[proving]' the latter is contingent on 'not focusing' on the former.

For Alexis who is in her late thirties and a drummer, she says that 'I've never [tried] to link, or [tried] to put this two together. Maybe I have tried but it's not something I like to do. So I obviously, just put it aside. I don't think about it' [10:106 (1578:1598)]. The effects of compartmentalizing, of not '[trying] to link, or [trying] to put this two together' work for her as attempting to reconcile both is, as she has come to realize, 'not something I like to do' given the reality that there are no easy answers. In the like manner, CK reiterates the axiom of '[putting] God aside' [17:40 (474:483)] (as discussed in the previous section). That sexuality and spirituality are non-reconciliatory stems from the absolutism, as CK believes, of 'He wants you [to] just put away everything and just be with Him'. The effects of compartmentalizing both are ambivalent for CK. On the one hand, self-defeatism seems apparent in his articulation of 'I do not want to go through the struggling or the pain by denying myself and follow God'. On the other hand, self-indulgence also seems apparent as he apologetically concedes that 'I want to stay in my own comfort zone. Sorry'.

Janic's narrative shows an eventual departure, over time, from compartmentalizing sexuality and spirituality which in retrospect had been a means to the end of self-actualization where they have come to recognize that sexuality and spirituality are mutually constitutive. However, for Alexis and CK, they are still caught up in compartmentalizing their sexuality and spirituality by '[putting] it aside'. In their narratives, 'it' refers essentially to the 'struggling or the pain' of '[trying] to put this two together' in the hope of resolving this inherent incompatibility in particular and spiritual impasse in general. An ambivalent sense of self-alienation and self-fulfilment prevails where Alexis '[doesn't] think about it' and CK '[wants] to stay in [his] own comfort zone'. Compartmentalizing sexuality and spirituality becomes as such, an end in itself.

An adjunct of 'incommensurability' of becoming queer and religious is the standpoint of incompatibility between the discourses of sexuality rights and proscriptive religious discourses that are often used to position heteronormativity at the centre and non-heteronormativity at the periphery. The narratives here have yet to begin queering Christianity, disrupting the sexual ethics of gender complementarity that is premised on the naturalness and rightness of male/ female, masculine/feminine who desire the opposite sex. It is little wonder that GLBTIQ persons are deeply conflicted in private spaces given their systemic marginalization at public spaces. At the International Women's Day celebration in Kuala Lumpur, Malaysia, when the LGBT community marched alongside women for 'a dignified minimum wage, a ban on child marriage (within the Muslim and indigenous communities), and an end to patriarchy and violence based on gender and sexual orientation', they were accused by Muslim conservative parties of '[misusing] democratic space' (Reuters 2019). The road to gender justice for queer persons is a long and hard one and a longer and harder one for queer and religious persons.

Adopting celibacy

Does celibacy divest or invest one with agency? The narratives discussed in this section avoid neat answers to this question and point instead to the ambivalence inherent in one's adoption of or attempt to adopt celibacy. On the one hand, celibacy to most, when taken as an expression of repressing one's sexuality, divests one of agency as it, among other reasons, curtails one's full enjoyment of the breadth of sexuality rights. Sexuality rights include the right to participate in sexual activity, the right to pleasure, the right to sexual (and reproductive) self-determination, the right to self-definition, the right to self-expression, the right to self-realization, the right of consent to sexual practice in personal relationships, the right to freely choose our sexual partners and the right to publicly recognize sexual relationships (Richardson 2000). Within a hetero-patriarchal worldview where procreative sexuality is overvalued, non-heteronormative women and men are proscribed celibacy, particularly within a Christian framework, as a prerequisite to acceptance and belonging as the Church loves the sinner not the sin.

On the other hand, celibacy to some, when taken as an expression of upholding one's sexuality, invests one of agency as it manifests one's full enjoyment of the breadth of sexuality rights, among others, i.e. the right to *not* participate in sexual activity as articulations of the right to self-expression and the right to self-realization. Sexuality within a hetero-patriarchal worldview is often reduced to sexual activity and one's worth measured against one's compliance to self-objectification even commodification for the heterosexualized pleasure of the hegemonic male subject. In that regard, non-heteronormative women and men resist such co-optation of their bodies and sexualities by embracing 'erotic celibacy' that Isherwood articulates as a 'new pleasure seeking [that] has brought many to a new understanding of mutuality, imagination and selfhood ... [that is, within a Christian framework, a] reflection of the self giving love of Christ' (2000: 162). Based on the complex ways in which celibacy is understood and practised by interviewees in this study, the narratives in this section are further thematically clustered where celibacy is equated with the most extreme form of suppressing sexual desire, is equated with abstinence from sexual pleasure due to religious observances within the Hindu tradition, adheres to yet redefines sexual orientation and unsettles the religious injunction to love the sinner but not the sin. These narratives of 'mutuality, imagination and selfhood' potentially embody a 'transgressive sexuality…[that mirrors yet is differentiated from] cloistered withdrawal' that more intimately engages the self and the outpouring of the self to others in more honest encounters (Isherwood 2000: 163).

Celibacy as loving the sinner not the sin

The narratives of Peter, AY, Andy and Ling Jackie highlight their encounter, either directly or indirectly, of the church's tolerance of 'deviant' sexualities from heteronormativity. 'Heteronormative', according to Peletz (2007: 43), refers to 'hegemonic (or dominant) expressions of gender and sexuality…[that emphasize] the heterosexual relations and desires that are normative for the majority of the population'. Peter, who is a fifty-year-old divorced Malaysian professional, with Roman Catholic religious background, mentions an e-group that he 'occasionally participated' in when he was working in the United States, called 'Queer Asian Fellowship…which was for gay Asian people who are related with Christianity' [1:36 (447:459)]. As a father to a twenty-something-year-old son and daughter who is in her late teens, Peter was also involved with a 'gay married men's' support group before returning home to Malaysia [1:63 (744:756)]. On surveying a couple of 'gay affirmative' churches in New York where he was based, he notes, 'And in fact if you read the notice and they say they have a ministry for gay people … but the purpose is so that … you have to be celibate … or that they must tell you that being gay is this thing' [1:28 (336:347)]. Peter makes visible that acceptance or affirmation that is extended by these purportedly 'gay affirmative' churches is contingent upon one '[having] to be celibate' or being counselled on how 'being gay is this thing'.

AY, who is currently dating, adds: 'I know Catholic churches have the stand of love the sinner not the sin. And they've accepted the fact that well, you don't choose to be gay. You get born as gay. But um, so you can live your life as a gay person. You can have a gay relationship as long as you don't have … sex which is strange in a way … but I guess that's their coping mechanism' [*laughs*] [20:58 (740:754)]. Here, AY guesses at the Catholic Church's theological 'stand of love the sinner not the sin': that it arises from the compassion of not condemning the sinner (as 'You get born as gay').[1] This compassion extended by the church is contingent upon 'gay' persons becoming celibate ('you don't have … sex'). The nature/culture or birth/choice dichotomy is apparent: 'you don't choose to be gay. You get born as gay'. Agency thus lies in the 'choice' of '[not having] sex' in one's 'gay relationship'. In recognizing that those who 'get born as gay' are 'born as gay [by God]', the church finds itself in a 'strange' moral dilemma: it is damned if it does and damned if it does not condemn both the sinner and the sin. So the church's 'coping mechanism', as AY quips, is to condemn the sin but not the sinner or 'love the sinner not the sin'. Sexual intercourse becomes constructed as the reserve of heterosexual relationships not 'gay [relationships]' and, in doing so, further naturalizes heterosexuality that is predicated on oppositeness (of sexual partners) (Dyer 1997: 266). In a 'gay relationship', one has to contend with becoming celibate.

Pastoral counselling for GLBTIQ persons and their families is premised on the standpoint of loving the sinner but not the sin: a gay Christian (who is a sinner) can be loved but not if he or she fulfils his or her sexual desires, the practice of which is deemed a sin. As such, self-identified Christian GLBTIQ persons are exhorted to live his or her life in celibacy and the reward of embracing such a life-long chaste love is to be deemed not a sin, i.e. tolerable. For Andy, this is questionable even objectionable as 'that sort of chaste love' is tantamount to the denial of one's self as 'you don't actually, fulfil your sexual desires' for a lifetime. The incongruity between a religious injunction and secularized sexuality rights, which includes among others the right to universal enjoyment of human rights; the right to equality and non-discrimination (Principles 1 and 2 of the Yogyakarta Principles); and the right to freedom from criminalization and sanction on the basis of sexual orientation, gender identity, gender expression or sex characteristics (SOGIESC) (Principle 33 of the YP+10), is also made apparent. This incongruity is not only 'strange' as AY graciously describes but rather a violation of one's personhood as sexuality in its holistic sense – the inalienable right to live out one's SOGIESC – encompasses every aspect of one's being and becoming.

The incongruity between a secular and spiritual approach is more marked in Ling Jackie's experience. She is in her early forties, was awarded a PhD in an Asian country a few years back and is currently lecturing at a university in Malaysia. Ling Jackie has accepted her sexual orientation more than ten years ago but she is still single. She had succumbed to depression in the initial phase of her journey to reconcile her sexuality and spirituality. She sought and received double and contrasting doses of counselling: secular (psychiatrist) and spiritual. As she recounts:

> They gave me very different feedback. The psychiatrist in the hospital said that they didn't really consider this as an illness. They say they didn't have any medicine for me to overcome this problem. So the doctors just advise me to accept my own sexuality. And try to, um, know some friends that [are] like me. [18:4 (60:71)]

Where non-heteronormative sexualities used to be medicalized ('[having] medicine ... to overcome this problem') and, worse, pathologized ('they ... consider this as an illness'), Ling Jackie now benefits from a paradigm shift within the field of medicine where 'the doctors just advise me to accept my own sexuality' and 'know some friends that [are] like [her]'. She refers to the de-pathologization of homosexuality as a 'mental illness' with the removal of homosexuality from the *Diagnostic and Statistical Manual of Mental Disorders, Second Edition* (DSM-II) and in the DSM-III, a new diagnosis of 'ego-dystonic homosexuality' – the experience of conflict with same-sex attraction or behaviour – was also removed (Flentje et al. 2014: 1244–5). The disparity in advice from 'the counsellor in [her] church' is apparent: 'This is a sin. God won't allow it. So you have to pray for it and you have to change.' Homosexuality thus condemned as 'a sin', which entails repentance ('you have to pray for it') and sexual reorientation ('you have to change'), renders Ling Jackie '[feeling] very confused and exhausted' [18:6 (72:87)]. Praying the gay away is a self-imposed purging of sexual desire or DIY conversion therapy that in reducing one's sexuality into sexual practices thus negates how intimately and intricately interwoven one's sexual orientation, gender identity, gender expression and sex characteristics are.

To compound this confusion and exhaustion, she received further advice on managing her sexuality which is, as medically diagnosed, neither 'an illness' nor a 'problem' but is religiously classified as 'a sin' or 'as something [not] correct':

> Although the counsellor of a Christian organization whom I talked to in 2001 did not consider homosexuality as something correct, she did tell me that sexual orientation or the feeling of want to look for a partner or want to have an intimate relationship with someone is part of our lives. No matter how tough a person is, he/she will still have that kind of longing. However, she said that not everyone needs to get a partner to satisfy the longing. Some could spend more time with their family members (like parents) and some could diversify their energy and enthusiasm on charity works and other activities. In her point of view, homosexual people can have that kind of longing but they don't have to act

out. I would like to highlight here that unlike the counsellor from my church, this counsellor did not use any scripture in the Bible to counsel me. Initially I thought that her points made sense and tried to become a lesbian Christian that does not need to look for a partner. But the incidents that happened later (the non-Chinese girl issue in mid-2005) show that it does not work for me at all. [18:86 (1067:1079)]

For Ling Jackie who identifies as a 'lesbian Christian', coping strategies recommended to her by a 'counsellor of a Christian organization' comprise varied means to the same end, which is practising celibacy as 'homosexual people can have that kind of longing but they don't have to act [it] out'. Sexual desire or 'that kind of longing' which is inseparable from the being human, as it 'is part of our lives', need not be satisfied as 'not everyone needs to get a partner to satisfy the longing', according to the counsellor. So 'that kind of longing' can be deflected and dissipated through '[spending] more time with their family members (like parents) and … [diversifying] their energy and enthusiasm on charity works and other activities'. As the counsellor did not at the outset use the 'Bible to counsel [her]' or condemn homosexuality, Ling Jackie thought that 'her points made sense and [she] tried to become a "lesbian Christian" that does not need to look for a partner' – thereby embodying celibacy where she is accepted and loved as a sinner who denies 'that kind of longing' as '[acting it] out' is a sin.

But her 'longing' to 'have an intimate relationship with someone' prevailed and she has come to accept that those strategies '[do] not work for [her] at all' when she fell in love with a 'non-Chinese girl' four years later. During the intervening four years between receiving and attempting to adopt such advice in 2001 and finally disengaging from it in 2005, Ling Jackie realizes the paradox of loving the sinner but not the sin. The doer and the deed – Ling Jackie as a 'lesbian Christian' who wants 'to act [it] out', 'have an intimate relationship with someone' – are inseparable. To sever this whole, based on her lived reality, is not only ineffective (it did 'not work for me at all') but potentially disempowering, even harmful. Becoming a 'lesbian Christian' for Ling Jackie is to realize her deep desire 'to look for a partner … have an intimate relationship with [a woman]'. She adds that with regard to her current relationship status, 'I hate to say that I am still single, still do not have a chance to get involved in a romantic relationship … [I] plucked up my courage to confess my feelings for them (different women that she had crushes on over the past years) but all of them rejected me as they only treated me as a friend'. Nurturing and bringing to fruition this desire, 'that kind of (inherently "sinful") longing' is constitutive of who she is as a human person. Essentially, the doer, like the deed, is not naturalized but constructed:

in paraphrasing de Beauvoir (1989), one is not born a 'lesbian Christian' but becomes one.

On the one hand, these narratives of Peter, AY, Andy and Ling Jackie seem to exemplify how religion becomes 'the *justification* for sexual regulation' (Jakobsen and Pellegrini 2004: 16). Far from *being* (naturally) celibate, they are called upon by 'gay affirmative' churches, and pastoral counsellors in their various lived experiences, to *become* celibate. *Becoming* celibate entails the unlearning or surrendering of one's sexuality towards the moral imperative of '[You] don't have to act [it] out' as the conditional premise to being accepted – the sinner is loved but not the sin. On the other hand, in becoming celibate, they show how it is 'pretty much [not] OK' to comply with such religious regulation of their sexuality that seeks to dichotomize the doer and the deed. In becoming a 'lesbian Christian' or gay Christian, by embracing both the doer and the deed, loving the sinner *and* loving the sin, they radically suggest how 'religion [can become] the ground of sexual freedom, rather than the *justification* for sexual regulation' (Jakobsen and Pellegrini 2004: 16) (to be further developed in Chapter 9). They do so because they are challenging the incongruity of becoming queer *and* religious in their everyday realities: navigating between both states that are untenable – refusing to choose between either becoming a sinner (in loving as a sin) or not becoming a sinner (in not loving).

Celibacy as suppression and realization of sexual desire

That fine line where 'religion [can become] the ground of sexual freedom, rather than the *justification* for sexual regulation' (Jakobsen and Pellegrini 2004: 16) resonates with the process of becoming celibate discussed in this section through the narratives of Joe, AY and Janic. Where becoming celibate is perceived and experienced as the repression of one's sexuality, agency is divested and sexuality rights contained. Where becoming celibate is perceived and experienced as the liberation of one's sexuality, agency is potentially restored and sexuality rights realized.

According to Joe:

I thought, after reading Paul Monet's book *Becoming a Man* that I thought I could keep my love sexless and my sex loveless [*smiles*]. And there you know, that [I] could be a happy, what do they call this, um, heuristic distinction or something like that. So I thought and ... obviously I couldn't. By that point when

I left church, I was out to myself but … I didn't have any … gay friends. And I hadn't experienced sex … with someone. [27:11 (110:117)]

The 'heuristic distinction' that Joe alludes to in '[keeping] my love sexless and my sex loveless' encapsulates succinctly a way of life that he had once considered embracing: of not having sex with a man whom he loves (keeping 'my love sexless') but having sex with a woman whom he cannot love (keeping 'my sex loveless'). His lived reality then – 'I left church, I was out to myself but … I didn't have any … gay friends. And I hadn't experienced sex … with someone' – facilitated the possibility and sustainability of living out such a way of life for one who self-identifies as Christian and gay and was deeply conflicted. In the intervening years between 'So I thought and … obviously I couldn't' – where Joe had '[found] church' in the form of the GLBTIQ-affirming Free Community Church, 'was out to [others]', had many 'gay friends' and '[had] experienced sex … with someone' – lies the process of becoming celibate which begins with the intent to become celibate and choosing not to follow through with it.

AY also considered embracing celibacy. He says:

> When you are at that point in your life and you're struggling with that, of course then you would say, 'OK, if this is God's way and God's word, then you know, that's what I choose, not for myself-lah. So I would say that I was not accepting of who I was. And I think in terms of my spiritual, my sexual journey, um, it was veering more towards just being a straight person and … if in the event I have to live myself as celibate then, so be it. [20:32 (416:429)]

The preparedness to become celibate is similarly evident in AY's narrative as it is in Joe's. In 'struggling with that' – to come to terms with his sexuality and religiosity – AY commits his sexuality to God and chooses what he perceived then as 'God's way and God's word'. His fidelity to 'God's way and God's word' finds expression in unlearning or surrendering his sexuality through becoming celibate and 'a straight person' as being Christian and gay is deemed to be incompatible. On the one hand, agency is manifest in his obedience to God as succinctly articulated in 'so be it'. On the other hand, by his own admission, AY chooses to become celibate 'not for [himself]'. And his cognizance that '[he] was not accepting of who [he] was', becoming celibate at this juncture of his journey, marked by struggle, self-resistance and sacrifice, defers the realization of his personhood. Agency is, in this sense, divested.

Janic's journey towards 'self-realization' resonates with AY's journey where becoming celibate is not easily compartmentalized as either the suppression or the expression of sexual desire. Janic, who was a missionary in the field then and subsequently worked at a Tibetan Buddhist centre, says: 'But for the longest time, for about seven years out of that 12 (that she was away in the US for studies)...I wanted to be celibate. I was very, very deep into Christianity and I just wanted to concentrate on that' [7:82 (1061:1072)]. She adds: 'I want to study everything I could about Christianity as well as its meditation, as well as...its works. So that was why I was also out in the field (as a missionary). So I didn't have to answer to anyone about my, you know, sexuality'. The moral imperative to becoming celibate for Janic, 'for about seven years out of that 12', rises out of the incompatibility of being Christian and lesbian and being compelled to hold the latter in abeyance. Through full immersion in being 'out in the field', she did not need to be 'out' in terms of her sexuality, as she 'didn't have to answer to anyone about [her] sexuality'. The 'field', on the one hand, becomes the site of self-realization for Janic as she embodies '[wanting] to be celibate [and going]...very, very deep into Christianity'.

The 'field' for Janic resonates with Sara Ahmed's theorizing of the 'field' in *Queer Phenomenology* (2006b: 87) where she says:

> A field can be defined as an open or cleared ground. A field of objects would hence refer to how certain objects are made available by clearing, through the delimitation of space as a space for some things rather than others...Heterosexuality in a way becomes a field, a space that gives ground to, or even grounds, heterosexual action through the renunciation of what it is not, and also by the production of what 'it is'.

Janic's being 'out in the field (as a missionary)' was not to be out as either heterosexual or homosexual. It was to eschew being sexual, as she adds, 'So I didn't have to answer to anyone about my, you know, sexuality'. Being 'out in the field' was to eschew both 'heterosexual action' and homosexual action in the sense of realizing SOGIESC. Where the 'field' in the way that Ahmed makes sense of it connotes 'heterosexuality' given that it is the normative sexuality practised by the majority and certainly by the faith community of missionaries that Janic was surrounded by then, she inadvertently subverts heteronormativity. She opens up the 'field' by challenging its delimiting space as 'a space that gives ground to, or even grounds, heterosexual action through the renunciation of what it is not' (homosexual action and objects). She does so, paradoxically, by refusing to opt for the either/or limitations imposed by that heterosexualized space – she produces a celibate body that is neither 'what it is not' (homosexual) nor what 'it is' supposed to be (heterosexual).

On the other hand, the 'field' also becomes the site of self-denial for Janic, as she adds:

> So it was my internal struggle – who am I you know, as far as my sexuality goes because of course, I go out, I get attracted to people even though I wanted to be celibate that time. Maybe because I felt condemned. If maybe, I didn't, maybe I wouldn't be celibate, I don't know. [7:83 (1072:1092)]

Her 'internal struggle' was two-fold: within herself and with a friend whom she had lived with for those seven years who, as Janic says, 'gave me trouble [as] in the Christian context she was trying to condemn me'. Apparent in her narrative is a self-reflexivity that questions, on the one hand, her reasons for '[wanting] to be celibate' and, on the other, 'who I am'. In this instance, where becoming celibate amounts to the suppression of one's sexual desire and arises 'because [she] felt condemned', Janic's agency is, to some extent, divested. Clearly, '[wanting] to be celibate' for Janic is not the absence of sexual desire as she '[got] attracted to people' then. Instead, '[wanting] to be celibate' for Janic possibly stems from the presence of religious guilt, as she adds: 'If maybe, I didn't (feel "condemned"), maybe I wouldn't be celibate, I don't know.'

Attendant with religious guilt was depression which accompanied Janic's journey in becoming celibate, as it was fundamentally 'having to put a side of me on hold ... [which was] painful in the sense of having to shelve that part of me' [7:105 (1369:1384)]. The reiterated imperative of 'having to put a side of me on hold' and 'having to shelve that part of me' at other junctures in her narrative shows the extent to which Janic exacted on herself the discipline of desire to the desired end of the production of a celibate self. This resonates with Foucault's 'docile bodies' which are discipline-produced 'subjected and practised bodies' (Foucault 1977: 138) – where the policing of her sexuality in the 'field' by her friend, subsequently internalized, led to the self-policing of her sexuality that she had 'put ... on hold' and '[shelved]' for seven years. Janic became the 'principle of [her] own subjection' (Foucault 1977: 203). The seven-year regulation and, in fact, suspension of her sexuality were sustained by the 'hope' that she 'will finally realize the other one actually doesn't exist, meaning me you know, being attracted to the same-sex people, it actually doesn't exist, it's just an illusion or delusion'. The suppression of her sexuality and denial of her personhood which encompasses 'being attracted to the same-sex people' lead to a divestiture of agency that she willed herself to repress as a mere 'illusion or delusion'.

The divestiture of agency paradoxically leads to a reclamation of agency for Janic. The power of surveillance in the 'field is productive and gives rise to a new subjectivity – Janic's coming "out in the field" as a Christian and lesbian at the conclusion of the seven-year hiatus. Janic attributes coming out of that field' to 'looking for what is it that I'm missing that is why you know, I am the way I am'. The search for 'what is it that [she was] missing' eventually leads her to embark on a 'different path' [7:86 (1116:1132)] in her circuitous journey. She then willingly exposed herself to the queer hermeneutics of 'gay churches' where 'how they interpret each and every verses… [leads to] the acceptance of homosexuality'. The radical 'split' in coming out from that 'field' of self-denial and into self-realization is evident as she says: 'I go back to exploring that part of me. And… I felt much more at peace in a sense because for the longest time, I kinda like put myself on a shelf.' This marks her transition from becoming celibate as a means of purging religious guilt to becoming whole and '[feeling] much more at peace', where 'peace', in turn, becomes a signifier of God's grace. The recuperation of the self was, however, not an overnight occurrence as Janic adds: 'It took great effort to put the other side of me on hold. But because I've done that for quite some time, to slowly integrate that in… it took a while, I think maybe about four… years before I totally felt at peace, totally at peace' [7:92 (1186:1200)]. The abundance of life that is signified by becoming 'totally at peace' is further marked by the reconciliation of sexuality and religiosity extended by 'many Christian friends whom [she] actually was in the field with and [who] supported [her]' in her journey towards self-realization.

Self-realization in the narratives of Joe, AY and Janic is paradoxically realized through self-denial – the experience of becoming celibate. *Doing* celibacy encapsulates the process of becoming celibate: that one is not born celibate but becomes one. This process begins with the mind-body-spirit preparedness to 'keep my love sexless and my sex loveless' in the case of Joe or 'being a straight person and… [having] to live myself as celibate' in the case of AY. For Janic, it was because she 'felt "condemned"' by a Christian as a Christian. Becoming celibate as shown both divests and invests one of agency as the processes of self-denial and self-realization in becoming straight, becoming celibate and becoming sexual are intimately integrated. Celibacy is thus redefined as it becomes both a denial and realization of self. Redefining celibacy then calls to question not only the heterosexualization of desire but also its sexualization. As such, through the lived experiences of Joe, AY and Janic, becoming celibate or doing celibacy, in denying or realizing the self, is an expression of one's fidelity to God. The consequence of surrendering to God one's sexuality ('so be it') and recuperating one's self ('this is who I am') lies in the blessings of happiness and peace, as markers of an abundant life, in having emerged from 'conflict', depression and guilt. To deny oneself is paradoxically to find oneself. Their narratives of becoming celibate echo Isherwood's prophetic wisdom on 'erotic celibacy' where achieving 'equality' within a hetero-patriarchal world 'is as much a matter for transgressive sexuality as it is for cloistered withdrawal' (2000: 163).

Celibacy as redefining 'sexual orientation'

The narrative of AY in this section emphasizes how celibacy calls to question the heterosexualization of desire and the sexualization of desire that are endemic in a hetero-patriarchal world, already intimated in discussions above. Doing celibacy unsettles the sexualization of desire, as it suppresses or holds in abeyance the expression and practice of sexual desire, as Janic puts it: surrendering to the moral imperative of 'having to put a side of me on hold' and 'having to shelve that part of me' [7:105 (1369:1384)]. Doing celibacy more problematically unsettles the sexualization of desire as it is also an expression and practice of sexual desire. Doing celibacy becomes the realization of sexual desire.

Doing celibacy unsettles the heterosexualization of desire as one disavows being desirous of the opposite sex and/or acting on it. This goes back to the 'heterosexual matrix' (Butler 1990: 5) which dictates that it follows that one born a man ought to be gendered masculine and desirous of a woman and one born a woman ought to be gendered feminine and desirous of a man. So when AY says that 'in terms of my spiritual, my sexual journey, um, it was veering more towards just being a straight person and ... if in the event I have to live myself as celibate then, so be it' [20:32 (416:429)], he unsettles the heterosexualization of desire in two ways. Firstly, AY considers becoming 'a straight person' as a self-identified gay man. In doing so, he denaturalizes heterosexual desire; that born a man, he does not naturally desire a woman. The work involved in passing as 'a straight person', in desiring a woman, effects the semblance of an effortless adherence to the gender script of the 'heterosexual matrix'. Secondly, for AY, to 'live [himself] as celibate' seems to follow from 'veering more towards just being a straight person'. To '[veer]' towards desiring women as 'a straight person' is seemingly aligned with 'veering' towards neither men nor women in his preparedness to 'live [himself] as celibate'. The heterosexualization of desire is thwarted in both these ways.

In another but related instance, AY makes reference to his former pastor who is 'lesbian', albeit 'celibate', as he recounts her categorizing him as a 'person that's struggling with homosexuality' [20:43 (544:561)] which resulted in his being stripped off a national youth award. As he recounts:

> I was supposed to receive an award as a youth leader. But one of the pastors who's lesbian but I guess she decided on a celibate life. Anyway, I say she's lesbian anyway [*both laugh*]. She brought up the fact that you know, why are we giving an award to a person that's struggling with homosexuality when ... it's a national award and other young people will be looking up at him. [20:43 (544:561)]

I find it insightful that AY recognizes the pastor as being 'lesbian anyway' although she had 'decided on a celibate life' because in doing so, he further destabilizes the (hetero)sexualization of desire. The sexualization of desire presupposes a love object where the heterosexualization of desire presupposes a love object that is of the opposite sex. This in turn is aligned with 'sexual orientation' where one born a man naturally desires a woman or 'unnaturally' desires a man, and one born a woman naturally desires a man or 'unnaturally' desires a woman. You are who you desire despite the seeming incongruity of the labels of 'lesbian' and 'celibate' with reference to the same person, in the above quote. The pastor, as one born a woman who *naturally* desires a woman, pre-empts the sanctions that she herself imposes on people like AY who are 'struggling with homosexuality', by making invisible her 'sexual orientation' (in 'veering more towards' women) through '[deciding] on a celibate life'. Within the imposition of heteronormativity, she is presumed by others, AY excepting, to be 'straight'. In doing so, she enjoys the reward for compliance (as either a straight woman or a celibate lesbian) and escapes the sanctions against noncompliance to 'compulsory heterosexuality' (Rich 1980), whereas AY, who had been exposed by her as a Christian gay youth leader, receives the sanctions for his noncompliance to 'compulsory heterosexuality' by being shamed, stripped and cast aside as an ineligible role model as 'other young people will be looking up at him'.

In making visible a 'queer phenomenology', Sara Ahmed states that becoming sexually oriented as straight 'means not only that we have to turn toward the objects given to us by heterosexual culture but also that we must turn away from objects that take us off this line' (Ahmed 2006a: 554).[2] In the case of the 'lesbian' albeit 'celibate' pastor whom AY encountered, where she naturally does not 'turn toward the objects (men) given to [her] by heterosexual culture', she masks '[turning] toward the objects (women) [not] given to [her] by heterosexual culture' by adopting 'a celibate life'. In doing so, she neither '[turns] toward the objects given to [her] by heterosexual culture' nor '[turns] away from objects that take [her] off this line' by virtue of her sexual desire for women that she does not act on. She thus destabilizes the heterosexualization of desire and the sexualization of desire. That the pastor is 'lesbian anyway' where AY is concerned shows the limits of 'sexual orientation' – the classification of one's sexuality based on one's 'veering more' towards either the opposite or same-sex love object, where being 'off [or on] this line', is obfuscated when she had 'decided on a celibate life'.

Where AY was prepared to 'live [himself] as celibate', his former pastor did: 'she decided on a celibate life'. Where AY had considered 'veering more towards just being a straight person', his former pastor's heterosexuality is implied or assumed by virtue of her 'celibate life'. And becoming 'lesbian' but 'celibate' coheres with the loving-the-sinner-not-the-sin theology of some churches (National Council of Churches of Singapore 2004). The heterosexualization of desire is challenged in these instances where a Christian gay man almost wills himself to become 'a straight person' thereby making visible the work invested in becoming straight: heterosexuality as such is not naturalized. But the heterosexualization of desire is reified when a celibate lesbian is co-opted as an implied heterosexual and feted accordingly (given the clout that she had in persuading others to strip the 'national award' off AY). The sexualization of desire, however, as challenged by 'a celibate life' potentially makes visible the limits of 'sexual orientation' (and GLBTIQ labels by extension), in making sense of one's sexuality. Ultimately, celibacy itself as a label points to the paradox of sexuality: the crossing of boundaries (through becoming straight, becoming celibate) is made possible by the hardening of these boundaries (sexual/celibate, heterosexual/homosexual) that in turn are scripted by 'sexual orientation'. Queering the field (Rooke 2010; Schippert 2011), through the praxis of celibacy that is grounded in these lived realities of doing celibacy, shows not only the potency of identity politics (based on the cogency of GLBTIQ labels) but also its limits.

Celibacy as religious abstinence

In this final section on celibacy, the narrative of Jagadiswari juxtapositioned against Janic's is highlighted. Her narrative resonates with Janic's practice of celibacy as religious abstinence, as discussed in the previous section, where she says: 'But for the longest time, for about seven years out of that 12 ... I wanted to be celibate. I was very, very deep into Christianity and I just wanted to concentrate on that. I want to study everything I could about Christianity as well as its meditation, as well as its works' [7:82 (1061:1072)]. Her desire to 'be celibate' for 'seven years out of that 12', was an integral component of the ascetic way of life that she embraced where she was 'very, very deep into Christianity...its meditation, as well as its works'. Her voluntary and full immersion into asceticism – a contemplative life ('its meditation') and praxis ('its works' which includes among others a three-month sojourn in Africa as a missionary) – is reminiscent of Jesus's first disciples who were invited to leave their kinsfolk and come follow him on the spiritual journey of spreading the good news that was the new Christian faith then. These 'seven years out of that 12' witness a transformation of self that is facilitated by a shift of space where she was 'away from [her] parents' and 'out in the field'.

The deeper effects of Janic's desire to 'be celibate' and concomitantly go 'very, very deep into Christianity...its meditation, as well as its works', are further elucidated, as she adds:

> But I was happy in the sense that I was gaining knowledge...in that teaching because there's a lot in...Christianity that's very, very good. So I don't despise it. I still embrace it. But in doing all that, I also saw how a lot of people within that faith misuse it...for other people and also for themselves. So because of all that, I think you know, I am able to speak a little bit more unlike other people who just believe in hearsay...maybe also when I was going through that period of time, thinking the more I study, the more I understand, the more faith I have in God, the more willingness I have in God to be who I am supposed to be, the other part of me will become lesser and lesser. [7:106 (1385:1395)]

Janic's 'being attracted to the same-sex people' [7:105 (1369:1384)], as she says elsewhere, is sublimated as sexual abstinence that she supports by 'gaining knowledge...in...Christianity'. This is apparent where she makes the connection that her sexuality is inversely proportionate to her religiosity: the diminishing of the former leads to the deepening of the latter. As she says: 'When I was going through that period of time (her seven-year celibacy), thinking the more I study, the more I understand, the more faith I have in God, the more willingness I have in God to be who I am supposed to be, the other part of me will become lesser and lesser.' Where the 'other part of me' – her sexuality and, in particular, her 'being attracted to the same-sex people' – '[becomes] lesser and lesser', the reiteration of 'more' is significant; where 'more...study...more...[understanding]...more faith I have in God...[leads to] more willingness...to be who I am supposed to be'. The mind/body dualism that characterizes much of Christian thought and theology is here espoused by Janic as she wills herself to 'be who [she is] supposed to be', a heterosexual woman and in the process of becoming, a celibate lesbian. The benefit of sublimating her sexual desire in the pursuit of 'gaining knowledge' in her self-study of Christianity is being 'able to speak a little bit (and with implied authority) more unlike other people who just believe in hearsay'. She also comes off with the gift of discernment in '[seeing] how a lot of people within that faith misuse it ... for other people and also for themselves'. And above all, that she 'was happy [thus fulfilled] in the sense'.

Sublimating sexual desire for women as a woman through celibacy is echoed by Jagadiswari, who in reflecting on her early Catholicism as she is now a Hindu priest, says: 'And I really wanted to join the sisters (Catholic nuns) ... Why am I going there? Because I felt that, OK, God gave me a gift and I couldn't be around women that I could really love and be intimate with. I might as well become a nun' [25:27 (213:224)]. That Jagadiswari attributes loving women as a 'gift' is significant given the privileging of heterosexuality and concomitant condemnation of homosexuality by the Catholic Church. Where being able to 'really love and be intimate with [women]' as a laywoman is delegitimated, she aspired then to 'become a nun'. In doing so, she would potentially sublimate her sexual desire for women as a woman within the sanctity of a monastic life and homo-sociality of a women-only religious congregation. She finally reconsiders as 'it's very difficult for me to do that ("become a nun")', having witnessed the pain endured by two women who 'loved each other so much' but one 'broke [the] heart [of the other] and became a nun'. A cautionary note on romanticizing 'erotic celibacy' arises as in that context of pain and suffering borne by those women, a 'cloistered withdrawal' is not as Isherwood posits, akin to 'transgressive sexuality' (2000: 163) but a negation of a fundamental part of one's being and one's relationality to another.

In contrast, being a 'full-time' Hindu priest is the vocation that Jagadiswari has committed herself to, as she says, 'I am a priest. I wear the threads wherever I go. I am vegetarian. I read the Vedas ... I do all the fun stuff.' She was celibate for five years before her current girlfriend 'came along', someone who is 'not Indian', a naturopathic doctor from the United States, but was referred to her (by her faith community) as she is someone who understands and is aware of 'the amount of energy that gets transpired through tantric work'. As a 'medium' or 'spiritualist' as she puts it, before her initiation as a priest in 2013, this discipline of the body for Jagadiswari includes periodic sexual abstinences, as she adds:

Now Hinduism, we're not very sexual in the way that, if there is a festival like *Thaipusam* (celebrated in honour of Lord Murugan and accompanied by devotional acts, e.g. piercing the body, carrying the *kavadi*, etc), you do not even hold hands. You do not have that [*clasps hands*], that intimate connection, ever. You sleep separate; you sleep on the floor, you fast. And that's a real luxury for me [*laughs*] because most of the women in my life don't understand the rules of, um, I could wake up next to them but once I have my shower and once I do, until I get here, my thoughts have to be here. I can't hold my girlfriend's hands, I can't do this. And she's such a blessing because she gets it. Even if I can't you know, so there's a great amount of discipline in this relationship. But she's perfect [*interviewer smiles*] because it's difficult for me to explain having to be that disciplined, I have to keep to myself sometimes and do my prayers. They don't expect purity of body, they expect purity of heart which is when you're humanly human, and you do this. [25:64 (619:631)]

Jagadiswari's reiteration of 'discipline' resonates to some extent with an adoption of a monastic way of life. It encompasses not only sexual abstinence but also 'that intimate connection' during religious festivals and the 'discipline' of not only '[sleeping separately]' but also '[sleeping] on the floor [and fasting]' by way of disciplining other bodily appetites. In her vocation as the 'embodiment of the Mother (Goddess Kali)' [25:9 (57:68)],[3] she inhabits the dual states of spirit – human as her body becomes a vessel that her Mother inhabits when she goes into trances. So 'they', her deities, 'don't expect purity of body, they expect purity of heart' in consideration of her 'humanly human' state. So whilst permanent celibacy is not expected but she needs to exercise a 'great amount of discipline in [her] relationship' in '[keeping] to [herself] sometimes and [doing her] prayers', for which she is grateful that her then girlfriend 'gets'. That the deities 'don't expect purity of body, they expect purity of heart' shows the non-dualistic thinking and practice of Hinduism that revere both expressions of erotic sexuality and chaste asceticism, as noted by Elizabeth Abbott in *A History of Celibacy* (2000: 164).

To conclude, Janic had embraced religious abstinence through the voluntary adoption of ascetic and monastic life within the Christian tradition, as a laywoman and Jagadiswari, who still does so periodically, as a Hindu priest. Their narratives afford a glimpse into their various faith traditions through the lens of celibacy. In the case of Janic, within the Christian tradition, celibacy is elevated as the zenith of apostolic life that she had imitated. That it is theologically premised on the mind/body dualism is apparent as Janic spent 7 years of the twelve in a metaphorical desert, willing 'the other part of [her to] become lesser and lesser' [7:106 (1385:1395)]. In the case of Jagadiswari, within the Hindu tradition, periodic abstinence from physical contact (clasping hands) to the intimacy of sexual acts is an imperative given her vocation as a conduit for her deities. Happily for her, the 'unified concept' of eroticism and celibacy within Hinduism (Abbott 2000: 164), does not necessitate either the repression of sexuality or the adoption of permanent celibacy. Their embodiment of celibacy shows how they sublimate sexual desire through prayer, meditation and good works as persons of faith. In this regard, doing celibacy for Jagadiswari resonates with Isherwood's notion of 'erotic celibacy' as 'the way we and others relate with our bodies sets the pattern for relations beyond the edges of our skin' (2000: 163). The discipline of the body through periodic abstinence of physical pleasures is a necessary reminder of the materiality of the body – that is not inferiorized to the mind or spirit – as a precondition for more honest and fulfilling relations with our bodies and sexualities and that of others.

Sublimating sexual desires through becoming celibate is not to be romanticized. The limit of subversive potential is, at least for Ling Jackie, keenly felt, as she says, 'I wonder if I continue living in Malaysia, I would end up spending the rest of my life as a spinster without any experience in romantic relationship.' This disenchantment is not just directed inwardly but also outwardly as it is compounded by the wider social-political climate in Malaysia post-GE14. She adds, 'I am still very pessimistic of the situation in Malaysia, even after the regime change in 2018. The public caning of two Muslim women in Terengganu under Syariah law for attempting to have lesbian sex is really outrageous. Things are not really good at all.' She refers to the recent controversy where a twenty-something and thirty-something-year-old Muslim women were caned six times each (on the back with a light rattan cane by a female prison officer) in full view of 100 witnesses (Palansamy 2018). This unprecedented punishment for alleged lesbian sex caused an uproar among various segments of not only Malaysian but also global society on the inhumanity of the treatment despite claims by religious officials that the caning was intended to 'educate' rather than 'harm' the women thus humiliated. GLBTIQ persons like Ling Jackie who is neither Malay nor Muslim (and thereby not subject to Syariah law in Malaysia) show how religious and secular laws (e.g. Section 377) in concert render the human, inhuman through her empathetic caring for the women who were caned, for exercising what the majority of the citizenry do, i.e. enjoy, among other rights, the right to sexual pleasure rather than, against their will, adopt celibacy or heterosexuality.

4

Facing condemnation and taboo

The struggle against the insistence of incongruity between becoming queer and religious that find expression in the narratives highlighted in Chapters 2 and 3 now becomes the struggle against gender-based discrimination and gender-based violence (GBV) that often follow from such intolerance not only of those who are queer but queer and religious. The embrace of celibacy has at its roots, notwithstanding its subversive potential, as demonstrated in the previous chapter, the sanctions that are meted out for noncompliance to 'compulsory heterosexuality' particularly by state apparatuses, e.g. legal, political and religious institutions which include one's faith communities, even families. The rewards for compliance include worldly ones such as the right to marry and found a family and otherworldly ones, e.g. made worthy to be loved by your Creator. The self-purging of sexual desire where sexuality is narrowly understood as consisting of sexual practices, in this chapter, finds darker expression in conversion therapy that gay-identifying men have been put through. In this chapter, narratives of GLBTIQ persons show how feeling conflicted, depressed, guilty and pain leads some to bargaining (with God), denying their selves, being intolerant of, condemning and demonizing their sexuality, or at best, pre-empting coming outs as sexualities remains a taboo subject.

Being conflicted

The first part of this chapter offers discussion of narratives based on related strategies to positioning sexuality and spirituality as incompatible and mutually exclusive that includes putting it aside, adopting celibacy, and compartmentalizing sexuality and spirituality. In the second part of the chapter, being conflicted about one's sexuality and spirituality as further expressions of positioning sexuality and spirituality as incompatible and mutually exclusive is a result of being demonized and condemned, being in denial, feeling guilt and pain, experiencing intolerance of others or being tolerated (for the sinner not the sin is 'loved') and repressing expressions of sexuality as it is taboo.

Articulations of being conflicted are diverse. For CK, '[being] like together' with another Christian gay man is doubly perilous, as he says:

> And there are other gay Christian…that ask, 'Are you interested to be like together or what?' Then I was thinking, 'How can…[*emphatically*] two Christians I mean be a partner. I mean it's like you call yourself Christian but then you're still living together or having a relation. No, I don't think so this is right'. [17:34 (402:407)]

Ling Jackie who has sought both spiritual counsellors and psychiatrists for her 'sexuality problem' says:

> Then I have no choice but I pray to God. I say, 'For this, for so many years, I try to pray for my sexuality problem. I try to change. And I went to see so many counsellors'. [18:9 (116:131)]

Joe, with the Free Community Church, in '[trying] to make sense of' his 'guilt', rationalizes:

> In terms of reconciling religion and sexuality…[there is] this one part that I can't make sense of…when I feel these urges, I feel guilty about it. And I feel bad about it…when I shouldn't. I think I shouldn't be…And there's this belief that…you shouldn't be in a state where you might like someone a lot you know. So that's one thing I try to make sense of. [27:51 (545:560)]

Peter who attributes a 'homophobic' church as being out of 'line with the Gospel' affirms:

> So talking about tensions between religious traditions versus sexuality…I think because of how I see faith and religion, it's not so much a tension within myself but within the social structures and how it's come about. And doing a lot of reading, etc., also made me more aware [that]…this whole homophobic approach is basically not really in line with the Gospel rather than the other way round you see. [1:30 (356:364)]

The pastiche of four narratives presented above begins with CK who mitigates his guilt (and perceived condemnation) by refusing the sexual advances of other Christian gay men. It ends with Peter who inverts the equation in assigning guilt to a 'homophobic' church as it runs counter to Jesus's values as codified in 'the Gospel'. The sum worth of the extracts in-between shows how being conflicted is paradoxically coming to terms with one's sexuality and spirituality. Where religious guilt is concomitant with being conflicted, these narratives offer individuated ways of coping through guilt management. Ling Jackie seeks to purge her guilt through prayer and both spiritual (church-based) and secular (psychiatric) counsel. Joe, to alleviate '[his feeling] bad about (sexual urges for men)... when [he thinks he] shouldn't be', cautions himself to not 'like someone a lot'. Guilt can potentially be transformative.

In the following narratives, Alexis, Jimmy and AY show how being conflicted is both a means to an end and an end in itself. In the former, there is some resolution to the incompatibility of sexuality and spirituality, and in the latter, there is little or deferred resolution. Beyond resolutions, the process of becoming is a journey that is not a straight path. Alexis, whose narrative was highlighted in Chapter 2 on compartmentalizing sexuality and spirituality, adds: 'It was quite a struggle I guess. I tend to separate them... I'm not sure if it's hypocrisy. And it's a struggle to me. And... I've made several attempts to change, try to because people interpret the Bible as you know, homosexuality is a sin' [10:34 (525:535)]. Her reiteration of it being 'a struggle' underscores her frustrated 'attempts to change' who she is before resigning herself to '[separating] them', her homosexuality and spirituality as a charismatic Christian where Biblical interpretation deems 'homosexuality [as] a sin'. So she is damned if she does ('change') and damned if she does not. The iterative cycle of religious guilt is apparent in her discomfort with the 'hypocrisy' or 'false' claim in self-identifying as Christian, as a lesbian.

The 'struggle' goes on as she deliberates if finding 'true love' [10:94 (1393:1408)] with a woman would mitigate her 'homosexuality [as] a sin', as she says:

And that maybe from there I don't know. I was just thinking that maybe that [I] could just escape from God's judgement. Because what would be considered sin would be then a person having sex with another person... like commit fornication... but if the relationship with another person, same-sex, I don't know if it leads to marriage [*laughs*]... can you know, reach up to that extent, after which whether it's acceptable to God or not acceptable. That's still, remains [*sighs*], a question. [10:95 (1409:1425)]

Alexis is aware of 'God's judgement' on her 'relationship with another person, same-sex'. But she hopes for an 'escape from God's judgement' if her 'relationship with another person, same-sex... leads to marriage'. She draws on the church's exhortation of chaste love that is levelled at any 'person having sex with another person (outside the sanctity of marriage)... [which amounts to committing] fornication'. The anguish of falling short and, by inference, being short-changed is evident as she knows that such hope is futile as her 'relationship with another person, same-sex' will not 'reach up to that extent' – it will not be 'acceptable to God' as 'homosexuality is a sin'. That it 'still remains a question' – 'whether it's acceptable to God or not acceptable' is hopeful as it opens up the possibility of not merely an 'escape from God's judgement' but possibly God's mercy, compassion and love in accepting a 'relationship with another person, same-sex'.

Yet self-alienation persists as Alexis comments on her lack of connection with the GLBTIQ support group that she is a member of, as she says: 'Maybe [I'm] still unable to accept this ... some people they are ... very proud of who they are. But ... I've not reached that level yet [*laughs*]. To me ... I just want to be comfortable feeling the way I feel' [10:99 (1477:1488)]. Gay pride is a distant reality for Alexis who at present aspires only 'to be comfortable feeling the way I feel' in coming to terms with becoming lesbian and Christian. She is also cognizant that 'God does not hate the person ... but hates his or her sin' [10:101 (1499:1513)]. And this has accentuated the impasse that is her lived reality, as she says:

> I wasn't too sure whether ... it contradicts my faith and so ... I haven't really sit down and think [of] what I should be doing. Whether I should just go ahead, change my lifestyle and stop feeling unsure if this is right or wrong, if this is what God wants. Or that I stick to my belief that this is not a sin [*laughs*]. This is, this way, just being true to how I feel. So I haven't really decided where to go. [10:100 (1488:1498)]

The metaphor of a journey is ever present for Alexis who is hesitating at the crossroads: 'I haven't really decided where to go.' Her options are either the sanctioned path which is to 'go ahead, change my lifestyle and stop feeling unsure if this is right or wrong' or the road less travelled which is to 'stick to my belief that this is not a sin'. The crossroads, in turn, signify dualisms that surface like contradictory signposts in her journey: sexuality as birth/choice, God's way/'this (my) way', right/wrong, heterosexuality/homosexuality, 'what God wants'/'how I feel' and 'change my lifestyle'/'stick to my belief'. The liminal gap in time and space between 'just [going] ahead' and '[sitting] down and [thinking]' is a critical generative pause for Alexis. It is akin to not dismissing the fracture lines in the wall of heterosexism in recognizing and eventually accepting that homosexuality 'is not a sin' (which the support group that she belongs to upholds). That she '[hasn't] really decided where to go' is less a state of stasis but rather a kind of contemplative action that in not foreclosing options potentially opens up possibilities of becoming.

Jimmy appraises his journey as one comprising 'a few [phases]' where he identifies as 'Christian … but [one who is] not so committed' [15:22 (307:317)]. And he casts the blame on his 'sexuality …. [as blocking him] from being too religious, somehow'. He remains closeted – he 'was very, very careful … about [himself] … about [his] thinking' – in the four years that he was with a non-denominational church where in '[following] the church … [he distracted himself] from [his] own self' [15:43 (599:613)]. In doing so, Jimmy self-policed his thoughts and actions in adherence to his church's teachings and practices. He was 'struggling in between religion and [himself]' [15:26 (347:359)] as 'the temptation … the desire … [of wanting] to have friends … is one part of [himself]'. He notes the duplicity between 'the things that [he says] … [and what's] still inside [him]' despite his 'focus in the church … [that keeps him] away' from himself. He affirms yet disavows his identity where he continues to secretly desire men 'friends' but is outwardly compliant. As he concedes elsewhere in the interview, 'My church was very strict that time, totally … not agree on [homosexuality] … it's very serious sin for them' [15:36 (499:509)].

Jimmy's self-policing reflects Foucault's '*anatomo-politics of the human body*', as one facet of 'biopower' which is 'centered on the body as a machine: its disciplining, the optimization of its capabilities, the extortion of its forces, the parallel increase of its usefulness and its docility' (1978: paragraph 139). His church in this case becomes that 'machine' that enacts that disciplining – which manifests as homophobia (with homosexuality being a 'very serious sin') – which Jimmy internalizes to optimize his 'capabilities' and 'usefulness' to the relevant church ministries that he contributes to. His body and sexuality, presumed heterosexual – 'his church was very strict' – is thus made docile.

The rupture of such docility (in the Foucauldian sense of regulation of desire) and compliance takes the form of being blackmailed by men who claimed to be the 'police' where he was threatened with exposure unless he paid them off [15:38 (526:537)]. Having paid them, they asked for more. As he recounts: '[I was] so scared to be exposed or to be *kacau*-lah (harassed) … because I was very particular in how people look at me … I'm very good boy in the eyes [of my church] … I mean … not so bad guy. So I feel like I cannot take it anymore' [15:39 (538:555)]. The fear of being outed as a 'bad guy' (Christian gay man) exacerbated by his alienation from his church members where he 'didn't have the friends to talk to' [15:37 (509:526)] compelled Jimmy 'to leave the church' and the blackmailing stopped.

In the subsequent phase of his journey, he says:

> Then now after three years, didn't go to church [*smiles*]. Just like that, mainly because of this issue (being blackmailed). I still cannot get a balance. I still cannot accept myself as a gay and a Christian. But now … I start to find a way-lah … Like try to see like it's not my sin … this is not the only thing that stop me from being close to God … But only thing like that, I am so weak or I don't want to go to church. From before that, this sexuality stop me from going. Now until it's like a habit maybe. Three years plus already what, so it's a habit. Right. Not like last time. [15:44 (614:630)]

Jimmy significantly '[starts] to find a way' having been forced off the road, metaphorically speaking, when he becomes accountable for his not '[wanting] to go to church' in the course of the next three years since the trauma of being blackmailed. He recognizes that whilst he 'still cannot accept [himself] as a gay and a Christian', he '[tries] to see like it's not [his] sin … that [stops him] from being close to God'. Staying away from church had simply become 'a habit'. He transitions from one who used to blame his sexuality – 'this sexuality stop me from going' – to '[starting] to find a way' home to his self and God. Where the first rupture to an unquestioning compliance came from an external source (blackmailers), this second rupture to habitual complacency (in not '[going] to church') comes from within. K begins to self-direct the course of the next phases of his faith journey.

His reflexivity is further marked when he recognizes that he has the propensity to 'categorize', to hold onto dualisms, that serve like an out-of-date roadmap, such as 'holy'/'unholy' or 'spiritual'/'unspiritual' [15:81 (1112:1121)] and 'good boy'/'bad guy' – the infantalization of 'good boy' against the maturation of 'bad guy' is noteworthy. He makes the link between falling prey to such dualisms and, by extension, falling prey to the blackmailers who reify the mindset that 'you're homosexual, you're not holy. You're bad, morally in the eyes of God'. In coming to terms that it is 'the guilt [that] actually hold me back from doing more for God', he hopes that 'one day I can really accept myself-lah, get the balance'. '[Getting] the balance' is akin to searching for more reliable navigational cues. Being conflicted as such is productive of a new subjectivity, the forging of a new path that begins with '[accepting] myself' and desiring to 'get the balance'.

Being conflicted and coming out from that also resonates with and finds full expression in AY's narrative. As he says: 'All this while I was very involved in church … you fool around a bit and then you feel really guilty about it. And then you vow never to do it again, and it happens again and … the whole guilt process goes over and over again. This struggle went on for many, many years'

[20:2 (22:33)]. The iterative cycle of guilt and repentance that 'goes over and over again' as experienced by others had also been AY's lived reality 'for many, many years' in his 'struggle' as a full-time youth worker then, coming to terms with his sexuality and spirituality. The rupture to this predictable rhythm of a 'struggle [that] went on for many, many years' is being outed by his former lesbian pastor, stripped of the national youth award and shamed before his congregation. In his bittersweet reflection of his journey thereafter, AY says:

> AY: It's like you do all the good in your life you know, but with one little speck of flaw and someone could just use that and wipe every good work, every good deed that you've done. And to me that was just so uncalled for.
>
> SAB: Do you feel that's a speck of flaw in your whole make-up?
>
> AY: Then I probably did-lah. Because I was you know, struggling... within and stuff. But now, no. I feel that it's who I am and I'm such a better person today in terms of knowing who I am... accepting who I am than I was before... to the point that if anybody... off the streets [were to] ask me if I was gay, I'll say, 'Yeah'. I've got no qualms about it. I've got nothing to hide you know. So I don't look at it as a flaw. [20:47 (601:614)]

There are striking similarities between Jimmy's and AY's journeys of faith: both have sought to transform their 'guilt' or overcompensate for that 'one little speck of flaw' through fidelity to their church's teachings and innumerable 'good work' and 'good deed'. And where Jimmy's carefully crafted image as a 'good boy' not a 'bad guy' was threatened, AY was outed and faced dire consequences. Both reacted by leaving their churches. AY's resilience is noteworthy as he '[doesn't] look at it (sexuality) as a flaw' and that he is a 'better person today in terms of knowing who I am... [and] accepting who I am'. Today, both have freely come out to those whom they trust and love. That guilt is not only transformative but also liberating is evident, as AY says: 'I've got nothing to hide.'

CK, Joe, Peter, Alexis, Jimmy and AY show how religious guilt as concomitant to being conflicted is potentially transformative: the mind/body breakthrough is paradoxically effected by a mind/body breakdown. The prolonged iterative cycle of religious guilt is ruptured by traumatic turning points (blackmailers in the case of Jimmy and being outed in the case of AY) that, in turn, precipitates an awakening that finds expression in Jimmy's desire to 'start to find a way' or AY's self-acceptance, 'I've got nothing to hide' in being proud and gay. And in the absence of a rupture to the seeming stasis, in not 'really [deciding] where to go' in the case of Alexis, ways of becoming are opened up and not foreclosed. Being conflicted is revalued as both a means to an end and an end in itself.

Bargaining

In this section, Ling Jackie and Janic as self-identified Christians bargain with God in the process of making sense of why they are who they are. The perceived Godly indifference resonates with Janic's narrative, as she recounts:

> That was when it started, very, very young, 10, 11. And I was already started asking God … 'If you make me then help me to stop doing this, help me to stop feeling this way', ever since then you know, as young as I could remember. So if it was so natural for me to feel that way, from nowhere, why wasn't it natural enough for it to be taken away you know, if I accept it so easily, if it's not meant to be? And with all the effort I put in to stop it you know, asking help from wherever until you know, so much later in years, I was still asking the same question but never, never. Whenever I felt OK, if, not like I hear a voice or anything but in all my prayers, if I wanted to know something important, I will always feel like OK you know … I know what I needed to do. But in this case, the only question is, is it because I'm willing, unwilling to listen, that is why I never heard? But I've asked a million times. But why the other stuff I ask I always understood? I always got it. But why this one, nothing at all you know? [7:110 (1433:1445)]

Janic's prolonged frustration arises from 'all the effort … put in to stop it' and 'asking the same question … a million times' and not 'never [hearing]' answers. Janic singles out God's muteness on this one prayer: 'why the other stuff I ask I always understood? I always got it. But why this one, nothing at all you know?' So Janic's bargaining with God, since she 'very, very young, 10, 11', has been: 'If you make me then help me to stop doing this, help me to stop feeling this way.' Having exhausted her resources 'to stop it', even the consideration that she might have been 'unwilling to listen', she calls on divine intervention. In doing so, Janic throws the gauntlet at God 'to stop it': 'So if it was so natural for me to feel that way, from nowhere, why wasn't it natural enough for it to be taken away you know'. That what is 'natural' is God-given results in a sophistry that comes full circle as Janic rationalizes that 'if I accept it so easily … it's … meant to be'.

The divergence from torment to self-realization resonates with Ling Jackie's faith journey, as she says:

> I went to see psychiatrist. And yet this problem … still exist. It didn't change at all. So I … told God that, 'If you're willing, then I will plan to find some other

different ways to handle this issue. Because all this while, I have tried all sorts of ... so-called proper ways to handle it but still, it didn't work at all'. So I told God that, 'If you're willing, I'm going to start [to] know some of the friends like me' So 'If you're willing, I hope that you'll open a window for me as soon as possible' [*laughs*]. [18:10 (132:141)]

Ling Jackie who now identifies as a non-dogmatic or non-fundamentalist Protestant Christian had sought both spiritual and secular counselling to redress the 'problem' of her sexuality and was on the brink of despair as her desire for women as a woman 'didn't change at all'. Her bargaining with God humorously positions God as a matchmaker in '[opening] a window for [her] as soon as possible' as she desires to be in a relationship to 'start [to] know some of the friends like [her]'. Having exhausted 'proper ways to handle it' but to no avail as they 'didn't work at all', Ling Jackie manifests resilience in not being defeated but rather resourceful in outsourcing 'different ways to handle this issue' to God!

In the two narratives above, God is interestingly positioned as a counsellor (Janic) and matchmaker (Ling Jackie), through the diverse bargaining tactics deployed. The weight of the 'bad [thing]' of being homosexual is mitigated by '[trying] to change', being '[willing] to listen', finding 'different ways to handle' the 'problem', observing the tenets of one's faith and choosing one's profession well.

Demonizing sexuality

Praying the gay away for both AY and CK is consonant with secularized sexual orientation change efforts (SOCE) that go by different terms such as '*sexual orientation therapy, reorientation therapy, conversion therapy,* and *reparative therapy*' (Flentje et al. 2014: 1244). The aims of these therapies, regardless of the term used, are to alter one or more of these 'domains' ('sexual identity', 'sexual attraction', 'sexual behaviour' and 'social connection') so that one may stop identifying as 'LGB', stop engaging in non-heteronormative sexual behaviours, stop finding same-sex persons attractive and stop associating with them altogether. Despite the removal of homosexuality as a 'mental illness' from the DSM-II and 'ego-dystonic homosexuality' from the DSM-III, clinical and spiritual interventionists insist on de-pathologizing and demonizing homosexuality, respectively. That these are not evidence-based therefore sound interventions is apparent given the scientific evidence that show how these practices are not only ineffective but also harmful, even unethical (Flentje et al. 2014: 1261) with short-term harms (e.g. depression, anxiety, shame, guilt, self-hatred) and long-term harms (e.g. suicidality both attempted and completed).

In this section, AY's and CK's experiences of having the 'demon of homosexuality' cast out from them, within the Christian context, will be discussed. As AY recollects:

> But the strange thing was this. You know how a lot of people say that... it's born of... Satan and the spiritual thing... but every time I was prayed over, because I was in a charismatic church, seminary... it's supposed to cast the demons out of you. But nothing actually happened you know. And it didn't feel like I changed as a person. It didn't feel like my desires changed because they were still there. Even though they said, well you have to surrender it and all that, I've done all of that. And nothing changed... to be you know, truly honest. They were still there. [20:33 (429:442)]

'I've done all of that' that AY attests to here encompasses: being 'prayed over' to cast the 'demons' of homosexuality from him; and in the quote before [20:32 (416:429)], 'veering more towards just being a straight person'; and 'living... as celibate'. The gamut of ways of becoming that he had adopted or was prepared to adopt is evident – 'you have to surrender it' – your will, to the perceived will of God, for love of God, as indoctrinated by the 'charismatic church, seminary' that he was a part of then. The promise of '[casting] the demons out of you' on condition that you 'surrender it (your desires)' did not materialize, as 'nothing actually happened you know. And it didn't feel like I changed as a person. It didn't feel like my desires changed because they were still there'. The reiteration of 'nothing changed' marks the fracturing of that promise that eventually leads to his 'truly honest' realization that who he is, is not 'born of... Satan'. In being 'truly honest', his transformation of self is effected albeit not overnight and in the way his pastors intended it to: AY 'changed as a person' paradoxically through accepting that 'nothing changed'.

AY's survival account of conversion therapy resonates with the testimonies of ex-ex-gay individuals who note the following reasons for identifying as LGB after reorientation therapy that include, inter alia, the acceptance of and being honest about being gay or lesbian, the realization that one cannot change one's sexual orientation, 'religious integration (rather than dissonance) with LGB identity', desire of or finding intimacy in same-sex relationships (Flentje et al. 2014: 1260). In short, it is the happy failure to meet any or all of the objectives of sexual orientation change efforts designed to facilitate one's becoming heterosexual! One's sexuality, as AY shows, is immutable.

The immutability of one's sexuality is also resonant in CK's narrative that compels divine intervention in casting out demons. He recollects:

> Sometimes... [the] church pastor would say, people chose to be a gay or homosexual because they are misleading by friends, by the media... But a lot of gays will not agree with this because who wants to be gay or homosexual when they have a choice. We feel like we are born, I mean when we're young boys, you know, when I'm sharing with my friends... they already started to have this tendency to love men more than women. I mean how can this be an influence when you are at a very young age when you don't know what is a relationship or what is sex... So I believe that what they say is inaccurate. I mean, they try to pray for you, to cast away the demons. I don't really quite agree with their point in this matter. [17:17 (210:229)]

The dualisms of nature/culture and birth/choice in relation to sexuality seemingly complement each other but are, in fact, contesting positions in the way that they are used: the former by the 'church pastor' and the latter by 'a lot of gays' like CK. On the one hand, the dualism of nature/culture arises from the mindset that, as a child of God, created in God's image and likeness, one cannot then be 'gay or homosexual' as God's creations are perfect, not flawed. One wilfully '[chooses] to be a gay or homosexual because they are [misled] by friends, by the media'. So one is not born 'gay or homosexual', to paraphrase de Beauvoir, but becomes one through the 'corruptible' influences of friends and the all-powerful media. So heterosexuality becomes naturalized and homosexuality, demonized. As nature (God's creation of the straight human person) is privileged over culture (human creation of the 'gay or homosexual' person), it occupies the first term of the binary.

On the other hand, the dualism of birth/choice arises from CK's belief and 'a lot of gays' through his 'sharing with [his] friends' that 'we are born [gay]', thus created by God and in God's image and likeness. As CK rationalizes: firstly, given the sanctions imposed on those who veer away from 'compulsory heterosexuality' (Rich 2004) in the context of Malaysia in particular, he questions: 'who wants to be gay or homosexual when they have a choice'. Secondly, the embodied narratives of CK and his friends show that they 'already started to have this tendency to love men more than women... at a very young age when [they did not]... know what is a relationship or what is sex'. So one is born 'gay or homosexual' which leads CK to privilege the naturalization of being born 'gay or homosexual' over the 'lifestyle' choice of becoming gay. Birth, as such, occupies the first term of the binary.

In the context of the quote above, within the dualism of nature/culture, one is deemed essentially straight, and within the dualism of birth/choice, one is deemed essentially 'gay or homosexual'. However, as shown in preceding discussions, one also *becomes* gay as the process of becoming is a journey that is rife with pain and joy, rejection and acceptance, confusion and recognition, and self-negation and self-actualization. This process of becoming demystifies the contesting dualisms of nature/culture and birth/choice as it blurs the points of departure. In the dualism of nature/culture, one becomes gay through choice that is culturally and socially mediated through the media and one's friends. Becoming gay is a cultural construct. In the dualism of birth/choice, one becomes gay in the everyday living out of what it means to *be* gay: one chooses, for instance, to come out or not and to whom and when and on whose terms. Becoming gay is embodied. In that sense, one *chooses to become* gay (in the like manner that some have chosen to pass off as straight or become celibate or be in a gay relationship). Through the lived experiences not only of CK but also of 'a lot of gays', one is born 'gay or homosexual' *and* also becomes one. The shared narratives of CK and his friends authenticate this collective lived reality and in so doing, destabilize the dualisms of nature/culture and birth/choice as they show that nature–culture and birth–choice are mutually constitutive states of being and becoming.

At this juncture of CK's journey, his agency is marked by his resistance of the dualism of nature/culture. He believes that what the 'church pastor' says is 'inaccurate' and he calls to question thereby invalidating quick-fix 'solutions' such as '[praying] for you, to cast away the demons (of homosexuality)'. And his process of becoming 'gay or homosexual' as a self-identified Christian and gay man continues, as he goes on to recount a particular exorcism episode where he says: 'So I was there and I was very afraid ... [and] embarrassed that my friends [will] know that I am gay. And I started to confess my sin ... on that moment' [17:20 (249:262)]. With heightened anguish on being outed in front of his church friends, he was filled with much trepidation when the invited speaker-pastor

[pointed his finger] at me. I was like, 'Oh no'. But actually just the man behind me started to vomit. So when you have demon or something, or spirit or something with you, and you started to vomit, it's like more or less you are the person. And I was saying, 'OK, I'm safe' ... So I'm not sure [whether] ... he's praying referring to me or that man behind up to today. [17:21 (263:272)]

The mutually constitutive states of being gay and becoming gay as discussed above that destabilizes the dualism of birth/choice are at work here. CK's spirited defence of being (born) gay [17:17 (210:229)] does not foreclose the process of becoming gay: *becoming* gay is living out on a daily basis what *being* gay means. In this extraordinary episode, CK, at the threat of being outed, renounces his sexuality and repents ('I started to confess my sin') as he 'was very afraid ... [and] embarrassed that [his] friends [will] know that [he is] gay'. Although he defends being (born) gay – that it is naturalized (created by God) and not constructed (culturally and socially mediated) – CK remains conflicted as he deems homosexuality a 'sin'. In the climactic moment recounted, CK's relief at not manifesting the mark of the 'demon', as 'the man behind [him] started to vomit', makes him feel 'safe', unexposed, for now. Becoming gay for CK henceforth is to remain tormented 'up to today' as he bears the mark of the 'demon' internally, due to his own misgivings about his sexuality, regardless of whether or not the preacher was 'referring to [him] or that man'. The vomiting serves as an externalization not of the mark of the 'demon' but rather self-loathing and shame which one could, in this context, read as CK's projection of his own repulsion onto the 'man behind [him who] started to vomit', which is more marked in the following account. He adds:

CK: But today I still saw this man on and off in [my hometown].
SAB: Right.
CK: He's thirty-something (10 years ago from today) and I think he's unmarried. So I'm not sure whether he's a gay or not. But that was a very bad experience for me. I mean, every time when I go to church or other camp and when they have this prayer session or body ministry know, to cast out the spirits ... or healing, I'll tell God, 'This is just between you and me'.
SAB: Yeah.
CK: 'So if you want to like say something to me or what, let's do it privately and not let ... the speaker ... prophesy through someone else' ... So up to today, I still have this fear.
SAB: It's a fear of?
CK: Being known by others. [17:22 (272:287)]

This 'thirty-something ... unmarried ... not sure whether he's a gay or not' man, whom CK sees 'on and off' the familiar streets of his hometown, becomes what Kristeva in *Powers of Horror* (1982) terms as the 'abject' or 'other' for him. The marking off of a psychic boundary between CK and that man constitutes abjection. As Kristeva explains:

> We may call it a border; abjection is above all ambiguity. Because, while releasing a hold, it does not radically cut off the subject from what threatens it – abjection acknowledges it to be in perpetual danger. (Kristeva 1982: 9)

The regulation of this border accounts for CK's feeling 'safe'. Yet 'abjection itself is a composite of judgement and affect, of condemnation and yearning, of signs and drives' (Kristeva 1982: 10). So the abject, what is deemed other to and expelled from the self, continues to both fascinate and repulse the subject. This is apparent in CK's unarticulated repulsion of the man (who is a cast of) yet articulated fascination in him as he wonders if his being 'unmarried [means that] he's a gay or not'. And more significantly, he is still haunted – as the abject is 'not radically cut off' – by whether or not the pastor was in fact 'referring to [him] or that man behind'. His regulation of the border of public exorcism/private confession is clearly marked when he bargains with God: 'This is just between you and me ... So if you want to like say something to me or what, let's do it privately and not let ... the speaker ... prophesy through someone else.'

The immutability of sexuality that one is 'a gay or homosexual' by birth and not choice, as an effect of nature not culture, is evident in both AY's and CK's narratives. Both have encountered first-hand being prayed over to exorcize the 'demons' of homosexuality from them: AY directly and CK indirectly. Ways of becoming 'a gay or homosexual' for both men who self-identify as Christian diverge. AY is 'changed as a person' paradoxically through accepting that 'nothing changed': he has reconciled his sexuality and spirituality. For CK, however, 'nothing changed' too as he remains 'safe' in not being outed as 'a gay or homosexual': he is, as discussed elsewhere, keeping in abeyance the reconciliation of his sexuality and spirituality.

Being in denial, diverting oneself and shutting off

These strategies of being in denial, diverting oneself and shutting off share the desired effect of delaying, even resisting the negotiation of one's sexuality and spirituality, and are, at different junctures, either adopted or noted by Jimmy and Ling Jackie.

Seeking diversions from one's self, as a corollary strategy to denial, finds expression in Jimmy's and Ling Jackie's narratives. Jimmy who belonged to a 'non-denomination church' says that 'they claim to follow the Bible. So many things like we cannot do ... I was very, very careful about myself. About my thinking like that. So really-lah, follow the church. So distract me from my own self, just like that lor' [15:43 (599:613)]. Where his desiring other men is part of '[his] own self', Jimmy suppresses that by distracting himself with rigid adherence to his church's teachings. And he was 'very, very careful about [himself]' to '[maintain] the fiction of unity' that there are, as inferred, given the 'many things like we cannot do', no gay Christians in his church. Through denying himself, he becomes complicit in the 'ignorance' that sustains this 'fiction of unity'. Ling Jackie willed herself to '[stop] thinking about this problem. [She] concentrated on [her] works and studies'. This self-denial was tenable until she fell in love with a woman from a different ethnic group. This served as a disruption to the 'fiction of unity' that she had preserved – the normality of her personhood with the 'problem' buried. Wrecked with confusion and nervousness, she is compelled to not only resurrect but also deal with herself (sexuality and spirituality) that is doubly problematized, as she says: 'So again, this problem (her falling in love with a woman who is differently ethnicized) also make me [feel] that I will have to start finding some ways to handle this problem (being lesbian and Christian)' [18:7 (88:100)].

'Maintaining the fiction of unity' (Bailey 2007: 83) through strategies such as being in denial, distracting oneself from oneself and shutting off, evident from the narratives of Jimmy and Ling Jackie as self-identified Christians, are seemingly premised on 'ignorance'. Ignorance in this sense as borrowed from racialized discourses 'is a form of not knowing (seeing wrongly), resulting from the habit of erasing, dismissing, distorting, and forgetting' parts of one's lived realities, essentially, parts of one's self. The narratives discussed above show that firstly, 'maintaining the fiction of unity' is made possible through the complicity of those like Jimmy and Ling Jackie who within their deeply heterosexist faith communities opt or are compelled to not challenge the 'fiction of unity'. The 'fiction of unity' in this regard is the multilevel institutional (e.g. familial, governmental, religious, legal) construct of a unified, heteronormative subject: that being gay and Christian is a contradiction in terms. Secondly, the fragility of this 'fiction of unity' is made visible when it is disrupted by the refusal to remain ignorant, albeit reluctantly, as shown by Ling Jackie. In embodying these forms of *strategic ignorance* – for the sake of face or self-preservation (Jimmy) and for the sake of sanity (Ling Jackie) – as an effect of the flux of such processes of becoming, they *queer* time, as 'life is a circle' and one's sense of self, indeterminate.

Negotiating the condemnation of homosexuality, intolerance and taboo

The realization of self and living out an abundant life are tempered by incomplete 'interpersonal routinization' and incomplete 'institutional routinization' (Seidman et al. 1999: 11). The former 'indicates informed ways individuals integrate homosexuality into their conventional social lives, e.g. disclosing to family members or co-workers'. 'Institutional routinisation', on the other hand, 'refers to incorporating policies and practices into organisations that do not subordinate non-heterosexuals'. Incomplete 'interpersonal routinisation' is the result of being demonized resulting in GLBTIQ persons being in denial and experiencing guilt and shame, as discussed in previous sections of this chapter. Incomplete 'interpersonal routinisation' in not being able to reconcile one's sexuality and spirituality is indelibly linked to incomplete 'institutional routinisation' which I extend to include familial, relational, spiritual, or instructional and ideological institutions that impact one's sense of self, sexuality and spirituality. The following narratives that mark out expressions of intolerance and condemnation of homosexuality and its repression as taboo show how these rest on a continuum of practices of othering sexualities of GLBTIQ persons. Highlighted are interviewees' responses and coping strategies that show the connectivity between these practices of othering ('incomplete institutional routinisation') and their coming to terms with their own sexuality and spirituality ('interpersonal routinisation').

On sexuality as taboo

The silencing of the topic of sexuality is apparent growing up in Malaysia and Singapore. In this instance, Mary Douglas's thought-provoking thesis, that 'dirt is matter out of place' in her seminal text *Purity and Danger: An Analysis of Concept of Pollution and Taboo*, is instructional, as she states:

> If we can abstract pathogenicity and hygiene from our notion of dirt, we are left with the old definition of dirt as matter out of place. This is a very suggestive approach. It implies two conditions: a set of ordered relations and a contravention of that order. Dirt then, is never a unique, isolated event. Where there is dirt, there is system. Dirt is the by-product of a systematic ordering and classification of matter, in so far as ordering involves rejecting inappropriate elements. ([1996] 2002: 44)

The 'set of ordered relations' is the binary of normative sexuality/non-normative sexualities or, as state rhetoric puts it, 'right'/'wrong' sexuality that finds parallelism in the binary 'matter'/'dirt'. That 'dirt' is 'never a unique, isolated event... [but a] system ... [and] the by-product of a systematic ordering and classification of matter' solidifies the connection between 'dirt' and 'matter'. Interestingly, 'matter' takes shape through 'dirt' which is filtered from it and 'matter' as valued against the devaluing of 'dirt' as undesirable rejects or 'inappropriate elements' within this schema. Fundamentally, the indelible connection between 'matter' and 'dirt' remains. The 'contravention of that order' is inevitable as there arises in any cultural system of values, what Douglas categorizes as, 'ambiguity' and 'anomaly': 'an anomaly is an element which does not fit a given set or series; ambiguity is a characteristic of statements capable of two interpretations' (Douglas 2002: 47). The field of sexuality is ambiguous given the diversity of desires, intimacies and practices, and within a heteronormative ordering of sexuality, what is filtered out are anomalous non-normative sexualities that are deemed as 'inappropriate elements'.

Where culture 'in the sense of the public, standardised values of a community, mediates the experience of individuals', there exists 'various provisions for dealing with ambiguous or anomalous event' at public and private (individual) levels (Douglas 2002: 48). Douglas maintains that revising or negotiating shifting boundaries between 'matter' and 'dirt' at an individual level is more easily facilitated as 'categories [are] more rigid' at a public level precisely because there is a greater compulsion to manage aberrations at a public level in order to maintain its authority in prescribing such communal values that in turn inform private values. In terms of treating 'anomalies', Douglas suggests that 'negatively, we can ignore, just not perceive them, or perceiving we can condemn'. But 'positively, we can deliberately confront the anomaly and try to create a new pattern of reality in which it has a place'. Other strategies include 'settling for one or other interpretation' to reduce ambiguity, avoiding anomalous events which then 'affirms and strengthens the definitions to which they do not conform', labelling them as 'dangerous', or use 'ambiguous symbols' (in ritual) 'to enrich meaning or to call attention to other levels of existence' (Douglas 2002: 48-9).

I posit an inherent paradox in the 'systematic ordering and classification of matter' which renders 'dirt' its 'by-product' that Douglas proposes which is here applied to sexualities. The greater the need to harden defining lines distinguishing 'dirt' (non-normative sexualities) from 'matter' (normative sexuality), the 'stickier' (borrowed from Sartre's essay on 'stickiness' cited in Douglas 2002: 47) the connectedness between 'dirt' and 'matter' is. As such, many consider it an imperative to negate (e.g. suppressing as taboo) and/or condemn ambiguous or anomalous sexualities (e.g. condemning homosexuality) which threaten this defining line. The proscription of heteronormativity is sustainable only through designating other sexual intimacies as 'wrong' or anomalous where sexualities by virtue of their resting on a continuum of choice and practices are, in fact, ambiguous. The division between what is 'right' and 'wrong' becomes marked and, when confronted, can potentially call to question where it was previously obfuscated thus uncontested. It is to 'try to create a new pattern of reality in which it (dirt) has a place' (Douglas 2002: 48).

To illustrate, Peter identifies two other taboos – one sociocultural, the other, religious – that he had to overcome in his sexuality journey, in '[trying] to create a new pattern of reality' (Douglas 2002: 48) for himself:

> I think social, cultural context where … tenderness being shown … between men … is something very taboo, I think. [1:33 (394:412)]
>
> The question of getting divorced in the church because that is also another taboo … On the other hand, if you look at the whole understanding of marriage itself and this dispensation of marriage thing … one of the things is … whether both persons were fully aware, had full knowledge of what it was and it appears that both of us did not have that knowledge, neither me nor her realized that (his homosexuality). [1:83 (965:979)]

Peter's observation that 'tenderness being shown … between men … is something very taboo' and his 'not [having] that knowledge (of his own homosexuality)' that would have facilitated his 'dispensation of marriage' are related. Elsewhere in the interview, Peter admitted that he initially dis-identified with gay men as he was susceptible to stereotypical media representations of gay men as 'more feminine', 'people who cross-dress' and he 'didn't really see in that men could share tenderness with each other' although that was what he desired: 'to have a meaningful relationship and that I wanted tenderness'. So he rationalized that 'emotionally [he] wasn't gay' [1:9 (107:124)]. When he begins to identify as gay (aided by psychiatric counselling), he comes out (late, by his own admission) to his self and to his then wife, as he recollects: 'I had a strong feeling that I couldn't bear going through this life not living as a gay person … So I think the push to come out was more the emotional needs, even more than the sexual needs, to have an emotional, romantic relationship with a man' [1:21 (253:260)]. The veil of ignorance is finally lifted – his not being 'fully aware [and] ... not [having] that knowledge' of himself – and this led to the breaking down of two 'taboo[s]': that 'tenderness ... between men' can happen as he eventually discovers for himself and the severance of his marriage that unburdened both him and his then wife as they were both unfulfilled in their marriage.

Demystifying sexuality taboos constructed by familial and religious institutions and the media, as instances of 'incomplete institutional routinisation (institutional practices that subordinate non-heterosexuals)', potentially liberate as they make visible the schema of 'matter'/'dirt' that correlate with naturalizing the binary of 'right'/'wrong' desires, intimacies and relationships. As such, Peter effects 'interpersonal routinization' (Seidman et al. 1999: 20) for himself. And in shifting the defining lines between 'matter' and 'dirt', at a private, individual level, he begins to effect 'a new pattern of reality' (Douglas 2002: 48) for himself by firstly confronting then revising – and not without struggle – his perception of what he is told constitutes 'dirt' by familial, sacred (church) and secular (media) institutions.

On the religious or spiritual condemnation of homosexuality

'Negatively, we can ignore, just not perceive them, or perceiving we can condemn', observes Douglas, in our treatment of anomalies (Douglas 2002: 48). Negative public treatment of anomalies constitutes 'incomplete institutional routinization (institutional practices that subordinate non-heterosexuals)' (Seidman et al. 1999: 20). And the narratives highlighted below show the extent to which 'incomplete institutional routinization' shapes 'incomplete interpersonal routinization'. They call to question, in descending order, that 'culture in the sense of the public, standardised values of a community, mediates the experience of individuals' (Douglas 2002: 48).

For Andy, to condemn non-normative sexualities as anomalous is to 'keep stabbing sexuality'. It is also noteworthy that she makes a division between incompatible public (institutional) and private (individual) value systems, the latter translated as practices 'out of the institution', as she says:

> There are so many pressing issues out there, why keep stabbing sexuality? ... if I don't question whether or not you had sex this morning before you go to the communion table, why should you be questioning what I do in my life out of the institution? ... Am I stepping on your toes by doing this? [2:121 (1428:1438)]

The reiteration of 'struggle' in Alexis's narrative, in '[making] several attempts to change', is apparent. She does this in compliance with the Biblical condemnation of homosexuality as 'a sin' – 'dirt as matter out of place' (Douglas 2002: 44). The ambiguity of 'living a life' where she '[tends] to separate them (her sexuality and spirituality)' leads her to label her life as 'hypocrisy' as these boundaries are less maintained than they are polluted. As she says:

> It was quite a struggle I guess ... I tend to separate them. And it's like I'm living a life, um, I'm not sure if it's hypocrisy ... And it's a struggle to me ... I've made several attempts to change, try to because people interpret the Bible as you know, homosexuality is a sin. [10:34 (525:535)]

Where Douglas suggests that 'negatively, we can ignore, just not perceive them, or perceiving we can condemn' (Douglas 2002: 48), in treating anomalies, Jimmy does that literally by '[putting the Bible] in the cupboard'. In a bid to ignore the 'Bible [that is] always against homosexuality', he closets it! He rejects the Bible in the like manner that his 'heart [is] already lost' in knowing that he is 'rejected' despite his piety – 'no matter how good, no matter how close I can do':

> I wish that I can continue reading Bible [*laughs*] ... I like put in the cupboard. I took it out. I start want to like read again. But like I say it's like, used to it already-lah, like the heart already lost already because for me, like I always see that Bible always against homosexuality. So means like no matter how good, no matter how close I can do ah, I also feel rejected like that. [15:80 (1094:1111)]

That 'culture in the sense of the public, standardised values of a community, mediates the experience of individuals' (Douglas 2002: 48) is quite apparent in CK who insists on '[judging himself that] ... being gay or being in a homosexual relationship is wrong', despite being exposed to queer theologizing espoused by GLBTIQ-friendly networks and churches that he is aware of:

> I judge myself [that] ... being gay or being in a homosexual relationship is wrong based on my teaching that I have when I was young ... what is stated in the Bible. [17:37 (436:449)]

The boundary between sacred/secular is blurred in the case of Ling Jackie when she draws parallelisms between institutional heterosexism conveyed through secular counselling that merely reconfigures spiritual counselling that '[uses] the Scripture to oppose [her] sexuality'. Douglas's suggestion that 'negatively, we can ignore, just not perceive them, or perceiving we can condemn' (Douglas 2002: 48) in treating anomalies finds expression in Ling

Jackie's interpretation of the counsellor's advice as 'the best choice is you don't get involved in this gay life'. The anomaly of a Christian lesbian self is thereby negated in purging the 'dirt' in 'not [holding] this sexuality issue so hard':

> Unlike the church counsellor ... she didn't really immediately use the Scripture to oppose my sexuality. She, after hearing my problems, she told me that I have a lot of choices. I can either accept my difference ... compared to other straight friends or I can try to change it. Or I can concentrate on other activities and works. So she said, I have a lot of choices and it's up to me to choose ... what I feel comfortable with ... But ... I felt that ... in her point of view, the best choice is you don't get involved in this gay life ... So after that, I try to concentrate to other things and ... I try not to hold this sexuality issue so hard. [18:8 (100:115)]

In the narratives of Andy, Alexis, Ling Jackie, Jimmy and CK, what is more apparent is the negative treatment of GLBTIQ sexualities as anomalies. Highlighted is the tension between public and private treatment of GLBTIQ sexualities. The attempted resistances and compliances to treating 'dirt as matter out of place' leave one feeling defensive (Andy), hypocritical (Alexis), 'rejected' (Jimmy), judgemental of oneself (CK) and dejected (Ling Jackie) as she says elsewhere: 'During that time, I also felt that I would like to give up ... I felt very tired, tired in my mind during that time' [18:32 (369:379)]. Discussed also in this chapter is the demonization of GLBTIQ sexualities where 'dirt as matter out of place' needs to be expunged, through repentance (in the case of AY and CK who experienced having had the demon of homosexuality cast out of them), conversion (in the case of Jimmy who encountered the Real Love Ministry led by an ex-gay pastor and AY who resolved to 'live a straight life, have a family and stuff') [20:7 (77:87)], and erasure (by opting for celibacy in the case of Janic and AY, among others).

The narratives in the next section, however, show how a positive treatment of GLBTIQ sexualities can potentially 'create a new pattern of reality in which it (dirt) has a place' (Douglas 2002: 48).

On overcoming intolerance and condemnation

Andy hopes for societal tolerance rather than bigotry, as she says:

> Idealistically, I wish things could have been a lot easier for people like us. And you can't force society to accept things just like how some people can't be forced to eat durians [*interviewer laughs*]. But that's as trivial as how I would put it.

> But...for sure, some amount of tolerance would be good. I think it's all about tolerance. Like I said, do I want the church to one day accept it?...it's not an incredible need of mine that the church must accept it because at the end of the day, the church is just made up of people. Am I about to rewrite the Bible? No, I'm not. But what do I hope? I just hope that people would just ease off a little bit more. [2:90 (1102:1110)]

According to Andy, if 'people would just ease off a little bit more', that would potentially 'create a new pattern of reality in which it (dirt) has a place' (Douglas 2002: 48). This aspiration is borne from the acceptance of the fallibility of the largely heterosexist church, as 'the church is just made up of people'. Hence, 'it's not an incredible need of [hers] that the church must accept it'. Similarly, she does not seek to 'rewrite the Bible' as a clear distinction is made between 'incomplete institutional routinization (institutional practices that subordinate non-heterosexuals)' (Seidman et al. 1999: 20), practised by churchgoers who do not 'ease off (in "stabbing sexuality")' and complete 'interpersonal routinisation' where she has reconciled her sexuality and spirituality. As such, 'culture in the sense of the public, standardised values of a community' does not completely '[mediate] the experience of individuals' like Andy (Douglas 2002: 48) who, alongside 'people like [her]', stands apart from society.

And she adds with humour: 'You can't force society to accept things just like how some people can't be forced to eat durians (a local fruit dubbed "the king of fruits" that smells pungent even repugnant to some)'. Her advocating for 'some amount of tolerance' with humour is noteworthy as, according to Asian feminist theologian Gemma Cruz who applies James Scott, 'hidden transcripts' or 'weapons of the weak' strategically employed by the marginalized affirm the subversive potential of humour, as 'prophetic in that it breaks the mould of thinking and provides a designated radically new alternative behaviour pattern' (Cruz 2011: 103, 109). The subversive potential in Andy's advocating for tolerance without 'an incredible need of mine that the church must accept it' and the Bible must be '[rewritten]' lies in the maintenance of ambiguity: that the sexuality of 'people like us' is at once wrong *and* right. Tolerance embodies this blurring of defining lines between what constitutes 'matter' and 'dirt'. Hence, 'a new pattern of reality in which [dirt] has a place' (Douglas 2002: 48) is envisioned and created.

Adam, who is 45-year-old filmmaker, married and a Muslim trans man today, and then a Buddhist, on making sense of Buddhist ideological biases, says:

> But in our belief also, the female gender is, you're a woman because you did something bad...because you're a lower status than men, so there is this

discrimination. It's still a very sexist way of looking at things. And if you're a transsexual, that means you did worse things-lah [*laughs*] ... you might have, I don't know, raped somebody, now you have to suffer you know [*laughs*]. You are born in a wrong body... what can I do?

   If I did something, I can't correct what I've done. I'll just live with it. And I don't know if I actually believe that it's [*laughs*] because I did something wrong that I've become like that. I think it is harder ... but I also think that it makes you a stronger person ... [in] being able to accept people, diversity, accept people of you know, whatever race, religion ... because I am one of those minorities. So I don't necessarily think that it is a bad thing. [22:41 (482:495)]

The 'systematic ordering and classification of matter' that Douglas speaks of (2002: 44), of which 'dirt' is its 'by-product', resonates with the cycle of rebirth that is central to the Buddhist 'belief'. The 'systematic ordering', where man is ascribed with a higher status, and woman, a 'lower status than men', transsexuals as being 'born in a wrong body' in contrast to heterosexual men who are born in the 'right' body, as inferred, is hierarchically and oppositionally ordered. Aligned with this 'systematic ordering' is the degree of suffering of which sexism and heterosexism are extensions, that is in store for you: 'because you did something bad (in a previous life) ... now you have to suffer (in the present one)'.

Adam's disavowal of 'this discrimination [as it's] still a very sexist way of looking at things' is striking as he was then transitioning from a Buddhist radical lesbian to a female-to-male transgender person. His subversion, which like Andy's is laced with humour, begins with labelling the 'systematic ordering and classification of matter' (Douglas 2002: 44), as '[discriminatory]' and 'sexist'. Secondly, his casting doubt on the 'belief' of suffering as proportionate and cause and effect – 'I don't know if I actually believe that it's [*laughs*] because I did something wrong that I've become like that' – inverts the negativity of being a transsexual as one 'born in a wrong body'. Thirdly, Adam's making sense of his life as 'harder' (which echoes many interviewees' assessment of being heterosexual as 'easier') leads him to nurture his resilience and inclusiveness in embracing the connectedness among human persons, as 'it makes you a stronger person ... [in] being able to accept people, diversity ... because I am one of those minorities'. In doing so, he repositions the marginality of 'minorities' as imbued with the potentiality to contravene the 'set of ordered relations' (Douglas 2002: 44). Hence, 'dirt as matter out of place', as Douglas contends, is, as Adam shows, not 'necessarily ... a bad thing'.

In the narratives of Andy, as a self-identified Christian, and Adam, as a self-identified Buddhist then (now, Muslim) respectively, they show how 'positively, we can deliberately confront the anomaly and try to create a new pattern of reality in which [dirt] has a place' (Douglas 2002: 48). They do not succumb to the negative confrontation of anomaly by '[ignoring], just not [perceiving] them, or perceiving we can condemn', in this case, the sexuality of GLBTIQ persons. They systematically undo the 'systematic ordering and classification of matter' (Douglas 2002: 44) by doubting, calling to question, laughing at, destabilizing, inverting thereby subverting not only the defining lines of 'matter' (heterosexuality)/'dirt' (the proliferation of non-normative sexualities) but also the order in itself. In doing so, they show the limits of 'culture, in the sense of the public, standardised values of a community, [that] mediates the experience of individuals' (Douglas 2002: 48). They do not romanticize these subversive strategies as 'it is harder' to agitate for social reform from the margins as one of the 'minorities', as Adam puts it. Where ambiguity is not reduced nor anomaly disregarded, the ways in which GLBTIQ persons negotiate the tension between their sexuality and spirituality become enriched. In '[trying] to create a new pattern of reality in which [dirt] has a place' (Douglas 2002: 48), they begin to carve a place within the 'system' for themselves as they redefine the parameters of that 'system'.

5

Dealing with guilt, shame and pain

In this chapter, an extension of strategic ignorance discussed in the previous section, are 'strategies of engendering guilt, shame and embarrassment' (Inglis 2002: 15) as effects of naturalizing the constructed binary of heterosexuality/ homosexuality; the former is made normal and good whilst the latter is made deviant and sinful. Through the narratives highlighted below, these strategies paradoxically serve as both acts of acquiescence and resistance; the former is reactionary whilst the latter is generative. In the former, guilt is manifest as an effect of transgressing the construct of heterosexuality whilst in the latter guilt potentially engenders peace.

The face of guilt is multifaceted: arising from some narratives are 'sex guilt', religious guilt, relational and familial guilt. In the first instance, 'sex guilt' is defined as a 'generalised expectancy for self-mediated punishment for violating or anticipating violating standards of proper sexual conduct' (Mosher and Cross 1971 cited in Murray et al. 2007: 224). For some, 'sex guilt' and religious guilt are sometimes intertwined for self-identified Muslim, Christian and Buddhist GLBTIQ persons. The 'standards of proper sexual conduct' are heteronormativity that are being transgressed in becoming sexual and spiritual for GLBTIQ persons. The transgression of such 'standards of proper sexual conduct' is also the basis of relational and familial guilt that are not always aligned with religious guilt: they include, among others, the guilt of falling in love with a person of the same sex or pretending to with a person of the opposite sex, the guilt of infidelity and for the sake of (family) face and for the sake of peace.

On sexual guilt and religious guilt

Joe rehearses the representation of guilt as the direct effect of homosexuality, as 'painted' by his church and 'which [he] believed' then: that 'one, it's deviant, two that it's an addiction. Three; that it's against the design. Four; that it's a sin and the consequence of that sin, is separation from God' [27:8 (81:93)]. The experience of guilt is clearly reactionary as he goes on to add:

> There are no two ways about it ... like all other sins, the moment you do it, you're guilty. And if you feed it, it becomes an obsession and then your whole calling and your whole life will be ruined. And the ultimate fruit of that is that you go to hell, you'll be separated from God forever. [27:8 (81:93)]

Jimmy recognizes his dualistic mindset, as he admits to 'always [wanting] ... to like categorize, like holy or spiritual ... unholy, unspiritual ... you're homosexual, you're not holy, you're bad, morally or in the eyes of God ... So it's like guilt inside. So the guilt actually hold me back from doing more for God ... So I wish like one day I can really accept myself-lah, get the balance' [15:81 (1112:1121)]. Guilt as represented in these narratives is obstructionist as it deters Joe and Jimmy from reaping the 'ultimate fruit' of heaven as a reward for heterosexuality, 'from doing more for God' and from 'coming out'.

The naturalization of heterosexuality (that it is not 'deviant', not 'an addiction', not 'against the design' and not 'a sin') and concomitant denaturalization of homosexuality (that it is 'deviant', 'an addiction', 'against the design' and 'a sin') rest on the construct of guilt as a 'natural' effect of denaturalizing homosexuality. Guilt props up the 'fiction of unity' (Bailey 2007: 83) of the naturalization of heterosexuality where its construct is made invisible. AY says:

> All this while I was very involved in church ... And so it was always one of those things that ... you know, you play around, you fool around a bit and then you feel really guilty about it. And then you vow never to do it again, and it happens again and ... the whole guilt process goes over and over again. [20:2 (22:33)]

As 'a youth worker for more than a year and full-time', AY's iterative cycle of 'the whole guilt process' – the depth of anguish of guilt and its purging through repentance ('vow never to do it again') – is directly proportionate to his depth of '[involvement] in church'. So 'men and women with a strong religious interest', as research shows, 'had more sexual guilt than those with weak religious interest and infrequent church attendance' (Murray et al. 2007: 224).

Desisting from 'maintaining the fiction of unity' – the naturalization of heterosexuality and denaturalization of homosexuality – effects a disruption of experiencing guilt as a 'generalised expectancy for self-mediated punishment for violating or anticipating violating standards of proper sexual conduct' (Mosher and Cross 1971 cited in Murray et al. 2007: 224). This disruption that is expressed as ambivalence is evident when Andy makes a distinction between 'religious guilt' which she does not feel and '(non-religious) guilt' which she does, as 'put on [her]' by her then partner, for Andy's culpability in 'leading [her] down the wrong path ... [as she feels] very stuck ... very caught' [2:47 (577:590)]. In a similar vein, Alexis says:

> I didn't quite buy it (demonization of homosexuality). But it's logical to think that way because society at large you know ... are unable to accept that, what more if it's God you know. And because it's not normal for a person to have a relationship with a same-sex, otherwise God would have created Adam and Adam and Eve [*laughs*] and Eve, in a way. So this is how I sort of concluded that yeah, maybe it's a sin. [10:35 (536:553)]

When Alexis 'sort of concluded that yeah, maybe it's a sin', she disrupts the 'fiction of unity' – that heterosexuality is naturalized by making visible the process of internalizing its 'logic'. Firstly, she casts doubt on the 'logic' of the binary of heterosexuality/homosexuality which she 'didn't quite buy'. Then, she 'quite [buys] it' given the naturalism of heterosexuality as ontologically 'natural' 'otherwise God would have created Adam and Adam and Eve [*laughs*] and Eve'. Thirdly, her conclusion is at best provisional, '*sort of* arrived at, that '*maybe*, it's a sin' (emphases mine), thereby suggesting a possible mindset change later. Alexis's acquiescence to the 'logic' of the 'society at large' is therefore performative as it deconstructs the naturalization and immutability of heteronormativity.

Managing guilt also effects a disruption of the 'fiction of unity' that is heteronormativity. Alexis adds:

> If I were to interpret from my experience with God because to me God, yeah, I believe ... has unconditional love. And from the Bible as well, if I were to have these feelings for women ... I believe that it's not a sin, unless ... I act it out. [10:41 (628:641)]

When Alexis affirms that '[having] these feelings for women ... [is] not a sin', she firstly deviates from the 'heterosexualisation of desire' (Butler 1990: 17) where if follows that one born a woman ought to be gendered feminine and desire a member of the opposite sex/gender. Secondly, she also deviates from the ontological naturalism of Adam and Eve created for each other based on her embodied experience of God's 'unconditional love'. Abstinence, she maintains, is equally applied to 'heterosexual couples [wherein] ... if let's say they're not married, if they were to engage in any sexual activities, that would [be considered] a sin, fornication. So it's at the same level' [10:41 (628:641)]. On the one hand, heterosexuality and homosexuality are 'at the same level' in so far as those who engage in both are, in particular contexts, subject to sexual misconduct which is 'a sin, fornication'. On the other hand, they are not 'at the same level' as sexual misconduct ceases for 'heterosexual couples [who are] ... married [and have the literal licence to] ... engage in any sexual activities (with each other)' whereas for '[homosexual] couples' who cannot get 'married', they would have to 'refrain [themselves] from that' indefinitely. Alexis's '[feeling] safe [that she's] not doing anything wrong' is contingent on the different perception and management of guilt for 'heterosexual couples' and '[homosexual] couples'.

Moderation of guilt is also evident in Joe's strategy, who says:

> When I feel these urges, I feel guilty about it ... when I shouldn't. I think I shouldn't be ... And there's this belief that, oh but if you really like someone, you shouldn't be in a state where you might like someone a lot you know. So that's one thing I try to make sense of. [27:51 (545:560)]

This is the differentiated accounting of guilt that Joe makes for 'gay people' like him as opposed to 'straight people'; the latter can be 'intensely physically attracted to someone or different people at different times'. But for 'gay people' like him, compensation is in order for the deviation from the 'heterosexualisation of desire': in moderating one's attraction for a person of the same sex, one moderates one's guilt. That is why, even if 'you really like someone, you shouldn't be in a state where you might like someone a lot'.

Through the narratives of AY, Jimmy, Joe and Alexis presented above, it is apparent that guilt is a construct. It is a strategy that props up the 'fiction of unity' (Bailey 2007: 83) – that heterosexuality is normal and good whilst homosexuality is abnormal and sinful. Where sexual guilt and religious guilt are experienced, acts of acquiescence are evident: there is a buying into the hierarchical and oppositional differences of heterosexuality/homosexuality. The vast majority understand, legitimize and reinforce the former as more dominant as it is natural and right and the latter as unnatural and an aberration and both are mutually exclusive, i.e. you can only be either heterosexual or homosexual. The experience of ambivalence instead of unadulterated and long-term guilt, the management of guilt and moderation of guilt add up to strategies of not only negotiation but also strategies of resistance to this 'fiction'. That it follows that one ought to feel guilty if one destabilizes the 'heterosexual matrix' – in these instances, being born man but desiring men and in being born woman but desiring women – the hesitation, thinking through and ultimately refusal to become guilty makes visible the construct of guilt as an effect of the construction of the binary of heterosexuality/homosexuality.

On relational guilt

Where 'sex guilt' is defined as a 'generalised expectancy for self-mediated punishment for violating or anticipating violating standards of proper sexual conduct' (Mosher and Cross 1971 cited in Murray et al. 2007: 224), the transgression of such 'standards of proper sexual conduct' is also the basis of relational and familial guilt. Unlike the narratives presented above, these 'transgressions' are not always aligned with religious guilt. Relational guilt includes, among others, the guilt of falling in love with a person of the same sex or pretending to with a person of the opposite sex or the guilt of infidelity. Familial guilt stems from self-blame of parents of those who have come out and those who opt not to come out to their families or parents in particular for the sake of (family) face and for the sake of peace.

At its most fundamental is ontological guilt and this is evident in Adam's, Juuk's and Andy's lived experiences. Adam says:

> When I was 11 years old, I had a crush on my classmate. And then I thought, 'Oh shit, maybe I'm a lesbian you know' [*laughs*] because the crush was so strong. It was like, 'Man, I'm falling in love with this girl and I'm not supposed to have these feelings'. So it was at once very exhilarating and at once very guilty. [22:4 (45:56)]

Adam manifests the child-like horror of discovery that he is becoming who he does not want to become at the tender age of eleven: so 'it was at once very exhilarating and at once very guilty'. And the representation of a lesbian as the abject by his aunt – a 'monster ... with dark glasses, really macho woman who like, takes women out [*laughs*] and then never take them back' [22:3 (31:44)] – exacerbates Adam's fascination yet repulsion of who he is becoming. As he adds:

> But ... it's just too much guilt-lah, too much fear ... or too much pride ... to actually say that I am ... because once you say you are that means you're condemned to be in that group. So it's strange in that in my secret life I look for affirmation through books. But in my social reality life, I refused to be lumped into that group. [22:14 (177:185)]

The marking off a psychic boundary between Adam and a monstrous lesbian resonates with Kristeva's abjection which as she notes: 'We may call it a border; abjection is above all ambiguity. Because, while releasing a hold, it does not radically cut off the subject from what threatens it' (Kristeva 1982: 9). That Adam is critical of his split embodiment retrospectively through the reiteration of excess – 'too much guilt-lah, too much fear … or too much pride' – in demarcating a 'secret life' and 'social reality life' where he dis-identifies *and* identifies with 'that [abject] group' is revelatory of his ambivalence towards himself.

Juuk who is founder of a website that is GLBTIQ-friendly, in recollecting the pain of losing her lover years ago, blames herself: 'You start to question whether, did you love wrongly? Or was it your fault … So I needed, I thought … a boyfriend, I could be clearer … Perhaps it's my fault to bring upon her death kind of thing' [9:17 (192:207)]. In the like manner that Adam says with self-recrimination, 'Oh shit … I'm not supposed to have these feelings', Juuk's self-doubts as a precursor to self-blame is evident in her believing then that her friend was possibly punished for her 'fault' in '[loving] wrongly', by deviating from 'compulsory heterosexuality' (Rich 2004), hence her penitent recourse to getting 'a boyfriend [in the hope that she would] be clearer': turn back to the straight path in having veered off.

And Andy says: 'I think guilt was probably one of the reasons why I broke up with my first girlfriend. The guilt of not letting her go out there and just be who she is' [2:43 (536:554)]. Relational breakups on account of guilt experienced in the case of Andy is the 'guilt of not letting her go out there and just be who she is', as one who is or could be 'naturally' compliant with the 'heterosexual matrix' which characterizes 'a hegemonic discursive/epistemic model of gender intelligibility that assumes that for bodies to cohere and make sense there must be a stable sex expressed through a stable gender (masculine expresses male, feminine expresses female) that is oppositionally and hierarchically defined through the compulsory practice of heterosexuality' (Butler 1990: 151). Andy as a masculine-identifying woman does not display a 'stable sex [that is] expressed through a stable gender' as she desires women not men. She veers away from the 'compulsory practice of heterosexuality'. And she adds: 'I always have got this problem with people stifling me and because of that I have got this problem with stifling other people as well. So whether or not I'm stifling someone else, I rather not take the risk or the chance' [2:43 (536:554)]. The 'problem with people stifling [her]' alludes to the compulsion of becoming heterosexual imposed on her by her relatives (i.e. pressure to settle down with a man). In being wary of becoming, even an inadvertent source of compulsion of becoming homosexual on her girlfriends, Andy forecloses that by breaking up with them to 'not take the risk or the chance'.

Feeling ashamed or feeling 'sexual guilt' for 'violating standards of proper sexual conduct' (Mosher and Cross 1971 cited in Murray et al. 2007: 224) is expressed by Stephanie who was a fifty-year-old Tibetan Buddhist bisexual woman and mother to a twenty-something-year-old son (from her previous heterosexual marriage). Stephanie passed away from a terminal illness in May 2018 and her epitaph in a blog dedicated to her memory reads: Loving Mother. Devoted Partner. Loyal Friend. Gifted Writer and Artist. Traveller. Dreamer. Oxbridge Society member. Soroptimist Sister. Pokemon Go Player. Word Game Addict. Big-Hearted Soul. Romantic Sentimental. Pure Spirit of Kindness. When first interviewed, on recounting, with remorse, her non-monogamy as sexual misconduct to her current partner, Stephanie says:

> In the end, I just felt really shitty about it. I mean it was different when it was with my husband because my husband knew about it right. But with Janic, it was not fair on her because she was the innocent one. She didn't know anything about it, so we broke up and for a couple of months, I began to rethink my priorities. [6:37 (407:418)]

Feeling 'sexual guilt' or 'really shitty' about her affairs with other women whilst desiring a committed relationship with Janic serves as a catalyst for a mindset change, where there was an absence of 'sexual guilt' whilst married to her then husband as he 'knew' and consented. Stephanie's '[rethinking her] priorities' facilitates the shift from an open relationship with her husband who 'didn't play around but [she] did' [6:8 (88:99)] to compulsory monogamy with Janic who also 'didn't play around but [she] did'. The deregulation and subsequent self-regulation of her sexuality are made manifest, as by her own admission, she is 'naturally not monogamous' [6:45 (512:520)]. She imposes an ultimatum on herself: 'I could either screw around and not have Janic or have Janic and not screw around'. In the case of Stephanie, 'sexual guilt' is productive of a new subjectivity where she '[made] that choice (to "have Janic and not screw around") ... for the sake of ... the relationship' [6:45 (512:520)].

Stephanie's relish of playing around resonates with the narratives of bisexual-identified practitioners of polyamory where a 'pluralistic sexual ethics' that imbibes qualities such as love, intimacy and friendship abounds in a 'responsible non-monogamy' as opposed to 'pleasure-centred forms of non-monogamy' (e.g. cruising, casual sex) (Klesse 2006: 566). Although there is no hegemonic discourse of polyamory, practitioners speak about a 'politics of differentiation' in aligning the pleasure of love and intimacy with non-monogamous (non-exclusive) relationships (Klesse 2006: 573). Stephanie eventually adopts an exclusive relationship with Janic and continues to enjoy the pleasure of love and intimacy with her, evident from Facebook postings of their trips abroad, anniversaries, her son's accomplishments, until her passing away in 2018.

That 'sexual guilt' arising from 'two-timing' is potentially generative is also experienced by 35-year-old Dave who works in a finance department shipping company and has been attached for eleven years, as he says:

> I feel so horrible and guilty… And… I felt very exhausted at that point of time because I felt that this whole two-timing thing is so exhausting physically and mentally. I'm like travelling to two places. And keeping two people company and having no time for myself and trying to please two people-lah. And, and [*laughs*] trying to not let my best friend find out. [29:40 (481:489)]

The reiteration of two is symptomatic of his double life: 'two-timing… travelling to two places… keeping two people company… trying to please two people'. This duplicity led to Dave's choosing his then older lover over his 'best friend' who did eventually 'find out' but who was so forgiving that ironically accentuated Dave's guilt: he 'broke down… [and] knew that… I had to break off with my best friend' [29:43 (506:512)]. Sexual guilt in the case of Dave becomes a catalyst for what he perceives as responsible action.

A different kind of double life that effects 'sexual guilt' is present in Kun's narrative. Kun, who is forty-five years old, a teacher and in a committed relationship with a man, says: 'I have this guilt, very strong guilt towards her. I avoided her and we were housemates… then I moved out from the house to… avoid seeing her because it will trigger all my feelings of guilt' [12:138 (1422:1435)]. In performing heterosexuality as a man who desires men but effects to desire a woman, his female housemate, Kun finds himself quite averse to any physical contact with her which has not gone beyond holding hands. Kun then realizes the price of conforming to heteronormativity, as he reflects:

> I conform to that. And there's no passion. And of course, we still can maintain as like a couple. But it was just to fulfil some of this social norm, expectation. And of course, we respect each other. I think we probably can pretend that [*laughs*]. But of course, I don't feel that's the right thing to do because I don't want to deprive myself or her for having a more meaningful relationship. [12:130 (1353:1362)]

His 'very strong guilt towards her' precipitates an act of resistance to conforming to the work involved in *doing heterosexuality* in the form of a passionless heterosexual coupling (in imitation of his parents' passionless marriage) with his former housemate 'just to fulfil some of this social norm, expectation'. In doing so, he affirms their personhood and the integrity of relationships in resolving to not 'deprive [himself] or her for having a more meaningful relationship'.

The 'double life and strategies of everyday sexual self-management' (Seidman et al. 1999: 10), apparent in the narratives of Stephanie, Dave and Kun above, find further expression in CK's narrative. CK comments on his 'strategies' in managing 'sexual guilt':

When we started together... we don't acknowledge that we are partners or couple; that we are just best friend. And we didn't have sex. I mean, not very frequent because he'll feel guilty after doing it. He'll feel very bad... we have agreement that... we'll try not to do anything with other people that will bring back disease you know, like AIDS or STDs that will cause harm to the other half. [17:46 (534:546)]

Such practices of not publicly, even privately, '[acknowledging] that [they] are partners or couple', not having 'frequent' sex to alleviate the 'sexual guilt' of his 'best friend', and mutually agreeing to having safer sex with other men so as to not 'cause harm to the other half', are CK's and his partner's 'double life and strategies of everyday sexual self-management'. These 'strategies of everyday' for CK 'aim to avoid the risks of unintended exposure ... [and] also create a "protected" space that permits individuals to fashion a gay self and facilitates the making of gay social worlds' (Seidman et al. 1999: 10). These practices serve as a counterpoint to the valorization of coming out narratives that sometimes undermine, even negate, the necessity of maintaining a 'double life' in strategically choosing to stay in the closet with certain people at certain times and places.

The final facet of relational guilt is expressed in Kun's narrative. Kun shows the limits of 'interpersonal routinization' (Seidman et al. 1999: 11) of his homosexuality in public/private spaces, as he says:

I have to be very realistic about it. And I think by nature... I'm not a very provocative [person] and... I don't really like to engage in a conflict. So it's difficult for me... to argue with any officers, 'Hey, give us our rights'... it's just not my way. Perhaps I'll write [in] some papers... I used to think that oh, I should be ashamed of myself. But after that I think [*interviewer laughs*], it is not me, just not me. So... I don't want to [*laughs*] beat myself up you know, like for not being able to act like an activist because this is not, I don't feel that I'm, can be that kind of person. [12: 102 (1058:1070]

There is a distinction made between 'inter-personal' and 'institutional routinization' (Seidman et al. 1999: 11), as reflected in Kun's narrative. The former 'indicates informed ways individuals integrate homosexuality into their conventional social lives, e.g. disclosing to family members or co-workers'. 'Institutional routinization', on the other hand, 'refers to incorporating policies and practices into organisations that do not subordinate non-heterosexuals'

(Seidman et al. 1999: 11). Kun is moving towards 'interpersonal routinization' in coming to terms with his sexuality as his relationship with his then partner has 'nothing much to do with [their] faith ... [and they are] kind of like more comfortable with [the] Buddhist point of view ... of the world' [12:83 (841:856)].

However, it is apparent here that Kun is resistant to effecting 'institutional routinization' as '[arguing] with any officers, "Hey, give us our right" ... it's just not my way'. On the one hand, relational guilt – 'I used to think that oh, I should be ashamed of myself' – is evident in his perceiving that he is not doing more for the gay community by '[writing in] some papers', for instance, to agitate for social reform. On the other hand, relational guilt between self and community, in the case of Kun, is also generative. It activates a process of becoming albeit not as a sexuality rights activist as Kun is 'not a very provocative [person] and ... [doesn't] really like to engage in a conflict'. It facilitates instead the transformation of guilt to self-acceptance of the 'kind of person' whom he is, as he says: 'So ... I don't want to [*laughs*] beat myself up you know, like for not being able to act like an activist'. Kun's personhood, of which becoming gay is an integral part, takes form in his negotiating the tension between 'inter-personal' and 'institutional routinization'. Where 'I used to think that oh, I should be ashamed of myself', he now chooses to not 'want to [*laughs*] beat myself up ... for not being able to act like an activist'. For Kun, 'it's just not my way' and 'it is not me'. Kun manifests not 'subjective ambivalence [which] is connected to incomplete interpersonal routinization' (Seidman et al. 1999: 26) but a 'subjective ambivalence' which is connected instead to 'incomplete [institutional] routinization'. As such, Kun's 'subjective ambivalence' becomes a *strategic ambivalence* as he sets the parameters of his engagement with the public/private domains of becoming gay: 'because this is not, I don't feel that I'm, can be that kind of person'.

In the narratives discussed above, relational guilt takes on many forms. At its most fundamental, it manifests as ontological guilt not only in straying from the straight path (for Adam and Juuk) but also in misleading others off it in the process of becoming non-heterosexual (for Andy). Yet relational guilt surprises in its generative effects: it potentially awakens Stephanie and Dave to accountability to their partners in opting for voluntary monogamy and fidelity; Kun to embracing the passion and sanctity of what constitutes a 'meaningful relationship'; CK to recognizing his 'subjective ambivalence [to homosexuality that] is connected to incomplete interpersonal routinization' (Seidman et al. 1999: 26); and Kun to arriving at self-acceptance in not facilitating 'institutional routinization'. These narratives of becoming dispel the linearity and reductionism of queer coming-of-age narratives where the closet is paradigmatic of the binary of either coming out or not coming out. Foregrounded instead is the circularity and complexity of this process that in being framed with *strategic ambivalence* shows up the 'double life and strategies of everyday sexual self-management' (Seidman et al. 1999: 10). Guilt then becomes an effect of these 'strategies of everyday sexual self-management' that, in the process of becoming, destabilizes the heterosexualization of desire.

On familial guilt

Relational guilt experienced in relation to family and coming out narratives will be discussed in this section. For Dave he was outed by his family, where they 'cornered me, went to my room, [closed] the door, [closed] the window... and started to ask me questions' [29:48 (564:578)]. And his reaction to the entrapment was, as he recounts:

> I just felt this urge to let it out once and for all, thinking at the back of my mind that ... you're my parents after all ... I've heard of those stories [where] you know, at the end of the day, you're still flesh and blood ... I mean I'm still your child at the end of the day-lah. So I decided to just blurt it out ... immediately there was this sense of guilt and disappointment that came over me ... as if I let down my parents. And I started to break down. And I started to say that, 'I'm sorry for being like that. I can't choose who I am and I just can't help it'. [29:50 (589:600)]

Dave articulates being overcome by 'this sense of guilt and disappointment'. And what he experiences is akin to *filial shame* in believing that he had 'let down [his] parents' by virtue of 'being like that' and not being able to 'help it'. For Dave, ashamed and shamed, his 'whole being is at fault' (Murray et al. 2007: 225). As this is a 'wrong' that he is unable to rectify – 'I can't choose who I am and I just can't help it' – he '[feels] condemned to [his] very core' (Murray et al. 2007: 225). On the one hand, disappointment is directed at himself for disappointing his parents by breaking up his five-year relationship with a woman whom they had approved of, in passing as straight, as he reveals elsewhere in the interview [29:48 (564:578)]. On the other hand, his disappointment is also directed at his parents for the disillusionment of knowing that his coming out story is bereft of the happy ending 'stories' that he had heard of where being 'still flesh and blood ... still [his parents'] child' is not a prerequisite for their unconditional love. Their rejection of his 'being like that' renders Dave's 'interpersonal routinization' – his coming to term with his sexuality – incomplete (Seidman et al. 1999: 11).

In the narrative of Dave, familial guilt as a form of relational guilt is manifest. Where others may underestimate the unconditional love of one's parents in not coming out to them sooner, this contrasts with Dave's being shamed in overestimating the unconditional love of his parents in being outed by them.

Guilt as a mediator to peace

Where guilt and shame can be kept in abeyance or overcome, guilt may serve as a mediator to peace. When one buys into the constructed binary of heterosexuality/homosexuality, guilt, as demonstrated in the above sections on 'sex guilt', religious guilt, relational and familial guilt, is manifest as an effect of transgressing this construct. In this sense, guilt and shame are often held at bay through acquiescence to the normalization of heterosexuality and demonization of homosexuality. When one stops buying into this construct, the act of resistance that this precipitates in turn potentially engenders peace which is the absence of guilt as a GLBTIQ person.

Dave says:

> I don't feel conflict. I would say that … sexuality and my faith is I guess reconciled in that sense … I don't feel guilty about who I am anymore. Whereas compared in the past, I always like you know, after having some encounter with a guy, after that I will like try and ask for forgiveness from God. But now, I kind of like don't do that. I don't view that as a sin anymore. Yeah. [29:79 (881:893)]

The journey of reconciliation of Dave's sexuality and faith is marked by his not '[feeling] guilty about who [he is] anymore … [and not viewing sexual intimacy with men] as a sin anymore'. The definitive ring to 'anymore' that is reiterated emphasizes his arriving at self-acceptance 'whereas compared in the past', he was perpetually penitent, particularly '[post-]encounter with a guy' in '*always*… [asking] for forgiveness from God' (emphasis mine). The departure from guilt markedly facilitates 'interpersonal routinization' (Seidman et al. 1999: 11) in Dave's not '[feeling] conflict' within his self. The alignment of then/now and guilty/not guilty shows how queer time operates in Dave's becoming gay through the adoption of 'strategies of everyday sexual self-management' (Seidman et al. 1999: 10); being deeply conflicted then and reconciled now are mutually constitutive states.

The transcendence of guilt is also apparent in J's narrative, who adds:

So that's when after much thought then I realised that I could come to terms with it. And when you can come to terms with it; that God made you the way you are ... you can just feel God like slipping back into your life. And you allow yourself to be used for His purpose. And so that's when I started like setting up Sunday school for the kids. And you allow yourself to be involved. You don't feel that you're being hypocritical or anything like that. And that's when you actually can feel ... happy, pure, pure, purely at peace with yourself. And in all honesty, if you don't feel that it's right, if the guilt is still there, you cannot, never feel that. So that's when you know that the guilt is gone already.... obviously it's not something that happens overnight-lah ... it can be quite a tough process. Yeah. [23:104 (360:372)]

For J, 'interpersonal routinization' (Seidman et al. 1999: 11), in '[coming] to terms with it', her sexuality as a Christian, affords an inversion of Joe's recounting his church's portraiture of guilt as correlated with homosexuality which is 'deviant', 'an addiction', 'against the design' and 'a sin and the consequence of that sin, is separation from God' [27:8 (81:93)]. In the case of J, her sexuality is not deviant as 'God made you the way you are'; 'it's right' and by inference, not a sin. And as a consequence, J's testimony of faith is thus expressed: 'you can just feel God like slipping back into your life. And you allow yourself to be used for His purpose' – in 'setting up Sunday school for the kids'. The 'interpersonal routinization' is complete as J not only knows that she is not 'being hypocritical' but more importantly she 'actually can feel ... happy, pure, pure, purely at peace with [herself]'. The association of feeling 'pure' and 'purely at peace' is significant as indicative of J's self-affirmation that is divinely sanctioned. This affirmation of the self is experienced and embodied as 'peace' which is the antithesis to guilt, as J says: 'if you don't feel that it's right, if the guilt is still there, you cannot, never feel [peace]'. Queer time is also evident in J's narrative of becoming as she attests to this journey as 'not something that happens overnight-lah ... it can be quite a tough process'. That 'it can be quite a tough process' alludes to the resistance (as J mentions elsewhere in the interview) to this act of resisting heterosexism.

In the narratives above, the transcendence of guilt and concomitant liberation from hiding and shame pave the way for reconciliation of one's sexuality and spirituality that is embodied in the experience of peace for Dave and J. Guilt and shame are overcome not because they have acquiesced to heteronormativity but paradoxically because they have resisted it through a fidelity to their selves. In doing so, they live out 'interpersonal routinization' (Seidman et al. 1999: 11) in coming to terms with their sexuality as self-identified Christians. Their narratives show how the closet can be reconfigured and what it means to go 'beyond the closet' (Seidman et al. 1999: 20) where everyday and individuated strategies of acquiescence *and* resistance are validated as these are often mutually impacting in the realization of self and living out an abundant life.

Going beyond the closet in claiming abundant lives will be tested for other Southeast Asians, particularly the GLBTIQ community in Brunei, Southeast Asia's only Islamic State, whose ruler in April 2019 mandated 'death for adultery and sex between men, as well as lashes for lesbian sex and amputation for crimes like theft' (Westcott 2019). The 'official silence' from neighbouring Muslim-majority nation-states like Malaysia and Indonesia, against the chorus of condemnation from Western nations, even celebrities as this 'draconian' law is a 'setback for human rights', is deafening. Political commentators conjecture that there is no political mileage to be gained by speaking up where silence would conveniently be construed as endorsement or even complicity in rising Islamic conservatism in the region. Malaysian LGBT rights campaigner Thilaga Sulathireh, with Justice for Sisters, a transgender-affirming NGO, says, 'All these things are creating a lot of fear for people and a lot of uncertainty ... What's going to happen to our lives and our future?' The LGBT community in Brunei remains ambivalent: there is fear on the one hand, and on the other, there is the refusal to believe that such archaic and barbaric practices would be enforced in Brunei Darussalam (meaning 'abode of peace').

The construction of binaries that align Western with human rights and Asia with rising Islamic conservatism or, worse, anti-human rights standpoint does not bode well for civil society in general, not just Muslims in the region. The 'unintelligible' (non-heteronormative) bodies and sexualities of GLBTIQ persons become intelligible (obvious) sites of contestation between these dualisms that include universality/relativism and secularism/religiosity: the '"*fundamentalism*" of human right [*sic*]' (Piechowiak 1999: 11) is pit against religious fundamentalism (Gellner 1992: 6). Human rights as a fundamentalist discourse are inherently secular, hence universal. And religious fundamentalism is 'secularisation-resistant', hence transcendent A deadlock ensues in the face of such competing discourses of absolutism that are acted out on GLBTIQ persons who are left with the untenable option of becoming either queer or religious within religious-political spaces that are hostile to them.

Negotiating ambivalence

Becoming queer and religious for GLBTIQ persons in this study finds parallelisms in becoming a postcolonial nation-state, the common denominator being the negotiation of ambivalence. In the same month that Brunei tightens the reins of the Islamic Penal Code by imposing the death penalty for anal sex between men, adultery, lashes for lesbian sex and amputation for theft, Pritam Singh, chair of the Workers' Party in Singapore, announced that his party will not call for the review of the Penal Code with regard to repealing Section 377A due to a lack of consensus within its party leaders (Au-Yong 2019). He cites the precedence of ambivalence held by Prime Minister Lee Hsien Loong (eldest son of the late Senior Minister Lee Kuan Yew), who 'took the position of an "uneasy compromise" on 377A, where the law will remain on the books but the Government would not enforce it'. The GLBTIQ community in Brunei similarly holds on to the fragile hope that the above-mentioned draconian laws will not be imposed.

As postcolonial nation-states, what can be inferred when Malaysia retains Section 377 (and all amended supplements), and Singapore, Section 377A? As discussed in the introductory chapter, the 'post' in postcolonial becomes problematic when sovereign nation-states, former colonies of the British Empire, latch on to this colonial legacy – 'medieval sexual ethos' (Chua 2003: 215) or 'colonial relic' (Lee 2008: 391) – in the name of 'Asian values'. The competing discourses between Communitarian and Liberal camps (Chua 2003; Lee 2008) continue to be rehashed with little resolution in sight. The Communitarians are described by Singh as a 'conservative, pro-family camp' who err on over-focusing on 'the tangential issue of 377A' in the face of more pressing concerns for the nation-state, e.g. 'young people delaying marriage, fewer marriages taking place, more divorces and infidelity' which impinge on the nation's drive towards development. The Liberals are described in oppositional terms, as 'pro-LGBT' with the tendency to '[weaponize] the concept of love' thereby alienating the majority who occupy the 'middle', i.e. non-committal position on the long-standing debate. The 'Asian values' construct that undergirds the Communitarian standpoint values the common good over individual rights, obedience to authority (familial, institutional; in Malaysia, this extends to the King) and, by extension of logic, compliance with heteronormativity, with progeny to build the nation. It is further buoyed by Islamic resurgence in Malaysia. It effects 'social cultural engineering' (Kuah 2018: 1) that exemplifies Foucauldian 'biopower' in exercising power over the life of its citizenry and produces an almost docile 'species body'.

In the previous chapters, narratives of GLBTIQ persons, as self-identified Buddhists, Christians, Hindu and Muslim who remain conflicted or whose sexuality is not affirmed by their selves, families and faith communities, are presented. In this chapter, narratives of in-betweenness are discussed which show the ways in which the 'species body' is sometimes compliant and other times resistant to the regulatory technologies of the body. The ambivalence of GLBTIQ persons as being more than conflicted and less than reconciled are evidenced through managing ambivalence, e.g. managing by not/denying the self, coping by not/lying to the self, accepting what is/not sexual misconduct, desiring to not/serve fully and desiring one's partner to not/be Christian.

Managing by denying and not denying the self

In this section, the narratives of AY, Andy and Jagadiswari show their varied responses to the call to deny themselves given the perceived incompatibility of their sexuality and religiosity or spirituality. AY says:

> Don't hate the church, 'cause I don't [*interviewer laughs*]. But I feel sad that the church has the stance that they do because with that, they have pretty much lost a lot of very talented, very gifted, very brilliant [people who are willing] to give back ... 'Cause I was very actively serving in church and all that. But because of my position, meaning that you know, me choosing my sexuality over what the church condones, basically what's happened is ... they now do not allow me to serve in church. [20:38 (490:496)]

AY alludes to the 'incomplete institutional routinisation (institutional practices that subordinate non-heterosexuals)' (Seidman et al. 1999: 20), that is practised by his former church in doubly constraining GLBTIQ persons like himself. The church 'condones' heteronormativity, and AY's transgression of that leads to his not being '[allowed] to serve in church'. He later receives further rebuke for noncompliance to 'compulsory heterosexuality' (Rich 1980), as discussed in the previous chapter, where he was stripped of an award for his contribution as a youth leader, ironically outed by a closeted lesbian pastor. AY's response is not only to make his 'position' clear, cognizant as he is, of the repercussions, indeed retribution, but also to not 'hate the church'. However, he regrets its 'stance' as it has alienated, hence 'lost a lot of very talented, very gifted, very brilliant [GLBTIQ persons who are willing] to give back' to the church as self-identified and committed Christians. He manifests 'interpersonal routinisation' (Seidman et al. 1999: 11) in actively 'choosing [his] sexuality over what the church condones' albeit at the cost of his discipleship, where he 'was very actively serving' within that church but is now denied this vocational channel.

Andy maintains a similar standpoint to AY's, as she asserts:

> To me, if anyone says, but how can you believe in your faith if your faith calls and terms this as wrong? There is a reconciliation factor. To me, there's nothing to be reconciled but I will tell the person-lah, 'If you don't have sin, you cast the first stone- lah'. To me ... I think my faith in God is [a] personal walk with God, it's a personal relationship with God. And like I said, when Judgement Day comes, I shall face Him. To me it's like, you ask me to deny myself, deny who I am and what I am, I also think I won't be living it to the fullest. [2:25 (293:302)]

Andy makes references to two Biblical verses: the first is Jesus's intervention in a public shaming and castigation of a woman for adultery (John 8: 7) where he says, as paraphrased by Andy, 'If you don't have sin, you cast the first stone-lah.' The second is also taken from the Gospel written by the apostle John (New Testament) who writes: 'I have come so that they may have life and have it to the full' (John 10:10) which is the basis of Andy's refusal to 'deny myself, deny who I am and what I am ... [as] I won't be living [life] to the fullest'. To rebut church members who insist on the incompatibility of her sexuality and faith – 'how can you believe in your faith if your faith calls and terms this as wrong?' – she responds: 'There's nothing to be reconciled.' Andy, as elaborated in the next chapter, maintains that her sexuality and spirituality are mutually constitutive, as she states: 'When it comes to guilt, I think I have dealt with my guilt. The guilt is still there ... it's already a part of who I am ... It really, really is no longer a problem' [2:44 (555:563)]. And her belief in the sanctity of her sexuality and relationships is clearly reflected in her readiness to be held accountable to God on 'Judgement Day' as she disavows being judged by others. The dichotomy between collective and individual faith is also emphasized, where her 'personal walk with God [and] ... personal relationship with God' cohere with her 'interpersonal routinisation' (Seidman et al. 1999: 11).

Jagadiswari, who is daughter to her deities whom she embraces as 'Mother' or here addressed as 'Ma', says:

> But I think the greatest gift Ma has given me is, sexuality is not the centre of my faith but neither is it absent. I don't have to hide it. I don't have to shout it at anyone's face but I don't have to hide it. There's a name *lalithasahasrama*, it's the litany of the Mother's name ... There is a form of Ma called *lokasikamarupini*- which means 'the Mother that is so divinely beautiful, she inspires desire in women'. That's a pretty good acknowledgement you know ... my faith is not just about this, I mean the real Hindu faith is poetic. It's not twisted. It's only now becoming that way. I mean, I come in here. I pray to them. I talk to them. I leave here. I go see my girlfriend. We go out for dinner. We go for a movie. This is a part of my life still that we're allowed to live our lives you know. [25:80 (844:855)]

In Jagadiswari's vocation as the 'embodiment of the Mother (Goddess Kali)', she inhabits the dual states of spirit–human when she goes into a trance or has 'conversations with [her] deities', as she puts it elsewhere [25:9 (57:68)]. As such, it is imperative that she maintains 'pollution rules' (Douglas 2002: 161) that prohibit physical contact and intimacy with her then partner (in addition to fasting) to ensure the purity of her body for the indwelling of her 'Mother' who possesses her. Douglas goes on to add that 'pollution rules do not correspond closely to moral rules. Some kinds of behaviour may be judged wrong and yet not provoke pollution beliefs, while others not thought very reprehensible are held to be polluting and dangerous' (Douglas 2002: 160). Although she acquiesces to the 'pollution rules' that are given to her by her deities on an everyday reality, she remains freed up from 'moral rules', upheld by most of society, that her sexuality is deviant and therefore wrong. As she asserts that 'the greatest gift Ma has given me is, sexuality is not the centre of my faith but neither is it absent ... I don't have to shout it at anyone's face but I don't have to hide it'. Where the divine beauty of her 'Mother ... inspires desire in women', Jagadiswari's sexuality is thus not only affirmed but also sanctified – 'that's a pretty good acknowledgement', as she adds. The negotiation of deity/human, freedom/restraint, is embodied in her as she sums it up: 'I come in here. I pray to them. I talk to them. I leave here. I go see my girlfriend. We go out for dinner. We go for a movie.' As such, her lived experience is that she is both (voluntarily) denying and not denying herself: 'This is a part of my life still that we're allowed to live our lives.'

Where 'by and large, the private conscience and public code of morals influence one another continually', as Douglas states (2002: 161), the narratives of AY, Andy and Jagadiswari discussed here reflect discrepancies more than reciprocity between 'private conscience' and 'public code of morals'. For AY and Andy who strongly identify as Christians, their 'private conscience' has moved beyond the sphere of influence of 'public code of morals' framed by their churches. Contrary to the 'public code of morals' upheld by their churches in condemning non-normative sexualities as 'wrong', Andy's 'private conscience' is moulded only by God whose faith is 'a personal relationship with God', whilst AY's 'private conscience' leads him to '[choose his] sexuality over what the church condones'. In the case of Jagadiswari, reciprocity is reflected between her 'private conscience' and the 'code of morals' afforded by her Hindu spirituality that is governed by her 'Mother' who affirms women loving women relationships in contrast to the 'Hindu faith … [that is] … only now becoming that way (twisted)'.

Accepting what is and is not sexual misconduct

Sexual and religious guilt experienced by GLBTIQ persons, as shown in the previous chapter, arise predominantly from the classification of non-normative sexualities as sexual misconduct. In the like manner that heterosexuality is constructed as normal and good whilst homosexuality as abnormal and sinful, so too is guilt a construct. Accepting this binary of normative sexuality/non-normative sexualities effects the feeling of guilt. Conversely, questioning or destabilizing this binary potentially effects an abeyance of guilt. Given the correlation between guilt and sexual misconduct, this iterative process of accepting-resisting this binary is facilitated by the opening up rather than foreclosure of what constitutes sexual misconduct. This process of reconstruction includes, among others problematizing the construct of non-normative sexualities as sexual misconduct and reconstituting sexual misconduct as infidelity or violence or other intentional acts that hurt one's partner.

The sexual and religious guilt that is manifest in AY's narrative shows his struggle with the classification of non-normative sexualities as sexual misconduct, as he vows to stop 'screwing up friendships'. He explains:

> I was experimenting with friends and stuff [*coughs*] in class, well one friend particularly. And I mean he is a Christian as well and Catholic. So it was something he was having difficulty dealing with as well and you know, likewise,

> I was… struggling… with religion already then. So… when you do something
> bad with a friend, when you think of it as something bad, you think, 'OK this
> is it. We're not going to be friends anymore. It's gonna change everything'. And
> when it's with such a close friend you know, then your whole world falls apart.
> [20:28 (354:369)]

AY's process of becoming gay is multilayered. And it encompasses here his
having to manage guilt that he experiences on at least two levels – personal
and relational – as expressed above. Firstly, he 'was… struggling… with
religion already then', cognizant as he was of the church's condemnation
of homosexuality as 'something bad'. The struggle to disengage his 'private
conscience' from the 'public code of morals' (Douglas 2002: 161), premised
on his then church's teachings, is evident. Secondly, this personal sexuality-
spirituality crisis is exacerbated by his '[doing] something bad with a friend' as
a result of 'experimenting with friends and stuff'. AY's recognizing that it would
potentially risk '[changing] everything' by threatening to sever the friendship
led to his anxiety that his 'whole world [would fall] apart'. The definition of
sexual misconduct is foreclosed here: it is non-normative sexualities that are
deemed as 'something bad'. To acquiesce or not to the binary of heterosexuality/
homosexuality effects guilt.

To not foreclose meaning is to open up meanings, both contested and
complementary, in relation to sexual misconduct, as is demonstrated in the
following narratives. The process of becoming is one that negotiates the tension
between what constitutes 'sexual misconduct' from the levels of a 'private
conscience' and the 'public code of morals'. It involves knowing and living out
what is ethically alright and might be morally wrong by societal norms. The
ensuing narratives of 'intermediate categories' (Esterberg 2002: 217) – beyond
the heterosexual/homosexual binary – such as bisexuality, transgenderism and
intersexuality, make more complex processes of becoming. These anomalous,
even chaotic 'intermediate categories' of sexualities as not only heterosexual
and homosexual render 'sexual misconduct' an even more contested category in
opening up its meanings.

Stephanie, who is a fifty-year-old Tibetan Buddhist bisexual woman and
mother to a twenty-something-year-old son (from her previous heterosexual
marriage), explains:

> I know that Dalai Lama does not condone homosexuality but our Lama, believes
> that it doesn't matter. Sexuality is just an outside, you know. It's like… our
> bodies… What's important is our mind. So… whoever you're sleeping with… as

long as you don't hurt anybody... like, i.e. sexual misconduct, is one of the vows when you take refuge. Sexual misconduct is defined as... being unfaithful to your partner... so it's regardless whether male or female, right... so if you're single and if you want to sleep around, that's your prerogative as long again, you don't hurt the people along the way, that kind of thing, which sounds good to me [*laughs*]. [6:55 (645:658)]

There are two levels of departure that are evident from Stephanie's narrative: the first, her Malaysian-based Tibetan Buddhist Lama's view on homosexuality differs from that espoused by the Tibetan-based Nobel Laureate 'Dalai Lama [who] does not condone homosexuality'.[1] And second, Stephanie's own view that is informed by her spiritual mentor's that 'sexual misconduct is defined as... being unfaithful to your partner... so it's regardless whether (your love object is) male or female'. Here, she emphasizes mutual consent which she extends to not only heterosexual and homosexual relationships but also open relationships, as she adds that 'so if you're single and if you want to sleep around, that's your prerogative as long [as], you don't hurt the people along the way'. Stephanie's relish of playing around (stated elsewhere), here '[sleeping] around', resonates with the narratives of bisexual-identified practitioners of polyamory with a 'pluralistic sexual ethics' that imbibes mutual consensus where 'you don't hurt people along the way'. These qualities of love, intimacy and mutual respect distinguish 'responsible non-monogamy' framed within Tibetan Buddhism for Stephanie, from more hedonistic 'pleasure-centred forms of non-monogamy' which would potentially 'hurt people along the way' (Klesse 2006: 571).

That this 'vow' that she '[takes] refuge [in]' 'sounds good to [her]' (if we recall her admission of being not naturally monogamous elsewhere) as she says laughingly is noteworthy, as she firstly dismantles the condemnation of homosexuality and secondly the stigmatization of bisexuality. In the first instance, she stands apart from those who '[do] not condone homosexuality' on the grounds that men-loving-men or women-loving-women relationships are ontologically constructed as a sexual misconduct. Instead, she would 'not condone homosexuality' on the grounds that it is not founded on mutual consent and respect in instances where one is 'being unfaithful to [one's] partner'. So infidelity and other acts that 'hurt the people along the way' become for her sexual misconduct. Stephanie embodies 'what's important in our mind' through a self-regulated sexuality that is practised on the body with the mindset change in becoming monogamous. Where she did not do so when married to her then husband, she willingly does so for Janic's sake, her partner and co-parent to her teenage son, as she candidly puts it elsewhere: 'I could either screw around and not have Janic or have Janic and not screw around' [6:45 (512:520)]. This mindset change is significant as by her own admission, she is 'naturally not monogamous' [6:45 (512:520)]. Stephanie manifests *bi pride* (as a variant of gay pride) in loving and living abundantly!

Secondly, her laughing literally in the face of social conventions that regulate sexuality inadvertently challenges the stigmatization of bisexuality: a 'bisexual menace' which collapses the 'hetero/homo divide ... into an unlabelled ambisexuality' (Esterberg 2002: 225), and, by logic of extension, unbridled sexuality. Stephanie's unabashed pleasure in loving abundantly both men and women within open relationships mostly is, as some would intuit, menacing as it unsettles multiple proscriptions: sexual dichotomization (she embodies neither hetero- nor homosexuality but ambisexuality), monosexism (she is neither exclusively opposite-sex nor same-sex 'oriented') and compulsory monogamy (where Stephanie's acquiescence to monogamy is voluntary and not obligatory). That all this fluidity of sexual desires and acts 'sounds good to [Stephanie]' potentially elicits 'bi phobia' (Garber 2000: 21) that is premised on *bi envy* and hostility, as a reaction to the *bi choice* (Bong 2011a) – in looking past sex/gender as a basis for attraction – that she has and lives out.

Adam, a 45-year-old trans man who formally converted to Islam upon marrying a Malay-Muslim in 2015, was then a thirty-something radical feminist lesbian and self-identified Buddhist and says:

> But it actually doesn't really make it OK for me to come out. It was still as bad. It's just that I know that ... I won't be condemned, karmatically and karma won't come after me just because I like a girl you know [*laughs*]. So ... if you're married and if you cheat on your partner, that's a sexual misconduct ... it's more of your integrity. And of course, rape is wrong. [22:9 (108:116)]

Adam knows that he 'won't be condemned, karmatically and karma won't come after [him] just because [he likes] a girl ... [*laughs*]'. He attributes '[cheating] on your partner ... if you're married' and 'rape' as 'sexual misconduct[s]'. As a self-identified Buddhist then, Adam reasons that 'it's more of your integrity' rather than proscriptions that ought to regulate one's sexuality in relation to others. His 'private conscience' and the 'public code of morals' (Douglas 2002: 161) are now aligned: he 'won't be condemned ... just because [he likes] a girl ... [*laughs*]'. The mirth that this revelation on recasting 'sexual misconduct' brings about further destabilizes the hegemonic alignment of sex/gender/desire that is contained within the binary of heterosexuality/homosexuality. What is revelatory about

Adam's narrative that resonates with Stephanie's (and later Jagadiswari's) is the breaking down of the reductionist dichotomy of heterosexual/homosexual as it erases the lived reality of bisexuals, transgender and intersex persons that are not contained by the binary.

Here, where non-normative sexualities are 'OK' as he discovers from his spiritual mentor that 'sexual misconduct... does [not] include homosexuality' [22:8 (99:107)], 'it actually doesn't really make it OK for me to come out', as Adam says in recollecting his moment of epiphany as sixteen-year-old. In fact, coming out is a recurrent refrain in Adam's narrative of becoming a transsexual. In his late teens and twenties, he came out to himself and significant others (e.g. his mother and foster family when he was studying in the United States) as a radical lesbian feminist: a woman loving women. In his early thirties, he has come out to himself and others as a female-to-male transsexual (FTM): a man in a woman's body who is sexually attracted and emotionally connected to women. To some extent, Adam may be considered a 'female-to-gay-male transsexual (FTGM)' or a 'female homosexual transsexual' (Rosario II 1996: 36): a woman in a man's body who is sexually attracted to men. He, however, self-identifies as 'bisexual' [22:70 (803:811)] as he is less emotionally connected to men as a man. He has been on hormone therapy and, ten years ago, was considering 'transsexual surgery' or gender reassignment surgery (Sullivan 2006: 553), as he says: 'I look back at when I was six years old and to my puberty age and I always felt that I was in the wrong body. I always felt that I was supposed to be a boy, supposed to be a man' [22:34 (416:425)]. The surgery is looked upon less as a corrective in righting a 'wrong body' but rather a realization of Adam's desire to become a man: 'I always felt that I was supposed to be a boy, supposed to be a man.'

Ten years later today, Adam has fully transitioned. In the intervening years, he yearned to be an 'invisible man' where becoming a 'visible man' with both top and bottom gender reassignment surgeries, including a hysterectomy, 'comes later'. By 'invisible man' Adam refers to 'passing as a male', just wanting to fit in like any 'Tom, Dick or Harry'. This was effected by his 'voice change', his 'second puberty', as he quips, following hormone therapy where before that his voice was 'feminine, soft' and he would receive 'second glances' from people, presuming that he is embodying 'female masculinity'. This reaction to gender ambiguity brings to mind what Judith Halberstam says of 'the cardinal rule of gender: one needs to be readable at a glance' (1998: 23) to mitigate the threatening effect of the incongruity of gender expressions with gender binaries (e.g. females gender presenting as feminine rather than masculine). He is out to both his elder sister and mother who have always known and accepted him for who he is, and the former told her children, 'Your aunty has become an uncle.' Where the 'kids are very good [in that they] accept you and they call you by the right pronouns immediately', Adam adds, 'And all the adults got them wrong.'

The fluidity of being and becoming is so pronounced in Adam's narrative that it cannot be overstated: Adam paradoxically elides as he proliferates sex/gender/desire categories. The hollowness of aligning sex/gender/desire within a hegemonic binary of heterosexual/homosexual is made apparent: he demonstrates that there is no neat or necessary alignment between gender identity, gender expression, sexual orientation and sexual aim. He does this as he manifests a 'bisexual positionality' or 'bisexual subject position', which subverts the false dichotomy of heterosexual/homosexual (James 1996: 219). This positionality – 'Because I feel I'm partly man or I'm going towards there. So in opening up to men also, [it] opens up to my transsexual self' [22:79 (891:898)], as he states elsewhere – engenders the following sexual misconducts. Adam firstly overturns 'compulsory monosexuality' or 'monosexism' which is 'the social ideology that demands of individuals a singular sexual object choice' (James 1996: 220). Secondly, his non-acquiescence to a polarized heterosexual/homosexual positionality or 'sexual dichotomization' (James 1996: 221) is manifest, as he contends (as does Stephanie) that 'the gender or the sexuality of the person [does not matter but it] is really the person [who does]' [22:70 (803:811)].

Jagadiswari, a 45-year-old Hindu priest who loves women, elaborates on what constitutes sexual misconduct as 'worshippers of the Hindu faith' and, more importantly, as a human mediator for her divine Mother:

> So as I told my girlfriend, no threesomes, no sharing, no open relationship, none because energy's very pure. The very energy I generate when I meditate or do my practices, is similar to what I have when I'm with her. So it's sacred. That's why we're not allowed to screw outside marriage 'cause you have to hold that sacred. [25:87 (926:936)]

Where 'it's more of your integrity' [22:9 (108:116)] according to Adam that provides him with a moral compass (his Muslim identity will be elaborated in the next chapters), for Jagadiswari, it is her fidelity to her Mother. The 'pollution rules' that Douglas posits (Douglas 2002: 161) in the case of Jagadiswari not only prohibit physical contact and intimacy with her then partner (in addition to fasting) at certain times but also with other partners at all times: so 'no threesomes, no sharing, no open relationship'. It is mutually incumbent on

Jagadiswari and her partner to maintain the purity of her tantric 'energy' as she says: 'The very energy I generate when I meditate or do my practices, is similar to what I have when I'm with her. So it's sacred.' As sacred and sexual energies are mutually constitutive, so too are the 'moral rule' of fidelity in the form of monogamy and 'pollution rules' wherein some 'kinds of behaviour [are] judged wrong and ... provoke pollution beliefs' (Douglas 2002: 160): as she asserts that 'we're not allowed to screw outside marriage 'cause you have to hold that sacred'.

The further alignment between 'pollution rules' and 'moral rules' brings to mind Jagadiswari's intersexuality at birth. Her parents disclosed to her at age twelve that she was 'misdiagnosed as a boy' – 'they thought I was a boy because I was born with a fused scrotum and it looked like I had a penis', she explains. Within a month of being born, she had pneumonia, and following an X-ray, doctors found that she had ovaries. It was only as an adult upon seeking a full medical examination as a prerequisite that enabled her to temporarily live abroad, did she know of her intersexuality. Her 'sexual ambiguity' (Chase 2003: 31) in being born both male and female was, in all probability, 'judged wrong ... [and provoked] pollution beliefs' (Douglas 2002: 160) as it led to, as she shared post-interview sex reconstructive surgery to 'correct' her anomaly – she 'did go through surgery. They did snip off some of the boy parts ... but they did a chromosome check and I was XXY', she adds. 'Paediatric genital surgeries', according to Cheryl Chase, an intersex political activist, 'literalise what might otherwise be considered a theoretical operation: the attempted production of normatively sexed bodies and gendered subjects through constitutive acts of violence' (Chase 2003: 31). I posit that it is the corrective surgery and not her 'nonnormatively sexed [body] and gendered [subject]' that constitutes a form of sexual misconduct: it is 'acts of violence' perpetrated on her body.

In the process of becoming, sexual misconduct is reconfigured. From the narrow definition of constructing non-normative sexualities as sexual misconduct, it is now broadened, through the narratives of AY as a gay-identifying man and Stephanie, Adam and Jagadiswari as a bisexual woman, trans man and intersex person, to include infidelity to one's partner and deity and 'constitutive acts of violence' towards one's body and sexuality and that of others. Significantly, their subjectivities show that there is no necessary association between gender identity, gender expression, sexual orientation and sexual aim, premised on the heterosexual imperative, that one born a man ought to desire a woman and one born a woman ought to desire a man. The narratives of bisexuality, trangenderism and intersexuality transgress, even the *homosexual imperative* or what Halberstam terms as 'compulsory gender binarism' (1998: 27) that one born a man ought to desire a man and one born a woman ought to desire a woman. In unsettling the symmetry of these categories – sexual orientation, gender identity, gender expression and sex characteristics (in the case of Jagadiswari) – they reconfigure and live out what constitutes sexual misconducts for themselves.

Desiring to serve and not fully serve

Making ambiguous what sexual misconduct means, as shown above, is destabilizing. In this section, desiring to serve as committed Christians for CK, AY and Joe and not serving fully as desired continue the narratives of ambivalence highlighted in this chapter. To what extent is the desire to serve and not fully serve strategic and invested with agency?

CK, who has ceased serving in his church that he continues to attend, says:

> I [stopped] serving in church because you know … how can you be a leader for
> the youth when you're a gay man having a relationship with a gay you know?
> Like they approach me before but then I just say no, I don't think so I'm suitable.
> I don't have time for all this. [17:73 (813:823)]

CK's not taking up the invitation to serve as 'a leader for the youth' in his church is double-edged: he is qualified to do so ('they [approached him] before') yet disqualifies himself from doing so ('how can you be a leader for the youth when you're a gay man having a relationship with a gay you know'). In doing so, he pre-empts the church's negation of his leadership potential and service if he were to be outed as a 'gay man having a relationship with a gay'. Cognizant as he is of his church's condemnation of homosexuality (as discussed elsewhere), CK demonstrates how 'by and large, the private conscience and public code of morals influence one another continually', as Douglas intimates (2002: 161). He feels unworthy in imitation of his church's judgemental stance (explicitly demonstrated as he articulates elsewhere) and this outweighs his desire to serve.

In distancing himself from the intimacy of serving as 'a leader for the youth … [as] a gay man having a relationship with a gay' (as opposed to the 'lesser evil' of being a gay man who is celibate or '[not] having a relationship with a gay'), CK brings to mind Douglas's notion of 'pollution rules'. For CK, his vehemence in withdrawing from a deeper contact and connection with the youth suggests that 'pollution rules do ... correspond closely to moral rules', wherein his homosexuality is a '[kind] of behaviour [that is] judged wrong and ... [thus provokes] pollution beliefs' (Douglas 2002: 160). CK's treatment of the anomaly of his sexuality is essentially, to find it condemnatory, as his church does. This coheres with Douglas's view that a negative treatment of anomalies would be to 'ignore, just not perceive them, or perceiving we can condemn' (2002: 48).

Joe advocates not being fixated on a gay identity per se but on the 'struggles' to live out one's desire to serve as an expression of one's fidelity to God, as he explains:

> Because your life has to be more multi-faceted than that. It can be a particular part of your identity that you're obsessed over. But you have to realize it is a part of your identity. And I say that because at the end of the day, I think you're on the right track if your struggles are the same as straight people. And that's the struggle to live close to your ideal of what you think is the call of God in your life and to want to seek the call. And when you finally think you have the call, to obey it or avail yourself to obey it. And this should be the struggles of everyone in faith. And I think I'm quite happy that I have these struggles because it means that in this part of my life I'm still making the journey. And it makes me feel alive that nothing that I know I can take for granted. So I think that's the struggle bit. [27:53 (576:589)]

Joe privileges 'the struggle to live close to your ideal of what you think is the call of God in your life and to want to seek the call' rather than being 'obsessed over ... a particular part of your identity'. He looks upon 'these struggles' as an equalizer between 'straight people' and GLBTIQ persons, as he posits that 'I think you're on the right track if your struggles are the same as straight people ... this should be the struggles of everyone in faith'. Through the 'struggle' of submitting to God's call to serve – 'to obey it or avail yourself to obey it' – Joe's 'journey' of becoming Christian and gay is sustained as these 'struggles ... [make him] feel alive'. Where he says that 'I'm quite happy that I have these struggles because it means that in this part of my life I'm still making the journey', 'these struggles' and 'the journey' become for him mutually constitutive, as is managing the tension between his sexuality and spirituality. In privileging 'the struggle' of submitting to God embodied in praxis or acts of faith (which includes but is not limited to serving in church), Joe demonstrates a positive treatment of non-normative sexualities as anomalies, as Douglas suggests that 'positively, we can deliberately confront the anomaly and try to create a new pattern of reality in which [dirt] has a place' (2002: 48). The 'new pattern of reality' created sees a democratization among 'everyone of faith', united as they are in their 'struggles' to recognize and realize God's will.

A more ambivalent approach of serving and not serving fully in his former church is offered by AY, as he recollects:

> In the sense that, um, I think if I had pushed my way, continued my way in wanting to serve ... I think they would have allowed it to a certain extent. It would have made it difficult for certain people within the church, elder, leadership that, you know, a gay person or an openly gay person is serving, let's say children's ministry ... And because of that I felt, well, I would not serve in, in those areas, like in worship in children's and youth ministry because I didn't want to put the pastors in a difficult position you know. I mean this is a life that I've chosen for myself. I know the church's stand. They don't have to elaborate it any more than necessary. And because of that, I stick by my stand ... for my life. But I respect the stand of the church as well so I pulled myself back from those areas. [20:41 (522:537)]

AY, who 'used to serve as a worship leader in church ... as well as ... used to do youth and children's ministry', has now chosen to disengage from fully serving in these capacities. And he has done so, by his own admission, because he is 'very sensitive to the church's need' [20:40 (510:521)]. On the one hand, AY's reasons for withdrawal resonate with that of CK's with regard to avoiding intimate contact and connection with not only the 'youth ministry' but also 'children's ministry'. In this sense, 'pollution rules' surface as they 'do ... correspond closely to moral rules', wherein his homosexuality is a '[kind] of behaviour [that is] judged wrong and ... [thus provokes] pollution beliefs' (Douglas 2002: 160). AY (like CK), who was once prayed over in a bid to cast out the 'demon' of homosexuality out of him [20:33 (429:442)], as a form of extreme ablution to cleanse his body and spirit, knowingly adds that 'I know the church's stand. They don't have to elaborate it any more than necessary'.

On the other hand, AY's stance departs from CK's as his withdrawal can be read as a form of closeting not *of* himself – as he is 'an openly gay person' and 'this is a life that [he has] chosen for [himself]' – but of the youth and children, *from* himself as a spiritual mentor. The closet here is paradigmatic of 'a protected space that allowed individuals to fashion gay selves and to navigate between a straight and gay world' (Seidman et al. 1999: 11–12). That AY consciously and conscientiously extends this 'protected space' to the youth and children, even the pastors and leaders of the church, in not '[pushing his] way' is noteworthy, as he says that 'I think if I had pushed my way, continued my way in wanting to serve ... I think they would have allowed it to a certain extent'. This ambivalence of acts of acquiescence and resistance in desiring to serve and not serving as desired, denying yet realizing his self, are expressed when he asserts that 'I stick by my stand ... for my life. But I respect the stand of the church as well so I pulled myself back from those areas'. AY thus serves his church paradoxically by not serving. And he adds:

> And I served in other areas-lah, like creative side of it, helping with church decorations and stuff like that, that you know, didn't involve me being an influence. Because as youth leader I have great influence on a lot of people in the church, so I didn't want to put the church in a difficult position. But in the way of how the church has expressed itself about homosexuality and the way it doesn't want you, you know that. [20:42 (537:543)]

The processes of engaging and disengaging and re-engaging come full circle for AY: his desire to serve finds a 'creative' outlet in his 'helping with church decorations and stuff like that' that does not involve him 'being an influence' to young, impressionable minds, hearts and souls. The reiteration of 'difficult position' in – 'I didn't want to put the pastors in a difficult position' and 'I didn't want to put the church in a difficult position' – renders the church a 'closet' that is sanitized of the 'polluting' agent, AY, who is imbibed with 'great influence', not unlike contagion, that is excised from the body of the church. Not only has 'the church ... expressed itself about homosexuality and the way it doesn't want [him]' but AY has also acquiesced and not 'pushed [his] way, continued [his] way in wanting to serve' [20:41 (522:537)]. Confronting the 'difficult position', in '[pushing] my way, [continuing] my way in wanting to serve' could have entailed the possibility of a different perhaps even positive treatment of non-normative sexualities, where, as Douglas suggests: 'positively, we can deliberately confront the anomaly and try to create a new pattern of reality in which it has a place' (2002: 48). By closeting himself, in not serving as a 'youth leader [where he has a] great influence on a lot of people' but instead 'helping with church decorations ... [which] didn't involve [him] being an influence', AY pre-empts this possibility.

In the narratives of CK and AY, agency is manifest in the ambivalence of their desiring to serve and not serving as desired in youth and children's ministries in particular as these ministries are the most pliable to the 'great influence' of gay spiritual mentoring. In the case of Joe, his 'struggle' lies in knowing and submitting to God's will on how to serve and how to live as his faith 'journey'. In all three narratives, the tension of acquiescence and resistance to not only God's will but also the church's tacit will tempered by their own will to serve show a self-reflexivity that shapes their personhood. In doing so, they firstly serve paradoxically by not serving as desired; secondly, they reconfigure the 'closet' as a 'protected space' for the young from themselves; thirdly, they manifest ambivalent treatment of non-normative sexualities; and finally, they show how by submitting to the will of God and church that their piety is an 'active submission and as a way of life' (Frisk 2009: 190).

Desiring one's partner to be and not be Christian

In this final section, ambivalence is reflected by CK's attitude on the religious affiliation of partners in same-sex relationships. CK adamantly does not desire his partner to be Christian, as he explains:

> In a way for me, I still want to be a Christian. I still want to be with God. I'm trying like to turn around … I still need God … in a way that when the other party … is not a Christian, at least I still know what I'm doing rather than when two gays are together and I wouldn't know that the other party, whether he's been like total leaving God and is no longer with God you know … I have a Christian friend … who doesn't go to church anymore and he's gay. And he ask me … do you want to start a relationship … Then I wouldn't want to be with someone who doesn't love God anymore you know. [17:43 (499:508)].

CK's reiteration of 'in a way' is noteworthy. He first expresses it in relation to his own spirituality: 'In a way for me, I still want to be a Christian. I still want to be with God.' He then expresses it in relation to a hypothetical non-Christian partner: 'in a way that when the other party … is not a Christian, at least I still know what I'm doing'. It serves as a qualifier for the depth of his piety as he tries to come to terms with his becoming Christian and gay hence he is '[Christian] in a way'. This, he extends relationally. CK's aversion to being in a relationship with a Christian partner lies in the avoidance of a double jeopardy which that entails. In the first instance, his 'wrong' sexuality is mitigated by his 'right' yearning to 'still want to be a Christian' and, in fact, his struggle 'to turn around' given his perceived incompatibility of his sexuality with his religiosity. Hence, his certainty and accountability of his own process of becoming are evident when he says 'at least I still know what I'm doing'. In the second instance, practising his 'wrong' sexuality is still mitigated by the 'right' kind of 'other party [who] … is not a Christian' as that frees him from being held accountable for the 'other party['s]' moral conduct. It is not incumbent on CK to be responsible for the 'other party': 'I wouldn't know that the other party, whether he's been like total leaving God and is no longer with God'. The inference being that if one is gay, one 'is no longer with God'.

Conversely, practising his 'wrong' sexuality, as a Christian and the attendant guilt which that breeds, can only be exacerbated with the 'wrong' kind of partner who 'is [also] a Christian'. CK's struggle to reconcile his sexuality and spirituality remains, as he projects his conflicted self onto his 'Christian friend (who had propositioned him) ... who doesn't go to church anymore and he's gay'. When he admits that 'I wouldn't want to be with someone who doesn't love God anymore', CK is, in fact, succumbing to the constructed incompatibility of becoming gay and Christian which he fails to reconcile hence his 'trying like to turn around'. The glimpse of disgust in his disavowal of not '[wanting] to be with someone who doesn't love God anymore' betrays his self-loathing at his inability 'to turn around'. The block in relating to himself is here extended to the block in relating to other gay and Christian men.

The narrative above shows that there is contiguity between reconciling one's sexuality and spirituality and tolerating differences that matter. For CK, his remaining conflicted about his sexuality as a Christian leads him to reject gay men who are Christian as potential partners. Unable and unwilling (as he admits elsewhere) to 'turn around', he mitigates his guilt by disavowing being involved with Christian gay men as a projection of his self-loathing. In the case of CK, where the defining lines are hardened in the binary of heterosexual/ homosexual, so too are they reified in the binary of Christian/non-Christian. So 'pollution rules' (Douglas 2002: 161) are constantly negotiated in the process of becoming.

Such contiguity is still lacking in public spaces where 'pollution rules' bracket off nonconformity. Joe's position of moving beyond an obsession with one's sexual identity (articulated in the section 'Desiring to serve and not fully serve') resonates with that of a prominent LGBT activist in Malaysia, Pang Khee Teik, who is editor of QueerLapis.com, a website for and by LGBT people in Malaysia, and also the programme manager for Innovation for Change-East Asia. Pang critiques the 'selective liberal outrage' against Brunei's Syariah Penal Code that specially singles out gays. He says: 'I am disturbed by this global trend of reporting which gives the impression that the killing of gay people is the only crime worth the outrage. Should we not be equally outraged by amputation of limbs, death for apostasy, whipping of children, and other crimes against humanity?'

(Pang 2019). Pang's standpoint is instructive as it jolts one of a myopic identity politics. It also points to the indivisibility of sexuality rights from the universal albeit secular discourse of human rights and the irreconcilable differences that these integrated rights pose to the Islamic Penal Code – to single out just two (from the Yogyakarta Principles) – the right to freedom from torture and cruel, inhuman or degrading treatment or punishment (Principle 20) and the right to freedom of thought, conscience and religion (Principle 21).

7

Queering time

In this chapter, the iterative process of becoming framed by a queer temporality is foregrounded. Time is, on one level, experienced as a linear progression comprising past, present and future. In this regard, narratives of becoming often begin with a sense of knowing as a child, hence a sense of the past – that one is 'different', differently sexed and gendered. And interviewees share their aspirations for the future that include finding a partner, getting involved, getting married, having a baby, adopting a child, emigrating to a safer space, coming out to their parents that come about in relation to present-day circumstances and events in their lives.

Yet their process of becoming is not only framed within a linearity of time; it is also iterative and, for some, cyclical. The process of becoming for GLBTIQ persons encompasses not only coming to terms with heteronormativity but also heteronormativity in religion. Pivotal to the reconciliation of one's sexuality and spirituality is the experience of guilt and individuated ways of managing in particular sexual and religious guilt, as discussed in Chapter 5. The everyday lived reality of GLBTIQ persons is an exercise in what I posit as *strategic ambivalence*: in negotiating the tension between one's sexuality and spirituality that are constructed as mutually exclusive or incompatible. As delineated in Chapter 5 on dealing with guilt, shame and pain, strategic ambivalence comprises both acts of acquiescence and resistance to hegemonic heteronormative norms. In acts of acquiescence which tend to be reactionary, guilt is manifest as an effect of transgressing the construct of heterosexuality. In acts of resistance which is potentially generative, guilt potentially engenders peace. Strategic ambivalence may be perceived as an extension of 'incommensurability' that Tom Boellstorff, a key scholar on gay Muslim Indonesian men, posits (2005a). Essentially, the nature of being gay and being Muslim (or religious) is incompatible, 'unintelligible', even 'ungrammatical' especially in public spaces (Boellstorff 2005a: 575).

The complexity and circularity of this process inadvertently reconfigure the spatiality of the 'closet': the closet is paradigmatic of the mutually constitutive acts of acquiescence-resistance to heteronormativity in religion. As such, coming in-and-out of the 'closet' is performed not only as a singular, one-off and distinctive act but one that is often repetitive, multiple and ambivalent. In privileging narratives of becoming rather than coming-out narratives, GLBTIQ persons show how temporalities and spaces are mediated by recognizing this process as a journey, coming to terms with their differences from the mainstream, educating others and being educated, making sense of one's sexuality in religion or spirituality, seeking psychiatric or spiritual counselling, and receiving signs from God. In the first section, queer temporality is embodied through their recognizing this process as a journey, coming to terms with their differences from the mainstream, educating others and being educated, seeking psychiatric and/or spiritual counselling, and making sense of one's sexuality in religion or spirituality. In the second section, as a precursor to reconciliation in Chapter 9, their experiencing peace is centred.

Recognizing this process as a journey

For J the temporality of then-and-now is marked. As she recollects: 'When I was very young ... I was already attracted to girls ... but, because I only understood that ... in order to like girls, you can only be a boy, so I always thought that there was no two ways about ... that dichotomy' [23:1 (6:22)]. Today, as a facilitator of LUSH (Lesbians United for Self-Help) and PLUSH (post-LUSH), outreach programmes for lesbians that explore the six Biblical passages or 'texts of terror' (Cheng 2010: 106) that are interpreted to condemn homosexuality, she has overcome 'that dichotomy' that 'in order to like girls, you can only be a boy'. And although she has come out to her brother (who 'was perfectly fine with it') and sister, she remains 'scared [that her] parents would find out'. And she adds that 'as for my parents ... it's still a long journey for me to come out to them' [23:4 (39:48)].

The trope of the journey is apparent in J's narrative. Firstly, the immutability of the binary of sex/gender – that 'there was no two ways about ... that dichotomy' – now rendered mutable for J, through unlearning and educating others in reinterpreting, with the effect of deconstructing, the six passages that sustain heteronormativity in religion. As these are six-month programmes that are held continuously (often with the same facilitators given the over-extended human resources), queering time becomes iterative and cyclical. Secondly, the finality of her narrative of coming out is deferred as she has come out to her siblings but not her parents, and by her own assessment, 'it's still a long journey' that lies ahead. This is her aspiration for the future as she holds herself accountable to her then partner in coming out to her parents for the latter's sake.

'A "queer" adjustment in the way in which we think about time, in fact, requires and produces new conceptions of space', as Halberstam puts it (2005: 19). LUSH and PLUSH are coded as sexualized and spiritualized spaces that are further radicalized as subversive, women-only spaces as queer-identifying participants engage in queer hermeneutics that unsettles traditional interpretation of the 'Texts of Terror' – from the Old Testament; Genesis 19.5, Leviticus 18.22 and 20.13, and from the New Testament, Romans 1.24–25, 1 Corinthians 6.9 and 1 Timothy 1.10 – as Biblical grounds for condemning homosexuality. The affirmation of queer identities and subjectivities within the safe spaces of the six-month LUSH and PLUSH programmes constitutes a coming out where the 'closet' is, as Sedgwick puts it, 'the defining structure for gay oppression in this century' (1990: 71).

Opting to come out to her siblings but not her parents coheres with the unsettling of coming out narratives that are valorized by most Western sexualities studies scholars that find expression in 'coming home' narratives first introduced by Chou Wah-Shan (2001) in his work on theorizing the cultural politics of *Tongzhi* (his use of the term refers to 'contemporary Chinese lesbigay people' in Chinese societies in East Asia, e.g. Hong Kong, China and Taiwan. 'Coming home', as Chou opines, 'can be explicated as a negotiative process of bringing one's sexuality into the family-kin network, not by singling out same-sex eroticism as a site for conceptual discussion but by constructing a same-sex relationship in terms of family-kin categories' (2001: 36). In practical terms, this opens the time and space for a gradual integration of a same-sex partner into the 'family-kin network' in the course of performing everyday activities, e.g. marketing, eating.

Coming to terms with their differences from the mainstream

Ling Jackie's narrative of becoming is juxtaposed against the narrative of becoming of a 'mainstream church here'. As Ling Jackie says:

> In my opinion, it is unwise for Christian to read the Bible literally. It will only cause some unnecessary problems if… Christian read the Bible literally. And this is my hope-lah although it is quite unlikely for the mainstream church here to consider… I hope that… the… people here try to educate the children

> Christians to read the Bible from different perspectives. For me...although I
> have become [a] Christian so many years, I only started to read the Scriptures
> from another perspective, um, around 2005. It took me quite some time to see
> the Bible differently. This is my hope-lah although I know that it's very unlikely
> for the mainstream church here to consider. [18:64 (775:789)]

For Ling Jackie, her own faith journey is not a linear one as it 'took [her] quite
some time to see the Bible differently' despite '[becoming a] Christian so many
years'. The year 2005 became a turning point for her where, precipitated by
her coming out to old school friends, she 'started to read the Scriptures from
another perspective' and not, as inferred, 'literally'. She maintains that the
'mainstream church here' should likewise undertake in its journey of spiritual
growth, '[trying] to educate the children Christians to read the Bible from
different perspectives'. However, her reiteration of doubt, despite the insistence
of 'hope', that 'it's very unlikely for the mainstream church here to consider [that
mindset change]', shows that the correlation between time and (institutional)
growth is not a linear one and, in the case of the 'mainstream church here', static
and not dynamic as her individual growth has been. The periodization of then-
and-now for the 'mainstream church here' is indistinct as it has indefatigably
maintained its stance in '[educating] the children Christians to read the Bible'
literally and not 'from different perspectives'. *Time as process* frames the micro-
narrative of a lesbian Christian but not the macro-narrative of the 'mainstream
church here' that she alludes to. She now identifies as a 'non-dogmatic or non-
fundamentalist Protestant Christian [who] still [believes] that Jesus Christ is
[her] Redeemer and still prays in His name. But [she is] not keen in converting
or proselytizing non-Christians'. She adds, 'I think that while looking for a
partner, it is important for me to become a Christian with empathy and who
respects other peoples' choices and decisions'. She continues to attend 'LGBT-
friendly churches' in Malaysia and Singapore.

Ling Jackie's narrative of becoming also refigures the spatiality of the 'closet'
in effecting a 'coming home' after 'all these years' in not needing to come out to
her father, as he had known 'all these years', as she says:

> On a positive note, over these years, I had plucked up my courage to come out
> to my father (that is most important), two aunties, one cousin sister, and one
> cousin brother, and they are accepting and supportive. Most importantly, I did
> not expect that my father already knew I was a lesbian all these years. When
> I tried to come out to him a few years back, even before I ended my second
> sentence, he already knew what I was trying to tell him. In fact, he asked me, 'So

you think you are a lesbian?' I was shocked for a while, but managed to respond by saying 'Yes'. Then he said, 'It is something in-born and not a problem at all. You don't have to see a counsellor or psychiatrist.'

Her father's acceptance of her lesbianism is significantly profound for Ling Jackie who had 'all these years' harboured the burden of unburdening to him as 'that is most important'. Although neither father nor daughter openly acknowledged her being 'a lesbian all these years' – the repetition of which reflects *time as process* – when she attempted to, it was received matter-of-factly. His affirmation that 'it is something in-born' and that she did not need to 'see a counsellor or psychiatrist', in light of her having seen both secular and spiritually-based counsellors in the far past, affords a closure on 'the problem' (as she terms elsewhere) which was not a problem at all for her father.

Queering time and space is uncannily experienced by Ling Jackie's father who with the intuition of a father knew of his daughter's lesbianism and had 'all these years' made connections between the naturalness of becoming queer as, in a time-space far removed, 'there was a Chinese emperor who was gay' and, in a time-space less remote, 'an elder lesbian couple' who lived in their hometown, where many knew of their relationship 'but they never openly talked about it'. Eschewing the need to 'openly talk about it' effects an I-know-they-know-I-know mode of inhabiting time and space that is queer. Although Halberstam maintains that 'reproductive time and family time are, above all, heteronormative time/space constructs' (2005: 26), in the case of Ling Jackie and her father's coming out to each other, 'family time' across the span of 'all these years' within the domestic space of home becomes de-heteronormalized.

Educating others and being educated

Time as process is evident in educating others and being educated as J's and Ling Jackie's narratives above show. Here, Andy addresses homophobic persons from her church who continually harp on 'sexual issues' and advocates that they constructively channel this obsession by either '[supporting] a just cause … like … stop war, stop famine' or '[teaching] Christians how to make love' instead. She thus challenges them with the rhetorical question: 'Is the faith always related to sex?' And she argues: 'There's so many other things for you to focus on … why, why [*emphatically*] sexuality, why always this?' [2:29 (344:355)]. Given Andy's protracted frustration, time seemingly freezes in the face of homophobia as an effect of 'incomplete institutional routinization (institutional practices that subordinate non-heterosexuals)' (Seidman et al. 1999: 20), given the rigidity of mindsets and hearts in not changing.

Joe, who like AY has had theological training as a layperson, offers his view on his role in educating others:

> But I think the core, the key takeaways of faith, I still keep with me (in having forgotten Greek and Hebrew learned as a theological student then); the ability to think clearly, sometimes too clearly, to intellectualise things, to form healthy debate. I think these are the skills that if I can transfer and allow other people to learn from it as I learn, I'm learning from it myself. I think that's what I want to do. I think I'll feel very happy if I can minister to people or through whatever little things that I do … help people to understand certain dimensions of their faith … I think I'll be happy enough for that. [27:73 (841:852)]

Joe's 'interpersonal routinization' that 'indicates informal ways individuals integrate homosexuality into their conventional social lives, e.g. disclosing to family members or co-workers' (Seidman et al. 1999: 11), is here expressed. He desires to share his 'ability to think clearly … to intellectualise things, to form healthy debate' with his faith community within the Free Community Church as a self-identified ministry. The mutuality proposed between 'interpersonal routinization' and 'institutional routinization' (incorporating practices that affirm GLBTIQ persons within the FCC) is evident, as he aspires to 'allow other people to learn from it as I learn, I'm learning from it myself'. Time as process is manifest as a long-term education of the self and others. It is sustained by 'little things that [he does]' in seeking to 'help people to understand certain dimensions of their faith'. And affectively, he would be fulfilled, 'be happy enough for that'.

Seeking psychiatric and/or spiritual counselling

Time as process is effected by those who have sought or continue to seek psychiatric and/or spiritual counselling in order to come to terms with their sexuality in religion or spirituality. The need for counselling is double-edged: it is to manage both the effects of disrupting and adhering to the gendered script of heteronormativity as a GLBTIQ person of faith. As shown in the narratives below, counselling is both received and given.

Jimmy, who was once blackmailed by threats to expose his sexuality to his church members, says:

Many church...very, very strict on this. Maybe because I myself-lah...put the stop there-lah...put the mindset...like they're against us, actually not [*laughs*]. We don't know. I never...ask for...counselling on...this issue...If I really ask the church, I mean the church leaders, his opinion, maybe I can get some counselling like that-lah. I never do it. Still is block for me-lah. [15:83 (1131:1146)]

The 'block' that Jimmy experiences effectively compels him to 'never...ask for...counselling on...this issue (of homosexuality)'. He pre-empts the 'church [leaders'] ...opinion' by not coming forward as he knows that they are 'very, very strict' – their insistence on the gendered script of heteronormativity and concomitant condemnation of homosexuality (stated elsewhere). Jimmy's reflexivity is however glimpsed as he questions his complicity in internalizing the binary of heterosexuality/homosexuality and 'church leaders'/PLU (People Like Us), as he says: 'Maybe because I myself-lah...put the stop there-lah...put the mindset...like they're against us, actually not'. 'Maintaining the fiction of unity' (Bailey 2007: 83) of a unified, heteronormative (Christian) subject is effected through Jimmy's reluctance to come forward, to come out as a survival strategy. As discussed, this constitutes *strategic ignorance* that in sustaining 'the fiction of unity' serves also as a 'block' for self-preservation. Jimmy's journey in coming to terms with his sexuality and spirituality is not a linear one. Instead, his 'closet practices' become 'extensive strategies of sexual self-management that created a protected space that allowed individuals to fashion gay selves and to navigate between a straight and gay world' (Seidman et al. 1999: 11–12).

Jagadiswari offers another insight on counselling, as she says: 'None of this would have happened, I don't think. They would have brought me to counselling. They would have locked me up [*interviewer laughs*] ...Maybe not lock me up...I could have started a nunnery' [25:93 (990:1013)]. Jagadiswari here recollects her Catholic past. She jokes about conversion therapy in being 'brought...to counselling...[and] locked up' by the church as one who has over time not only become divine–human but also lesbian. 'People think I'm *gila* (crazy) already' [25:92 (973:989)], as she candidly states elsewhere, given her gift of mediating between the here–now, supernatural–human realms. The elasticity of boundaries is apparent in her narrative: past–present, Catholic–Hindu, divine–human, straight–lesbian (she was born an intersex person) and sane–crazy. Madness becomes a trope for the multiple boundary crossings that she enacts in her sexual–spiritual journey which includes, as she quips, '[starting] a nunnery' in the embrace of asceticism (in the spirit of her 'favourite saint', St Theresa of Avila) given her openness to mysticism.

Ling Jackie turned to medical and spiritual counselling to deal with her depression in coming to terms with her sexuality as a Christian two decades ago. In addition to a psychiatrist and counsellor from her church, she sought the feedback of a 'counsellor from a secular counselling organisation'. This third counsellor 'did not consider homosexuality as a moral issue' but recommended that she consider trying to '"adjust" [her] sexual orientation' through 'homeopathy'. She went on to cite 'some cases (in the US) where homosexual people who received homeopathy became straight people later' [18:88 (1081:1090)]. She adds that 'the choice was totally up to me and it was fine if I did not want to try'. Ling Jackie explains her decision:

> I took a few months to consider her suggestion. For me, if homosexuality is a physical 'problem' that can be 'cured', I don't mind give myself a try. But I also believe that if it is really an in-born thing, I don't think it can be 'cured' by any treatment. And I told God that I don't want to spend too much time on dealing or fighting with this sexual orientation matter. After all, the psychiatrist that I saw in 1999 had already told me that there is no conventional medicine to 'cure' homosexuality. [18:89 (1090:1095)]

The conversion therapy that Jagadiswari mentions in passing resonates with 'sexual reorientation therapy' (Flentje et al. 2014: 1244) that was recommended to Ling Jackie by the 'secular' counsellor where 'homosexual people who received homeopathy became straight people later'. The binaries that surface in Ling Jackie's narrative are 'straight people'/'homosexual people', now/'later' (post-therapy), normal/'problem that can be cured' and 'in-born thing'/'choice'. Mindful of the psychiatrist's counsel eighteen years ago that 'there is no conventional medicine to "cure" homosexuality', Ling Jackie comes to her decision having long weighed secular and spiritual counselling received. The psychiatrist, as she recounts, 'didn't really consider this... an illness... So the doctors just [advised her] to accept [her] own sexuality'. The counsellor from the church told her that homosexuality 'is a sin. God won't allow it. So you have to pray for it and you have to change' [18:4 (60:71)].

Time factors significantly in her decision. In the course of nearly two decades of trying 'to change', in unlearning her sexuality, she succumbs to depression in the process. She also 'ended up being very confused', burdened with the conflicting counsel, and admits to wanting 'to give up' as she 'felt very tired in [her] mind during that time' [18:32 (369:379)]. In this time, although worn out physically, emotionally, psychologically and spiritually in 'dealing or fighting with this sexual orientation matter', she does not foreclose ways of becoming.

Her 'subjective ambivalence [which] is connected to incomplete interpersonal routinization' (Seidman et al. 1999: 26) is evident as she does not consider her sexuality 'an illness' yet considers it a 'sin', informed as she is by the conflicting counsel received that she proactively sought. As she is broken down (in desiring 'to give up'), she breaks down the gendered script of heteronormativity in desiring women as a woman. Ambivalence becomes productive in her refusal to '[fight] with this sexual orientation matter' any longer, having '[spent] too much time' doing so. She reclaims agency in accepting herself for who she is and, in doing so, facilitates a turning point for herself in her sexuality–spirituality journey.

Queering time leads to other kinds of temporality: queer temporality is not only individuated but also interpersonal and intergenerational, as evident from Peter's narrative of becoming where he sought counselling on account of himself, his then wife and son after coming out to them. Peter had come across a 'gay affirmative church' that had a 'special ministry for the gay people' [1:26 (316:329)] when he was working abroad (his family was also living with him then). There, spiritual counselling in the form of pastoral care was accessible to him. He also sought the aid of a 'psychotherapist or psychiatrist', who had counselled him through phone therapy and advised him that 'you are not comfortable seeing yourself as gay' and that, as Peter recounts, 'helped me become more comfortable after that' [1:20 (235:252)]. Prior to that, Peter thought that 'emotionally [he] wasn't gay' as he subscribed to the 'common stereotypes' which conflated gay men with effeminacy and transvestism where he desired 'to have a meaningful relationship and … tenderness … [with a man but] didn't really see in that men could share tenderness with each other' [1:9 (107:124)]. And quite apologetically, he concedes that he 'came out quite late' [1:4 (38:47)] to himself and, by extension, to others. In Peter's case, he lived out the gendered script of heteronormativity until he was compelled to recast it as he 'couldn't bear going through this life not living as a gay person, or at least not trying to live as a gay person' [1:21 (253:260)].

Queering time on an interpersonal level occurred when Peter 'wrote a long letter' to his wife and 'came out to her then' [1:22 (261:270)], as he says:

> There was quite a lot of tension because of all the stresses … going there (working and living abroad in the U.S.) and then coming out. The initial stage, the first time, the first night I'm coming out, we were quite close because it was like me sharing, talking about something personal. And then, she went into denial and into all the different stages, anger and all those things … And it was difficult to

talk to her. And I tried to like bring her to go for therapy together, for couples' therapy, and she refused. She went for once or twice and then after that, refused to … The psychiatrist tried to come to our house to see whether, still didn't work out. So nothing worked. We tried all sorts of things and then finally realized that actually, we felt that it's best we stay separately. And slowly she also came to that conclusion. [1:53 (662:675)]

Going for couples' therapy serves as a rite of initiation into a different way of being together and doing family. Peter's coming out to her on the eve of a New Year in 2001 significantly heralds an end and beginning not only for himself but also for his wife and children. The trajectory of their marital fulfilment has not been a linear one where the accumulated years together have not given rise to deeper happiness as the years together had been punctuated with 'a lot of tension because of all the stresses' and loneliness. And he counts that coming out night as one of the most intimate ones that he had shared with her: as 'we were quite close because it was like me sharing, talking about something personal'. The painful dissolution of their marriage follows unsuccessful attempts at couples' therapy, where they 'tried all sorts of things … [but] nothing worked', including a 'mixed orientation marriage (staying married with one or both having other relationships outside marriage)', as stated elsewhere, with divorce being the final not first course of action [1:24 (280:294)]. Her gradual resignation to the breakthrough of her husband's sexuality and the concomitant breakdown of their marriage is apparent: 'we felt that it's best we stay separately. And slowly she also came to that conclusion'. The queering of time, in this sense, becomes interpersonal as it extends to Peter's wife who lives out the consequences of his rewriting the gendered script of heteronormativity after fourteen years of marriage, where for both marriage had been the 'natural thing to do' [1:13 (164:176)] and sustaining it, a moral imperative as Catholics (given the taboo on 'getting divorced in the church') [1:83 (965:979)].

Queering time on an intergenerational level is precipitated by an external cataclysmic event. In the year that Peter decided to come out to his wife, he 'was in the lab when 9/11 happened' (he was then working in New York and witnessed first-hand the terrorist attack on the Twin Towers), as he recollects: 'that was just after 9/11 actually … where people were starting to think better do something, what is life all about' [1:16 (206:218)]. Contemplating 'what is life all about' and '[doing] something' about it jolt him on refocusing not only on the here-now but also there-then in factoring the well-being of his children, particularly post-divorce. On coming out to his children, he had to deal with the after effects, as he '[takes] them back (to Malaysia) every summer' as it is too expensive to fly over to the United States post-divorce [1:58 (721:727)]. Peter says: 'They're sort of familiar with me, seeing me staying with another guy, as well as familiar with me not staying with their mother you see ... my son was not happy with that ... We brought him to child psychiatry for some long time for a lot of therapy' [1:47 (581:590)]. Coping with reorientation intergenerationally calls forth not only professional counselling but also paternal counselling, as Peter's eight-year-old son then received:

> I did come out to my son, in a way, like telling him ... what homosexuality means ... it's not always a man and a woman but sometimes it's a man and a man. Not so much in sexual terms but more in relation terms. He seems to understand it but he doesn't seem comfortable talking about it ... And towards the later part I also showed him ... the video which ... actually talked about, not all parents are straight ... the kids talking about their parents are gay ... or their parents are divorced because they're gay ... and trying to get him to understand that-lah ... to see other children of gay people. [1:46 (565:580)]

The imagined community of 'kids [whose] ... parents are gay ... or their parents are divorced because they're gay' adds to the intergenerational ties that Peter and his children are now a part of. Peter's emphasis on his son's mental health lies in his holding himself accountable as his son's model of masculinity and fatherhood. In 'trying to get him to understand' that 'it's not always a man and a woman but sometimes it's a man and a man', Peter rewrites not only the gendered script of heteronormativity but also the familial script of heteronormativity. In this regard, Peter undoes 'family time' as 'heteronormative time/space constructs' (Halberstam 2005: 26). In 'envisioning family' (Oswald 2002: 380), as 'sometimes it's a man and a man' (or 'sometimes it's a [woman] and a [woman]', as in the case of Stephanie and Janic), Peter and his family, which includes his partner who is 'comfortable with (his kids)', as they are with him [1:42 (529:534)], *do family* differently. It is a constant envisioning and revisioning of what doing family means, which is also inclusive of the first generation, i.e. Peter's parents whom he is out to. Queer temporality in this instance becomes cyclical or seasonal given that Peter's parenting role heightens during yearly summers till today. Till today, his 23-year-old, job-seeking son 'still has issues'.

Queer temporality that is individuated, interpersonal and intergenerational is manifest through the formative role of counsellors and counselling in the narratives of becoming of Adam and AY. Adam fondly recalls his first coming out to a counsellor, when he was studying at a US college:

So when I was there, I went to see the counsellor. There's this counsellor ...
Monique, a [exaggerated] sweet person, very beautiful, very tall, I was so, 'Man,
I'm going to have a crush on her' [*both laugh*]. She was the first person ever
that I came out to ... I went to her and said, 'Monique, I'm gay'. She said, 'OK'.
She was still waiting for something else [*laughs*]. 'Yeah, that's it. You're the first
person I told'. (She said) 'OK' and gave me a hug. I remember I cried-lah. She
was saying, 'It's alright, it's alright'. It's like no big deal. She was really waiting for
what is it that I came to her but it was just that [*laughs*]. [22:21 (263:272)]

The figure of a counsellor embodies understanding, empathy, even compassion
for some GLBTIQ persons like Adam, as he had purposefully sought her out as
'the first person ever that [he] came out to'. Prior to coming over to the United
States for studies, Adam, on knowing that he 'was gay when [he] was 11 years
old', grew up, courtesy of her aunt, with the 'impression that lesbian is this
monster ... with dark glasses, really macho woman who like, takes women out
[*laughs*] and then never take them back you know' 22:3 (31:44)]. Burdened
with the ontological monstrosity of the lesbian body and subjectivity, Adam's
epiphany occurred when he 'felt this burden lifted', having questioned his
Buddhist teacher then that homosexuality does not, by default, constitute 'sexual
misconduct ... as long as there's mutual consent' [22:8 (99:107)].

His second epiphany with Monique, in coming out to another, in a different
time and space, led to such an unburdening of the heart that he broke down
and 'cried'. That the counsellor was nonplussed and 'was still waiting for
something else' is noteworthy as it shows that she does not operate within the
gendered script of heteronormativity. This first coming out, and the centrality
of the figure of the counsellor, precipitated a series of coming outs 'to everyone
with a vengeance' beginning with his 'host family'. As Adam recalls: 'The host
dad, was totally like, "OK, is that all?" ... the mum was like freaking out ... and
she started saying, "Oh by the way, Sara (her daughter) is not gay"' [22:27
(332:344)]. In 'envisioning family' (Oswald 2002: 380), the boundary of what
constitutes normativity is destabilized, queered. Adam's mission to 'just ... see
how people react to me ... just be in their face' reflects this intentionality to
unsettle the heterosexual imperative. In effecting ripples of 'epistemological
[jolts]' (Dyer 1997: 264) – with the propensity to interrupt the normalization of
heterosexuality – Adam becomes the embodiment of deviance – 'Yeah, I'm gay',
as he would defiantly declare.

Finally, queer temporality that is individuated, interpersonal and
intergenerational is also manifest through the formative role of parenting in
the narrative of AY, as he and his then long-term partner were approached to
mentor a gay teen:

We're also god parents now. Um, really strange...I think because of our nurturing ways and how we look at things and people...we had a teenager which we met...quite a few years ago, came up to us and said...'Can I call you pa?'...He was I think about 15 then...and is now 18 or 19 soon. And so, we've been a Godpa to a teenager. He's in Singapore. And...we've been helping him with his coming out and you know, his parents, and stuff. He's very assured of himself and who he is and all that but you know, again, typical family, difficult experience coming out to the family. So we've been counselling and helping him, supporting him in that sense. [20:89 (1112:1126)]

The desire not only to mentor but also to father as a gay man for AY is evident in his accepting the teen's invitation to parent him. Elsewhere, AY, who was then in a long-term relationship and also fulfilled through his own business, shares his desire 'to one day have [his] own family (through adoption)' and that he and his partner are committed to '[finding] ways and means to bless other people ... [such as giving to] children's orphanages' [20:88 (1099:1112)]. The ethic of care and responsibility finds resonance here through the varied ways in which AY and his then partner had dedicated their lives in the nurture of others. In serving as 'Godpa to a teenager', in 'helping him with his coming out' to a 'typical family' where the experience of coming out to them is a 'difficult' one, AY and his partner queer the family. Through their sustained 'nurturing ways' in 'counselling and helping him, supporting him', they embody 'resilience' in *doing* family which encompasses 'intentionality strategies to create and sustain family ties in the absence of much societal (indeed familial) support' (Oswald 2002: 379). Theirs is not a 'typical family' where an enabling environment rather than a forbidding one is created to facilitate the 'experience [of] coming out', as desired by the teen, whose readiness is suggested by his being 'very assured of himself and who he is'.

The narratives highlighted in this section – Jimmy, Jagadiswari, Ling Jackie, Peter (and his wife and son), Adam and AY – show how time is queered through receiving and/or giving counselling. *Time as process* is effected by those who have sought or continue to seek psychiatric and/or spiritual counselling in order to reconcile their sexuality with religion or spirituality. As Halberstam, the queer theorist, defines it:

Queer time for me is the dark nightclub, the perverse turn away from the narrative coherence of adolescence – early adulthood – marriage – reproduction – childrearing – retirement – death, the embrace of late childhood in place of early adulthood or immaturity in place of responsibility. It is a theory of queerness as a way of being in the world and a critique of the careful social scripts that usher even the most queer among us through major markers of individual development and into normativity. (Dinshaw et al. 2007: 182)

As 'way of being in the world', the narratives of Jimmy, Jagadiswari, Ling Jackie, Peter, Adam and AY show how time is, in the first instance, individuated as receiving and giving counselling serve to manage both the effects of adhering to and resisting the gendered script of heteronormativity as a GLBTIQ person of faith. This is apparent in the narratives of Jimmy who eschewed seeking counselling from his church elders, Jagadiswari who jokes about conversion therapy through counselling and Ling Jackie who for almost two decades considered it as means of effecting a change. In making sense of who they are, 'major markers of individual development and into normativity' are both adhered to and resisted at different junctures in their narratives of becoming. Time becomes circular in the reiterated attempts to change and the 'failure' to do so. Time becomes episodic, even fragmented in the multiple transitionings experienced, as 'major markers' constitute both coming out as a GLBTIQ person of faith as well as not coming out for the sake of the family and significant others.

Time becomes fluid as sexualities in religion or spirituality proliferate more than two '[ways] of being in the world' in manifesting 'the perverse turn away from the narrative coherence' of heteronormativity (i.e. one born male ought to be gendered masculine and desirous of women; one born female ought to be gendered feminine and desirous of men). They do this by redefining what it means to be responsible, as differentiated from an uncritical acquiescence to 'careful social scripts'. Time is also interpersonal as others are affected by these 'major markers of individual development and [deviation from] normativity', such as Peter's wife and son who went through couples' therapy and child psychiatric counselling, respectively, as effects of his coming out to them. Time is intergenerational through the ethic of care and responsibility demonstrated by Peter as a father to his children and AY who desires to father as a gay man. And time is sometimes linear in demarcating a then/now that is significant in the healing process of those who are diagnosed with clinical depression and for those who have willingly come out. Time becomes epiphanic in the case of Adam who turned to a counsellor as the first person whom he came out to and Peter who witnessed first-hand the cataclysmic event of 9/11 that prompted him to reassess his life.

Making sense of one's sexuality in religion or spirituality

In this penultimate section of the chapter that foregrounds the iterative process of becoming through the prism of queer temporalities, interviewees make sense of their sexuality and spirituality in the attempt to reconcile these facets of who they are.

'Queer time', according to Halberstam, 'is a theory of queerness as a way of being in the world and a critique of the careful social scripts that usher even the most queer among us through major markers of individual development and into normativity' (Dinshaw et al. 2007: 182). Andy is cognizant that 'levels of justification is always there [and you] try to justify yourself' as a Christian lesbian [2:26 (302:314)]. Her 'way of being in the world' is insisting on not '[being] the first to turn my back on Him … [as] God has not turned His back on me'. And she witnesses as a Christian lesbian to those who seek her help by '[ending] up with a prayer with this person'. In this regard, her marginalized identity, rather than perceiving it as a flaw, enables her to be empathetic to others similarly marginalized. Her 'way of being in the world', as Halberstam states (Dinshaw et al. 2007: 182), is thus to witness and reach out to people who are in need of comfort rather than condemnation.

For J, who is a facilitator at LUSH, 'a critique of the careful social scripts', as Halberstam maintains (Dinshaw et al. 2007: 182), resonates with the queer hermeneutics that LUSH engages in during the six-month weekly outreach sessions twice a year. As she testifies, 'LUSH taught me to read the Bible in a very different manner … where you take into consideration the context … of which the passage has been written' [23:28 (288:296)]. The disruption of these institutionally driven 'careful social scripts' heralds an 'epistemological jolt' (Dyer 1997: 264), as J says: 'You just suddenly see this whole transformation of how the Bible relates to you. And you don't feel guilty about it anymore … And you can actually feel God in your life … So that's like the greatest miracle I guess that has happened.' Her 'way of being in the world' (Dinshaw et al. 2007: 182) is to facilitate this epiphanic moment for other members of LUSH and, by extension, the FCC.

The 'perverse turn away from the narrative coherence' of heteronormativity (Dinshaw et al. 2007: 182), for Andy, lies in her embrace of her sexuality as a Christian where many deem that incompatible. It also lies in her revisioning what others consider a flaw into an advantage and she cultivates a new subjectivity for herself by harnessing her gift of empathy to be able to reach out to more people. And for J, it is to 'read the Bible in a very different manner' and by contextualizing the Bible in contemporaneous times and local spaces, she bridges the there-and-then with the here-and-now. In doing so, she effects the transformative resonance of the Bible in her life and potentially the lives of others whom she ministers to. Queering time and space is thus embodied in each of these narratives of becoming.

The processes of becoming that encompass managing incompatibility, adopting celibacy, facing condemnation and taboo, dealing with guilt, shame and pain, negotiating ambivalence and queering time are journeys that evidence time-space compression for GLBTIQ persons in this book. This journey, that is fraught by episodic adherence and disruption of the gendered scripts inherited that deem a queer sexuality and religiosity or spirituality incompatible, is necessitated. These constitute 'major markers of individual development [into and out of] normativity' (Dinshaw et al. 2007: 182), or GLBTIQ persons for whom making sense of who you are becomes a moral imperative in order to begin developing as a person and living life abundantly. And the rewards of embarking on such a journey are, among others, the experience of peace.

Towards reconciliation

Experiencing peace

The experience of peace is aligned with both the adherence to and disruption of gendered scripts inherited. In the former, GLBTIQ persons experience the absence of peace and the presence of 'sex guilt' and religious guilt (Murray et al. 2007) when deeply conflicted about fully living out their sexuality and religiosity or spirituality. So the adherence to gendered scripts – to not come out to one's parents, for instance, 'for the sake of peace' as stated by Stephanie (illustrated below) – renders peace as an effect of reifying heteronormativity. In the latter, GLBTIQ persons experience the presence of peace and the abeyance or absence of 'sex guilt' and religious guilt when they have reconciled their sexuality and religiosity or spirituality. So the disruption of gendered scripts – to come out to one's parents, for instance, not 'for the sake of peace' – recasts peace as an effect of destabilizing heteronormativity. As such, where being conflicted and becoming reconciled are mutually constitutive states, these effect the breakdown of peace and its paradoxical breakthrough. The multilayered experiences of peace are glimpsed in the narratives highlighted below that serve as an axis to the narratives of conflict and reconciliation of sexuality and religiosity or spirituality.

For Stephanie, she says that 'for the sake of peace, I just let it be as long as I can'. She alludes to her deferring her coming out to her parents whom she deems as 'real worriers' [6:92 (1119:1129)]. Her regret is not being able to, for many years, openly acknowledge her partner Janic who co-parents her son. So 'for the sake of peace', she seemingly adheres to the gendered script of heteronormativity by passing as straight also in relation to Janic's parents.

Her partner Janic, who was a Christian missionary in the field and now works at a Tibetan Buddhist centre, experiences peace as an effect of being 'willing to listen to God ... [rather than] ... still [wanting] to be who you are'. She alludes to her having 'pushed [herself] to a point' [7:107 (1395:1406)] in adopting celibacy for seven years in order to discover for herself God's will for her. And the fact that 'that part ... still was there ... does tell [her] something about [herself]': that her sexuality cannot be unlearned or expunged as it is God-willed.

Jagadiswari finds herself 'at peace' with herself as she asks: 'Am I gay because I'm being punished for feeling things? Or am I feeling things because I'm gay' [25:23 (170:180)]. By 'feeling things', she refers to her gift of being able to communicate with her Gods, in having 'conversations with [her] deities', as she puts it elsewhere [25:9 (57:68)]. She is now 'at peace with both of it': this ability to embody her Mother serves as both a bane and boon to her as it entails sacrifices.

As for J, facilitator at LUSH, she says: 'I know that ... I'm going the right direction [as] I will feel at peace with my heart' [23:97 (1189:1203)]. For J, 'feeling at peace ... [is] like a sign' from God that rewriting the gendered scripts for herself may, to others, constitute a 'perverse turn away from the narrative coherence' of heteronormativity (Dinshaw et al. 2007: 182), but for herself, it is a journey in 'the right direction'. And she adds that 'just believe that God shows people different things in different ways ... in different times as well ... That's a good gauge'.

The multilayered experiences of peace complement the multilayered processes of becoming. The absence and presence of peace are aligned with 'major markers of individual development [into and out of] normativity' (Dinshaw et al. 2007: 182), in being conflicted and becoming reconciled and the fluid degrees of separation between the two mutually constitutive states. Peace, as 'a sign' or 'a good gauge', as J puts it, signifies the ongoing journey (in becoming person, doing family) rather than, arriving (often benchmarked as coming out), as reconciliation of one's sexuality and religiosity or spirituality is neither absolute nor definitive (as shown in the next chapters). Peace thus sustains the queering of temporalities in the narratives of becoming of GLBTIQ persons of faith.

The narratives of becoming of GLBTIQ persons of faith manifest a queer temporality that is individuated, interpersonal and intergenerational that inflect the meanings of space, particularly the home, familial and spiritual (e.g. LUSH,

PLUSH). Queer subjectivities that inhabit these private spaces also circulate in public spaces and call to question 'reproductive time and family time' that remain 'heteronormative time/space constructs' (Halberstam 2005: 26). 'Reproductive time and family time' are produced by hegemonic discourses of nation-states in which the individual and the family as its organic principles are necessarily constructed as heterosexual, thus stable subjects. A heterosexualized person and family that are made natural are consonant with the drive towards modernization through the '*disciplines: an anatomo-politics of the human body*' and '*regulatory controls: a biopolitics of the population*' (Foucault 1978: paragraph 139).

The queering of time and space calls to question postcolonial time and space in the narrative of becoming a nation – how the liberated-from-colonization states (as former colonies of the British Empire) are managing not only ethnic and religious diversity but also gender and sexual diversity of the citizenry. Through entrenched heterosexism and 'social cultural engineering' (Kuah 2018: 1) premised on an edifying albeit static 'Asian values' buoyed by Islamic resurgence and Confucianism, the 'post' in postcolonialism in signifying the progress of a nation is contested by the lack of legitimacy accorded not only to ethnic and religious minorities but also gender and sexual minorities in Malaysia and Singapore. The prefix 'post' is thus prematurely celebratory (Ahmed 2000: 10) when benchmarked against the 'reframing of the sexual citizen' (Richardson 2017) by participants of this study as well as members of civil society who, on an everyday reality, continue to push the boundaries that mark off ethnic, gender and sexual minorities are quasi citizens. They navigate the interstices of what it means to exercise one's human rights deemed a Western-centric model of citizenship and reclaim the family and home deemed an Asian-centric model of citizenship through *both* coming out and coming home modalities of becoming. In doing so, they queer 'Asian values'.

8

Managing compatibility and inclusivity

Can the impasse of competing discourses be overcome? Can one become queer *and* religious? The narratives highlighted in this chapter diverge from Boellstorff's concept of 'incommensurability': that being religious and GLBTIQ is ontologically 'ungrammatical' or 'unintelligible', in private and public spaces (2005a: 575). They claim their citizenship, although not made equal by State rhetoric and practices that maintain such discursive strategies by according legitimacy only to heteronormative sexuality that, in turn, renders them as failed citizens. These non-heteronormative persons although not the subject of the production of the 'species body' in Foucauldian terms, of postcolonial nation-states, discursively, do and can exist. Through self-regulation oftentimes by internalizing homophobia and sexual reorientation therapies, they have been forced to fit into that 'grid of cultural intelligibility through which bodies, genders and desires are naturalized' (Butler 1990: 151). They have come to terms with such regulatory technologies enacted on their bodies (e.g. Section 377 in Malaysia and 377a in Singapore) that render their bodies as incoherent, unstable and unintelligible.

As gender and sexual outlaws, they offer oppositional standpoints corresponding to incommensurability, incompatibility and ascendency claims that make fuzzy rather than harden boundaries between sexuality rights and religious discourses. These standpoints include: commensurability in 'loving the sin' (Jakobsen and Pellegrini 2004), compatibility between sexuality and religious discourses, and eschewing ascending claims through re-visioning the mutuality of universalism and particularism. These queer (strange and unsettling) strategies show why to many both (sexuality) rights and religions matter and how they find the common ground between these where others insist are irreconcilable differences. These bodies of knowledge arising from the lived realities of becoming queer and religious are not only subjugated (previously marginalized) but also oppositional (potentially subversive) knowledge. This knowledge is founded on the fluidity and plurality of ways of knowing and doing: essentially, ways of becoming persons.

In this chapter, narratives of GLBTIQ persons who have in some way reconciled their sexuality and religion or spirituality are highlighted and discussed. Such reconciliation finds expression in the various coping strategies manifest collectively. They are: committing their relationships or sexuality to God or faith, believing that they are created by God or a deity and therefore no longer feel guilty in being gay, demystifying sexuality myths, having a mindset change, realizing that sexuality and spirituality are mutually constitutive, questioning and challenging religious interpretation, and essentially reconciling sexuality and spirituality.

Committing relationship or sexuality to God, deity or faith

Committing one's sexuality and same-sex partnership to one's God or deity is significant. It rests on spectrum in the process of becoming that is lived out by GLBTIQ persons managing conflict and ambivalence in seeking to make sense of their sexuality and religiosity or spirituality. Committing their selves and relationships to God marks the narratives of becoming of Ling Jackie, AY and Joe who are Christians. Ling Jackie as a postgraduate student abroad then both desires women and to be in a relationship. Despite the uncertainties that await her, she is steadfast in her faith, as she asserts that: 'I will let God make the ultimate decision and I believe that He will guide and lead me in this matter' [18:92 (1137:1144)]. AY, who was in a long-term relationship and is also fulfilled through his own business, reiterates the abundant blessings in his life. He says, firstly in coming out, that 'I was very blessed in that sense that I grew out of my insecurities with God's help and friends' [20:49 (624:634)] and, secondly, that 'we (AY and his then partner) wouldn't have done this ourselves (start up their own business) if not for ... the doors that God opens and the blessings that we've received from that' [20:73 (895:908)].

An 'experientially oriented or interpretive perspective in understanding agency', as Lois McNay posits, is to 'understand the effects of oppression and how it constraints or motivates action [by] first enquiring into its lived dimensions, that is, how individuals understand themselves and their position in the world' (Husso and Hirvonen 2009: 52). Agency thus framed finds resonance herein becoming queer and religious: submitting to God does not negate one's will. Their agency is nurtured paradoxically through their willing submission to God.

Ling Jackie is empowered in recognizing the interdependence of her spirituality (in loving God) and sexuality (in loving others), as she aspires to 'become a Christian who loves God (willing to know God better and have good behaviour) as [she believes] that a Christian who loves God will also know how to love His/Her loved ones' [18:92 (1137:1144)]. And AY, by his own admission, is 'quite a brave person [as] it doesn't really matter to [him] what people think (of his sexuality)' [20:49 (624:634)]. A transformation of self that embraces the mutuality of sexuality and spirituality ensues: Ling Jackie is relatively optimistic about her future as AY is thankful for his.

Joe, who like AY, has had theological training as a lay person. Where AY is thankful for God's blessings in his life, Joe lays claim to witnessing the 'presence of God in the relationship' [27:32 (352:364)]. He adds that: having been in ministry for five years before leaving it, 'as a young youth leader, I was quite sensitive to what I think is the move of God. So I felt that in a relationship. So it just, suddenly like threw me off'. Joe experiences an 'epistemological jolt' (Dyer 1997: 264); that disruption to church-sanctioned gendered script of heteronormativity and heterosexism. The 'presence of God' in his relationships 'threw [him] off' as it signifies for him an affirmation of his sexuality and relationships where he had resigned himself that 'this is wrong' or damnable. As he says:

> And both times it was when I wasn't looking for it, like I was already resigned to my idea that this is wrong and I can't experience God in a relationship. Yeah. So when I was in a relationship with two people, two different relationships, I felt this relational part that I see in heterosexual couples that are committed and have a fruitful Christian walk. So it just set me to be more open. And in a way, it again, um, ties back to my worldview of either my view of Christianity that it's both the written word and the way you understand the written word through your life. So it's two forms of learning: by textbook learning and through my relationships. [27:33 (365:373)]

Joe's testimony above is noteworthy as it demonstrates a mutual reframing of his sexuality and religiosity. He emphasizes his personalized 'worldview' of Christianity following the revelation of experiencing the 'presence of God' in his relationships: that the 'written word' or Holy Scriptures is embodied 'through your life', and by extension, your sexuality and relationships. Christianity for him is not an abstraction but centred on the praxis of 'two forms of learning: by textbook learning and through [his] relationships'. The transformation of self has led him to be 'more open' to recognizing the grace of God that is not bereft in gay relationships where like (some) 'heterosexual couples that are committed (to each other and to

God)', it is possible to 'have a fruitful Christian walk'. Sexuality and spirituality for Joe become mutually nourishing as he understands that gay relationships are not inherently sinful and they potentially embody the 'presence of God'.

In the above narratives of Ling Jackie, AY and Joe as self-identified Christians, committing their sexualities to God is essentially liberating as being sexual and religious or spiritual does not become a contradiction in terms. Reciprocity between an 'all-knowing God' and created beings lies in the various aspirations of the latter to become a worthy person in the eyes of God or humbled by gratitude for abundant blessings received and the 'presence of God' experienced. The following narratives by Jagadiswari and Stephanie highlight boundaries of proper conduct in adherence to Hindu and Buddhist precepts, respectively.

Jagadiswari, a spiritual medium then, now, a Hindu priest who loves women, explains: 'It's a challenge, sexual needs…I mean I'm as human and sexual as any other person. I'm not limited by it. There are certain days that we cannot be intimate…if I'm fasting…no sex, no meat [*laughs*]' [25:86 (913:925)]. In her vocation as the 'embodiment of the Mother (Goddess Kali)', she inhabits the dual states of spirit – human when she goes into a trance or has 'conversations with [her] deities', as she puts it elsewhere [25:9 (57:68)]. As such, it is imperative that she maintains the boundaries of purity/pollution (Douglas 2002) as a fitting vessel for the indwelling of her 'Mother': refraining from sexual pleasure or physical intimacy with her partner when she is fasting. Her human condition, however, is not a lower state of being as her deities love her unconditionally, as they tell her: 'It doesn't matter who you are and who you love. You're my daughter; I created you to do this work' [25:6 (40:44)]. The reciprocal devotion between Jagadiswari and her deities, who 'don't begrudge [her] the human condition' [25:70 (700:711)], is apparent and liberating.

In the case of Stephanie who was a Tibetan Buddhist bisexual woman and mother to a twenty-something-year-old son (from her previous heterosexual marriage), living a Dharma-governed life liberates her. As she candidly says: 'It's like karma's going to bite you in the ass, so [interviewer laughs] … you know, you better behave yourself. I wish I could have a karma holiday' [6:72 (870:876)]. To self-regulate her sexuality, as she is by her own admission, not naturally monogamous, she draws on 'Dharma principles' (i.e. where sexual misconduct includes hurting one's partner through infidelity) with the added disincentive of karma '[biting her] in the ass' if she 'misbehaves'. In being committed to her present partner, Janic who jointly parents her son, she duly commits her sexuality and relationship to 'Dharma principles' and '[draws] strength from that' to sustain her desire to be monogamous for Janic.

For both Jagadiswari and Stephanie, committing their sexualities and relationships to pleasing deities or adhering to Dharma principles demonstrates how sexuality and spirituality for them are mutually sustaining. The validation of plural bodies and sexualities finds further resonance within Buddhist and Hindu frameworks. The spiritualism of Buddhism upholds 'a mode of being that is genderless' in reaching Buddhahood or enlightenment, where sexual differentiation manifests our fallen human condition and is made irrelevant (Falk 2007: 44, 49–50). Despite the social realities of 'institutional androcentrism' (the privileging of monks over nuns) and 'gender complementarity' (the privileging of men over women) among the religious and lay Buddhist communities, the core teachings of the Buddha affirm 'soteriological inclusiveness' with all accorded equal access to enlightenment. Hinduism, unlike Judeo-Christian traditions whose theology of the body dichotomizes male/female and masculine/feminine, 'allows God to be visualised and worshipped as male, female and androgynous'. And quite significantly, Hindu deities have fluid genders and sexualities (Vanita 2005: 78) which is embodied through Jagadiswari's intersexuality as a Hindu priest (as discussed in the final section of this chapter).

Believing that you are created by God

In this section, the narratives of Jimmy, CK, Ling Jackie, AY, Joe and Jagadiswari are highlighted, as they speak of being created by God in trying to reconcile their sexuality in religion or spirituality. Twenty-something-year-old Jimmy is a self-identified Christian gay man, as he says:

> K: I like to go to church, to serve the church or what. Just like that lor.
> SAB: Do you still consider yourself, um, Christian?
> K: Yeah. I still, I think I still want to go back to church [*laughs*]. Don't know somehow I feel like in my heart, I still ... need God. I still think that, um, if God loves me ... I think because this not what, this is not what I chose. Ah, you can say I chose-lah but somehow I, I'm like that [*laughs*]. [15:45 (631:642)]

Jimmy's religiosity is apparent in his desire 'to go to church, to serve the church' and his spirituality is apparent in his yearning for God; 'I feel like in my heart, I still ... need God'. As such, he demonstrates a desire to be a committed and practising Christian. He had stopped attending church services at the point of the interview due to the trauma of being blackmailed for being Christian and gay at his previous church. In terms of his sexuality, he articulates the quintessential birth/choice or nature/nurture dichotomy of sexuality, as he says: 'I think because … this is not what I chose … I chose-lah but somehow I'm like that'. He is 'like that' as he is fundamentally created 'like that'. Although his sentence trails off in, 'if God loves me', it may be intimated that his lived reality is a daily making sense of how to fully live out his sexuality and spirituality, but not bereft of God's love.

The claim to God's unconditional love by virtue of being created by God quite strongly resonates in Ling Jackie's, AY's and CK's narratives. According to Ling Jackie, she says: 'And if you ask me how I handle my gay sexuality and my faith, um, basically now I would like to say that I didn't choose to become a lesbian. And I'm also a child of God. He created me and I should be proud of it' [18:14 (182:197)]. Where she had sought psychiatric and spiritual counselling to aid her in '[handling her] gay sexuality and faith', she is now 'proud of [being lesbian]' as she is 'a child of God'. AY says:

> Where religion's concerned and how I stand with religion and God, I feel that I know that I'm still Christian. That I'm still very much a part of God's family and someone that loves Christ and seeks his ways and lives according to that. And you know, the church will preach that God will not bless and love sinners and stuff like that. And really at the end of the day, God's hands of blessings and God's hands of love have not been any further from me than they were when I was in church and serving in the church … So then why preach the way they preach you know, because this is not what I'm experiencing as a child of God. [20:37 (477:489)]

AY's profession of faith is clear: 'I'm still Christian. That I'm still very much a part of God's family and someone that loves Christ and seeks his ways and lives according to that'. He too (like Jimmy) had left his (mainstream) church as he was discriminated against for being Christian and gay as a youth leader then. In drawing from the signs of God's love for him as 'a child of God', AY makes a distinction between institutionalized Christianity and his Christian faith. Whilst the church persists in '[preaching] that God will not bless and love sinners (such as homosexuals as he was once prayed over in a bid to cast out the demon of homosexuality from his body)', his lived reality of continuing to receive 'God's hands of blessings and God's hands of love', the affirmation of his personhood, then and now, is testimony of how he has redefined religiosity for himself. Likewise Joe, who is with the Free Community Church (FCC) in

Singapore, a distinction is made between one's religiosity and spirituality in coming to terms with one's sexuality in religion. He says: 'So even after I stopped attending church in a formal way, in my heart I still felt that I was Christian as in I was God's child but … I just had questions that I couldn't reconcile at that point in time, so I stopped attending'. His Christian spirituality remains intact as 'God's child', created in the image of God, *imago dei*, although the 'formal' church attendance as religious practice had then ceased.

Redefining Christianity as an extension of becoming Christian and gay finds indignant expression in CK's narrative. CK effectively questions God's design, as he says:

> So I know that being gay I need God more than anyone else in this world because I am a sinner. But one thing that I don't know, I don't understand why … God … doesn't allow … a relationship between man and man or woman and woman. Then why we are created this way. Seems like since the day we are born, we are robbed of the privilege to love and to be loved. [17:32 (389–396)]

Being 'created this way' as a 'child of God', seems callous as from birth, persons like CK 'are robbed of the privilege to love and to be loved' as 'a relationship between man and man or woman and woman' is, as he is taught to believe, prohibited by God. It is a belief that he knowingly retains despite knowing that alternative interpretations of the Scriptures exist that challenge Biblical grounds for condemning homosexuality. What is significant about situating CK's narrative here is not only that he remains deeply conflicted as a Christian gay man, in '[needing] God more than anyone else in this world because [he is] a sinner' but that he wrestles to reconcile his sexuality with his religiosity with much anguish. As a 'child of God' in being 'created this way', he claims the right to the Biblical promise of an abundant life[1] – in having 'the privilege to love and to be loved'.

In the narratives above, Jimmy, Ling Jackie, AY, Joe and CK as self-identified Christian gays and lesbian, believing that one is a 'child of God' because one is created by God facilitates varying degrees of reconciliation of one's sexuality in religion. This often results in: (1) one's departure from a mainstream church that discriminates gays and lesbians either overtly or tacitly; (2) distinction between formalized aspects of religiosity (i.e. church attendance) and a spirituality that is personalized; (3) scepticism of biased Biblical interpretations even God's design where some are seemingly more privileged than others. Yet what is consciously sustained, despite the pain of rejection by one's faith community, is a fidelity to one's faith and a sense of self that is not 'robbed' but reclaimed; (4) the materiality of lived experiences as a 'child of God' that authenticates the self and sexuality;

and (5) the need to make sense of one's religiosity (based on church teachings) and sexuality.

In the following final narrative in this section, Jagadiswari speaks as a daughter to her deities and how this impacts her sense of self as both human and spirit. She begins her journey of self-realization with her conversion of heart from Catholicism to Hinduism, as she recounts:

> My experience of my Mother … [is] a very maternal relationship. I've always had that experience of God. But many things in the church taught me that, 'Oh wait, how can God love me and not love me at the same time?' And that's something that I bring across to people now. I'm like, 'God is perfect and loving and without struggle. If you tell me that God has an issue with you, then you have no right to question His perfection. He cannot create anything imperfect'. So that was a real confusion because I knew that I was loved. But then I was told I wasn't lovable. [25:51 (447:460)]

The incompatibility of her sexuality and then Christian faith is apparent in the disparity between her personal belief and that espoused by the church in its condemnation of gay sexuality: 'I knew that I was loved. But then I was told I wasn't lovable'. As a 'child of God' created '(gay therefore) imperfect', her 'real confusion' was brought on by the contradictory messages of: 'how can God love me and not love me at the same time?' [25:51 (447:460)]. In contrast, her experience of God, Judeo-Christian and masculinized to her 'Mother' is 'a very maternal relationship' and one, where the divine 'is perfect and loving and without struggle' and does not have 'an issue with you'. As a 'child of God', daughter to her Mother, she rightly expects no less: the knowledge and experience of being loved and loved unconditionally.

Yet, as daughter to her Mother, there are familial expectations that run counter to personal desires, as she articulates:

> When I went back to Chidambaram (in India), she didn't say, 'You're my servant'. She just went, 'You're my daughter. I created you into this world'. And then I asked her, 'Ma, why can't I have a family? Why can't I get married? Why can't I have kids?' And she just said, 'If you had kids and family, who would love me you know? Who would love me enough to take care of the world, take care of my children?' [25:38 (333:339)]

> I felt loved and embodied but also realizing I wasn't going to have kids. I wasn't going to have marriage. Which is not a sore point but it also was acceptance. It was also, 'We know you're gay. We know you love women. We made you that way. We're at peace with you and you're at peace with us'. [25:39 (340:351)]

The reciprocity of devotion is noteworthy. To her Mother goddess, Jagadiswari is not a mere 'servant' but exalted as 'daughter' who 'is gay [and loves] women'; who is '[made] that way'. In return, they ask that she devotes her life to their care, thus forsaking her human desires of marrying and having children. That this is 'not a sore point but … acceptance' for her attests to the submission of her will to that of her Mother's. The divine that 'is perfect and loving and without struggle' that she yearns for which is absent from the God of her then Christian faith is now embodied in her Mother. Peace becomes a signifier for the mutual nourishment exchanged between Jagadiswari and her Mother, as: 'we're at peace with you and you're at peace with us'. As daughter to her Mother, she finds the long sought for solace of unconditional love. As daughter to her Mother, the realization of self comes paradoxically through the denial of self.

Demystifying sexuality myths

CK, Joe and Jimmy identify sexuality myths that need to be demystified in making sense of their own spirituality and sexuality. CK says:

> I used to be a strong Christian. And I believe in God and I've experienced God. And um, somehow maybe I don't blame God. But sometimes I'm angry with God, like why I'm created this way. So I want to meet up with you maybe to share with you and then maybe in your research, you can write up something which is like, um, more accurate. [17:16 (199:209)]

CK's being 'angry with God [in being] created this way' articulated here resonates with his questioning God's design as quoted above where he says: 'Seems like since the day we are born, we are robbed of the privilege to love and to be loved' [17:32 (389–96)]. His desire to come to terms with his religiosity is quite evident as he's torn between not '[blaming] God' and being 'angry with God'. His desire to come to terms with his sexuality as a Christian who has 'experienced God' and who 'used to be a strong Christian' is also apparent (he feels that he is a lesser Christian as he gives in to being physically intimate with men, as he intimates elsewhere). His coming forward to participate in this research project therefore stems in part from his desire to 'share' his journey with me in the hope that general understanding about gay sexuality would be 'more accurate' when it is based on lived realities like his. He refers to the day-to-day experiences of managing the conflict inherent in the sexuality in religion dichotomy of birth/choice as a 'child of God' albeit lesser 'child of God'.

The ways in which being Christian and being gay interrelate in individual lives lead to CK's ambivalent attitude towards God and Joe's pragmatic view of how Christianity is fleshed out in his life and relationship with his then partner. In committing his relationship to God, Joe says:

> I don't think that being Christian or not Christian would help us love each other more or less. I think it's a myth for people who don't really love each other to begin with, to think that if they go to church often enough, they might love each other more. It might help to a certain extent. But [not] if the fundamental attraction of love is not there. [27:45 (470:483)]

A faith-based relationship like his can be supported only by acts of faith such as '[going] to church often enough' if it is premised on a mutual 'fundamental attraction of love'. The limits of Christianity in his relationship are drawn. And his emphasis on human will in choosing to 'love each other' regardless of whether one is a Christian or not is made. He goes on to say that:

> I think our struggles are more than just about being gay, accepting ourselves. I'm not saying it's childish. I'm not even saying that you should move on. I'm just saying that we should look beyond what we're in. And try to examine and try to understand our faith and our relationships more than … just very narrow view that we're gay. How do we make sense of everything because we're gay? [27:58 (640:655)]

On the one hand, he critiques the over-importance that some members of his congregation (FCC) place on being Christian as being more naturally predisposed to transcend relationship woes. On the other hand, he also challenges Christian gay men, as one himself, to place into perspective the importance of being gay. The limits of sexuality are here drawn, as there is a need to: 'try to examine and try to understand [that] our faith and our relationships [are] more than … just [a] very narrow view that we're gay'. He intimates that it is not only a 'narrow view' but also over-indulgent to 'think [that] our struggles are [just] about being gay'. The journey of realizing one's personhood comes about in balancing the weightings placed on one's sexuality and religiosity or spirituality. For Joe, neither one category takes precedence over the other. The myth that either one category is the be all and end all of the meaning of a Christian gay man's existence is challenged.

By making visible his narrative as a Christian gay man, CK deconstructs a sexuality myth. He shows how it is a construct that many take as a given or truth claim: that sexuality is a lifestyle choice and those with 'deviant' or non-normative sexualities can and should change. Jimmy extends the deconstruction of this myth through recounting his experience as a volunteer at the Real Love Ministry (RLM) headed by a Christian pastor who is an ex-gay but is now contentedly married to a woman and seeks to convert gay men into becoming straight men. As Jimmy says:

> Not, not keen lor because later I found it's, um, not so correct-lah … start something from the gay and then to the objective right, turn the gay to straight. Married guy (pastor) like that. I think it's weird. It's too stereotype … too rigid-lah. Can be done but it's not so like preaching and then teaching can be done like that. I don't think so-lah. I mean the teaching I don't agree with. I didn't agree with that-lah. But they didn't know. I just quit like that … So the main thing is that I join the group-lah, now our group … it's a main turning for me-lah. [15:54 (754:774)]

Jimmy finds several aspects of the RLM objectionable: it is 'weird' to have a '(former gay now) married guy' preach to gay men; gay sexuality is 'too [stereotyped]' in the programme and the 'teaching' is 'too rigid (fundamentalist)'. Although it 'can be done' that one can opt to change one's sexuality, 'but it's not so like preaching and then teaching can be done like that'. What he means is that it is an incremental work in progress and not a total, instant or superficial conversion. His withdrawal from the gay-reforming group to the adoption of a gay-affirming group affords him 'a main turning (point)' in coming to terms with his gay sexuality as a Christian. This life-changing experience is precipitated by his radical refusal to be complicit (as a 'volunteer') to such 'homophobic bullying' and 'religiously based sexual prejudice' (Newman et al. 2018: 540) and gender-based violence – given that sexual reorientation or conversion therapies are a form of discursive and psychic violence to GLBTIQ persons. This gives rise to his self-awakening which, in turn, heralds several transitioning processes. Firstly, from trying to change or unlearn his sexuality, he begins to accept it. Secondly, he begins to question and reject 'the teaching [he doesn't] agree with' which is a marked departure from his attempt to imbibe the 'objective right' (interpretation of his faith that condemns homosexuality). Thirdly, he begins to realize his personhood in moving away from victimhood: he withdrew from his previous non-denominational church following the episode of being blackmailed for being Christian and gay. Jimmy thus makes visible the myth of dichotomizing sexuality and religion: one can only be either Christian or gay and in deconstructing the myth shows that one can be *both* Christian *and* gay.

Having a mindset change

The reiteration of 'I didn't agree with [the teaching]' as articulated by Jimmy above that led to his 'main turning [point]' resonates with the narratives on having a mindset change highlighted in this section by Janic. In making sense of her Christian religiosity as a missionary in the field then and now, a turning towards Tibetan Buddhist teachings, Janic says:

> Finally I got to the conclusion that is the answer. Maybe you know, you kept asking something that is totally irrelevant. When you're asking everything else for other people, have I not answered you? Have you not found answers on your own? So why is it that this one (regarding her sexuality), even if I see other people's interpretation, let's say alternative people interpreting the Bible in this way, why am I not accepting their views? Why am I just accepting views from one type of category of people? You know, so willingness, I must be open to anyone … to … consider their views. [7:111 (1446:1455)]

In her quest to reconcile her sexuality as a lesbian and Christian religiosity as a missionary then, Janic challenges herself on her resistance towards queer hermeneutics, the 'views' of 'alternative people interpreting the Bible'. The note of finality hinted at the opening phrase of this quote, 'Finally I got to the conclusion that is the answer', is revealing. She had become 'very depressed at one stage because of [her] sexuality', she adds, prompted by her partner Stephanie, who was present during her interview. Janic admits that: 'it goes back to me having to put a side of me on hold … being attracted to same-sex people … it can be quite painful … in the sense of having to shelve that part of me' [7:105 (1369:1384)]. The self-regulation of her sexuality found expression in adopting celibacy. She had compartmentalized her sexual self from her spiritual self as 'being attracted to same-sex people' and being Christian was incompatible to her. The denial of self in the suppression of her sexuality was an extension of 'accepting views from one type of category of people', essentially, Christians who condemn homosexuality. Her journey towards realizing her personhood, in finding fuller expression of her sexuality and spirituality, begins with the mindset change: leaving behind views that are 'totally irrelevant' and nurturing the 'willingness [to] be open to anyone … to … consider their views'. In doing so, she de-essentializes what it means to be Christian: to be Christian is not only to reject homosexuality but also to embrace it. And in living out that mindset change – 'I must be open' – she shows how being Christian and being lesbian are not mutually exclusive states.

Questioning and challenging religious interpretation

In this section, the narratives highlight the impetus to question and effectively challenge religious interpretation which facilitates a mindset change even moments of epiphany. Andy is past feeling guilty now about her sexuality as a woman of faith, as she says:

> Funnily enough, I also do commit some of the relationships to God, in the sense that in my own ways, I would pray for His blessings whilst I am there because I think that there are a lot of things in the Bible that is not clear, that is unclear to us … It's in grey areas, grey patches. People will say it's an abomination … and I'll say, 'Sure, show me the verse'. And they'll show me the verse, I'd say, 'You look at the context of where this verse came from. It was a point of where He was condemning Sodom and Gomorrah'. It's at that time, at that situation where they were having orgies, having a wild life in there … Then much later on, of course Paul condemned again. Why, simply because he believes in procreation. And this basically does not give rise to it. [2:27 (314:330)]

Like Ling Jackie, AY and Joe who are Christian; Jagadiswari who is Hindu and Stephanie, who is Tibetan Buddhist, as presented in the opening section of this chapter, Andy '[does] commit some of [her] relationships to God … [and] pray for His blessings'. On the one hand, she does not profess to have all the answers to her questions pertaining to her faith, as: 'there are a lot of things in the Bible that is not clear'. On the other hand, her standpoint, on the interpretation of certain problematic Biblical verses that some have used to condemn homosexuality as an 'abomination', is clear: 'You look at the context of where this verse came from'. Her emphatic response resonates with the queer hermeneutics used at LUSH and PLUSH. That homosexuality is inherently objectionable is questioned: as contextually, it was the 'wild life' practised in 'Sodom and Gomorrah' that is condemned, as is Paul's '[belief] in procreation' that led to his condemnation of gay sex. As such, 'this (her relationship with her then girlfriend) basically does not give rise to it'.

AY reinforces Andy's standpoint articulated above, in alluding to queer theologizing by 'people that do theology as a study'. As one who has had theological training as a youth leader in his previous church, he says:

> You know, so then the question for me when I put that back to the church, is then how then is that different you know? Of course, I've read other books as well, the ones written by pastors as well as people that do theology as a study. And they've actually come up with research and that says where stories like Sodom

and Gomorrah are concerned, that's not the sin of homosexuality that brought them the punishment that they had, more of the sin of inhospitality. And um, and then so with that in mind, then why is the church saying what it's saying with regards to sin because you know, they wanted to have sex with the other guys. It didn't matter or not whether they were men or women. It was the fact that they were inhospitable to a guest and that's why God you know, pronounced the punishment that He did. [20:35 (457:471)]

The 'question for [him] when [he puts] that back to the church' is 'why is the church saying what it's saying with regards to sin': that Sodom and Gomorrah is about 'the sin of homosexuality' rather than 'the sin of inhospitality', contrary to sound theology, as he imputes. Elsewhere he adds that:

so it makes you wonder and reflect on what the church has been preaching and all that. And why I feel then there's a huge injustice where that's concerned to the gay and lesbian community because they're just basically preaching what they feel they want, that they feel is right, another way of you know, human interpretation and not really what God wants. [20:36 (471:476)]

The fallibility, even corruptibility, of the church as fully human is pronounced here as an unsuspecting source of 'huge injustice' in relation 'to the gay and lesbian community' which he is a part of. The dichotomy between God's will ('what God wants') and human will ('they're just basically preaching what they feel they want') is marked. As one who had 'done all that' in a bid to reconcile his sexuality with his Christian faith – willed himself to become heterosexual, opted for celibacy, had the demon of homosexuality cast out of him, AY concludes:

But nothing's changed. You know, it hasn't changed who I am. It hasn't changed, um, what I want sexually. So when I decided eventually on embarking on this journey with my partner, I also realized one thing. It didn't change who I am you know, as a person. I'm still the same person. A person that's still very much who I am you know: giving, loving, I share, I do everything I can to help. But there weren't any demons involved. [20:34 (442:456)]

The various detours undertaken in his 'journey' as AY contends show both the mutability and immutability of one's sexuality as a man of faith. The mutability of his sexuality is evident as, at various junctures in his life, he desired to become straight, celibate and 'decided eventually on embarking on this journey with [his] partner'. Whilst the immutability of his sexuality is also evident as he says, 'it hasn't changed who I am. It hasn't changed, um, what I want sexually'. In '[putting] that back to the church', through questioning the church's interpretation of Scripture and taking on then abandoning the approved paths of normative sexuality, desiring to become heterosexual even celibate, he thus realizes his personhood: the knowledge that he is 'still the same person ... giving, loving', sans 'demons involved', as he quips.

Andy's and AY's queer theologizing serve as interventions to their mainstream churches' dichotomous stance of loving the sinner but not the sin. In embodying God, as *imago dei*, they unsettle the hard boundaries between doer and deed, in loving the sinner *and* the sin. That 'homosexuality is not a sin' and 'same-sex relationships do not violate the principle of love' is systematically and theologically argued by Malaysian-born openly gay pastor Ou Yang Wen Feng (Ngeo 2013: 175) who has dedicated his book *Gay Is OK!* to his husband, Phineas Newborn III. On returning home to Malaysia where he lives in New York with his American husband, their marriage abroad and wedding reception in Kuala Lumpur provoked the reaction that 'Malaysians of all races should protest en masse the practice of same sex marriages as they will erode the family institution' (Leach 2012). Identifying as gay and Christian embodies Cheng's (2010) four-point 'Christological model' (based on the redemptive figure of Christ who was crucified for all) that stands in contrast to the 'traditional legal model' (based on the Biblical 'texts of terror' that proscribe homosexuality) in rethinking sin and God's grace for GLBTIQ persons.

In this living vein of embracing and embodying gender diversity and inclusion, J who facilitates LUSH and PLUSH shares how the FCC is a safe space to question, as she says:

> So [everyone] comes from different denominations, different background and a lot of people have like even a worse story to tell, things like that. So that's when you really share, you really learn, like from each other, about their own perspective of what God is to them and why they even bother coming for something like that (LUSH). And when you go through the passages in the Bible and how you can look at it in a different way, how it's OK to question. When you go to a mainstream church, questioning is like one of taboo things that you should never do. You just take whatever that the pastor says as the Word from God. And that's when, I think that's, that's why I feel so like I've waste-, not really wasted but [been] so ignorant for like 20 over years of my Christian walk with God that everything I take, I do not question. [23:26 (270:280)]

The diversity of 'different denominations, different background' resonates with the mission of the FCC which is 'to be an inclusive community that celebrates diversity in living out God's love and promise of abundant life for all'. The embrace of diversity is aligned with its embrace of inclusivity and concretized in the Bible reading sessions where 'you go through the (six problematic) passages in the

Bible and ... it's OK to question'. J marks out this difference in faith experience
that she encounters in the FCC and 'a mainstream church' that she used to attend.
Elsewhere she labels such 'mainstream church' as 'a straight church' [23:53
(695:710)]. Where the FCC is an 'inclusive community', 'a mainstream church'
is not in her experience. She thus lines up several binaries: 'straight church'/
GLBTIQ-friendly church (FCC), 'mainstream'/'different', exclusive/inclusive,
pastor/lay leader (such as J) and 'do not question'/'OK to question'. The first
terms within the binary are positioned as the more dominant ones and aligned
with a 'mainstream church' whilst the second terms are aligned with the FCC.

Her regret in complying with the edict to 'not question' as it is 'one of taboo
things that you should never do' (as is having deviant sexualities) is evident in her
lament. She had, in effect, 'wasted' two decades of her 'Christian walk with God'
where she had knowingly been 'so ignorant ... [in] not [questioning]': not just in
taking the Bible 'point blank' or literally but also in uncritically '[taking] whatever
that the pastor says as the Word from God'. Her holding herself accountable in
her own faith journey, her 'Christian walk with God', in questioning, in learning
from those with 'a worse story to tell' and in discovering your 'own perspective
of what God is to [you]' are steps towards realizing her personhood.

The narratives above present a distinction between 'mainstream church' or
'straight church' and the diversity and inclusivity of the FCC, with corresponding
straight hermeneutics (that gives rise to 'huge injustice' for GLBTIQ persons)
and queer hermeneutics. Juuk, who is founder of a website that is GLBTIQ-
friendly, shares how she got past the disparity between 'religions [which] are
good' and 'religious teachers that make things so scary' (the fire and brimstone
variant) whom she had encountered in high school where she was first exposed
to Christian teachings. She had transitioned from questioning the Bible to not
questioning 'how it was translated by the religious teachers' as more pragmatic
emphasis is now given to 'trying to be as spiritual as [she] can [be]' [9:7 (64:75)].
In moving past the 'fear' of noncompliance, she now finds resonance between
her sexuality and eclectic spirituality (she dealt then in tarot cards as one means
of making a living), as she says that: 'I do not have much problems right now
with faith and sexuality because I believe there's God'.

Ling Jackie, who was 'angry at God' over twenty years ago, questions God's
will for her in creating her a woman who is sexually attracted to women: '(When
praying) I focus on why didn't He make me as a guy rather than why didn't He
make me as a straight girl' [18:47 (555:565)]. Her frustration in not being able to
realize her desire in being in a relationship with a woman, where 'straight guys

no need to wait until 20 years old (as they hook up fairly easily)' led her to ask of God: 'Why did you do this to me?' [18:46 (538:554)]. On trying to rationalize her queer desire to become a man, in order to access the male privilege of openly desiring and dating women, she says: 'I really don't know how to explain it. I think [it's] because I can't imagine the feelings of a straight girl towards a guy' [18:47 (555:565)]. Questioning God in anger although she '[doesn't] really feel that God really [answered her] question' facilitates a gradual coming to terms with her sexuality. With her anger at God now somewhat worked through, she is able to assert that: 'But one thing I'm quite sure that, um, it seems that God doesn't really want to change my sexuality'. And her search for a partner goes on till today.

Peter thinks that 'questioning the church's teachings about sexuality is helpful because it helps to dig to the very core of what faith is, to help people to really understand what the Bible actually is rather than what people say it is. And to, um, link it to real life I guess' [1:81 (951:954)]. Peter foregrounds the need to '[question] the church's teachings about sexuality' as that would 'dig to the very core of what faith is'. It would facilitate greater understanding among '[lay] people' as it would reveal the disparity between 'what the Bible actually is rather than what people say it is'. The test of authenticity, as Peter suggests, not only lies in opening up Biblical interpretation, often monopolized by an elitist few but also and more importantly lies in '[linking] it to real life'. It is contextualizing and making relevant Biblical interpretation to the praxis of everyday living out of one's faith and in this instance, one's sexuality. He adds that:

> I think from a faith perspective, I think it goes back to, if the core of Christianity is following Jesus and if you look at the person of Jesus who fights, who actually was one with those who are marginalized and then was killed because of that ... being one with the marginalized group itself is in a way, a faith experience. It helps to ... see ... what is so blessed about the oppressed [*laughs*] in a way ... And the wanting to change ... for a better world, for equality is there you see rather than maintaining the status quo, so questioning the status quo. So these would tie in with, be consistent with the values of Jesus, I think. [1:80 (936:950)]

Peter by his own admission 'came out quite late' (in his forties) to his self and then wife (he has since divorced) as he concedes at the outset of his interview [1:4 (38:47)]. In making sense of his gay sexuality and Catholicism, 'questioning the status quo' and by extension Biblical interpretation related to sexuality is a Christian praxis rather than 'maintaining the status quo' or not questioning Biblical interpretation related to sexuality. His Christian values are 'the values of Jesus' who through the way he lived and died 'was one with those who are marginalized and then was killed because of that'. Peter's identification with the figure of Christ – what he stood for, why he was crucified – resonates with the intersections of human–divine, material–immaterial which serve as the basis for Goh's 'Incarnational Theology' (2012b). The fluidity of immanence-transcendence is embodied in the figure of Christ who is 'the Word of God who "became flesh"' and lived among humankind. The incarnation of Christ, that evidences for humanity that 'God is *always* and *continuously* corporeally manifested on earth', affirms the inherent dignity and worth of all human persons, as they are created in God's image (*imago dei*) (2012b: 150).

Christian GLBTIQ persons continue the salvific mission of Christ. In this regard, Peter is able to relate to Jesus as a self-identified gay Catholic father, not only as a member of 'the oppressed' but also in 'being one with the marginalized group itself' through his participation in gay support groups (for Asian gay men and gay fathers when he was in the United States). He does not dwell in victimhood as, in being one of the 'oppressed' particularly in the context of Malaysia, he is affirmed as he '[sees] what is so blessed about the oppressed'. His embrace of his personhood is evident in his aspiration of 'wanting to change (the status quo) ... for a better world, for equality'. The sum of his 'faith experience' therefore lies not only in 'being one [of] the marginalized group', but also 'being one *with* the marginalized group (emphasis mine)' in agitating for a 'better world' for GLBTIQ persons through his life and writings. Agency for Peter is about enquiring into the 'lived dimensions' and living out these dimensions of oppression (Husso and Hirvonen 2009: 52).

In the narratives above, questioning Biblical interpretation and who decides this and for whom are embraced as interviewees quoted: (1) make visible Biblical interpretation that in demonizing homosexuality is a 'huge injustice' to the GLBTIQ community; (2) claim the right to question and, in doing so, open up the multiplicity of Biblical interpretations; (3) challenge the dominance of biased Biblical interpretations that endorse the 'status quo' of 'injustice'; (4) distinguish between an institutionalized or mainstream church whose treatment of GLBTIQ persons in its community is based on such biased interpretations and personalized faith that resists such treatment; (5) depart or withdraw from the exclusivity of 'straight [churches]' and affiliate themselves with the inclusiveness of GLBTIQ-friendly churches like the FCC and other support groups; (6) enrich their 'Christian walk with God' or 'faith experience' not only through the praxis of questioning the 'status quo' but also in being agents of 'change' as is 'consistent with the values of Jesus'.

That being liberated can sometimes come from questioning one's faith is also Adam's experience. Adam was then a self-identified Buddhist. Adam 'knew [he] was different since [he] was six years old' [22:1 (5:17)] which all interviewees testify to. He 'knew [he] was gay when [he] was 11 years old' and as he was 'very tomboyish', his aunt threatened him with the 'impression that lesbian is this monster like you know, with dark glasses, really macho woman who like, takes women out [*laughs*] and then never take them back you know' [22:3 (31:44)]. As a 'gender ambiguous individual' (Halberstam 2005: 38), as he was often perceived as embodying female masculinity, as form of failed masculinity in the early days of his transitioning, his desire for the same sex thus demonized and made not only predatory but monstrous, eroded his self-esteem then. As he recalls, such internalized stigmatization 'made me a loner actually when I was growing up because I had this big secret that I couldn't tell anybody' [22:5 (57:68)]. Emerging from the shrouds of secrecy and shame, in recalling his moment of epiphany, he says:

> And of course, in my mind, I know that you know, I cannot tell anybody because this is something really bad even though my religion doesn't actually say it's really bad. I don't know what my religion says. I go to Sunday school. I am a Buddhist. I think it's more of a cultural thing rather than my religion. Because ultimately I took up the courage to actually ask my Sunday school teacher in the temple and I think I was 15 or 16 at that time because we were doing the five precepts in Buddhism. [22:7 (86:98)]

That his sexuality 'is something really bad' is accentuated by: firstly, ignorance about 'what [his] religion says'; secondly, the then unfounded hope that '[his] religion doesn't actually say it's really bad'; thirdly, the consoling displacement of blame on culture rather than religion as it is 'more of a cultural thing rather than my religion'. At age fifteen or sixteen, he facilitated his turning point when he 'took up the courage to actually ask [his] Sunday school teacher in the temple' about the 'third precept [which] is not to indulge in sexual misconduct'. Adam adds:

> The first precept, I undertake the precept of not to kill; um, second one is not to steal; the third precept is not to, um, indulge in sexual misconduct; the fourth one is not to slander and lie and the fifth one is not to take intoxicants. So the third one I was very curious, sexual misconduct, so I asked my teacher, 'So does it include homosexuality?' And he said, 'No it doesn't, as long as there's mutual consent. Um, it's not, it could be any gender'. So at age 16, I was like, I just felt this burden lifted, like 'Oh' [sigh dramatically], 'It's OK' [both laughs]. So all these years I've been suffering but it's actually OK. [22:8 (99:107)]

The hope that '[his] religion doesn't actually say it's really bad' is now well founded as, according to his teacher, 'sexual misconduct' does not 'include homosexuality … as long as there's mutual consent … it could be any gender'. The shift from 'suffering' for 'all these years' with his ontological 'burden lifted' accounts for Adam's 'epistemological jolt' (Dyer 1997: 264): that right sexual conduct is 'mutual consent' regardless of the gender of one's love object or partner. With that hope that is akin to rebirth, 'it's actually OK', Adam begins his journey of realizing his personhood with Buddhism as a way of life reconciled with his queer sexuality.

Realizing that sexuality and spirituality are mutually constitutive

Becoming persons in the final section of this chapter that seeks to dismantle the incongruity of becoming queer and religious highlights the narratives of Adam as a Muslim-Chinese Malaysian trans man filmmaker who is married to a Malay-Muslim woman and Jagadiswari who is a Hindu-Indian Singaporean intersex priest with a current partner who is Hindu and American (non-Indian). Their highly intersectional subjectivities exemplify not only amorphous but also transgressive identity positions – how far transformed are they from intelligible bodies with stable sexes and stable genders.

The paradigmatic figure of gender and sexual pluralism is arguably, as Peletz opines, the "transgender" who is defined as 'individuals involved in customary behaviors that transcend or transgress majoritarian gender practices' (Peletz 2011: 661). This is made apparent as 'the vicissitudes of transgenderism index' the vicissitudes of 'gender pluralism' (Peletz 2011: 662) where there is not only gender diversity but also 'gender pluralism' in the sense of legitimacy accorded to the figure of the transgender in the history of early Southeast Asia, as he chronicles, before the onset of Christianity by European colonizers followed by Islamization in the region, largely a Malay archipelago with a flourishing maritime trade.

This precolonial time space sets the scene for what Halberstam theorizes as 'hypothetical temporality – the time of "what if"' in opposition to the 'time of reproduction' that heterosexualizes 'time-space constructs' (2005: 18, 26) which characterizes the investment that postcolonial nation-states and state apparatuses (e.g. familial, legal, social, religious) make in naturalizing genders, sexualities and families. What if Adam had lived in that time space? Would his journey of becoming queer and religious been easier and less protracted? His transitioning started with his becoming 'the father, going to work', as early as three years old, as his older sister (who stayed at home to cook), recollects during their role plays. Subsequently, through hormonal therapy, as discussed earlier, he went through a 'second puberty' with a voice change that made passing as an 'invisible man' – unnoticed – a significant rite of passage for Adam. The excision of his femaleness – his 'inauthentic' femininity masqueraded as tomboyism in his teen years – was effected through a hysterectomy performed in Kuala Lumpur and mastectomy, or 'top surgery' as he puts it, around 2008. The enactment of masculinity – masculinization of gender identity and expression – effected his transitioning from an 'invisible man' to a 'visible man' through a series of 'bottom surgeries' or 'Sexual Reassignment Surgery' between 2011 and 2013 in Thailand.

And Adam 'found God in this body'. He thus articulates the parallelism between his journey in becoming a man and Muslim:

> It's strange because … being on this spiritual journey … is something where you go beyond the material of the body or the external … And yet, at the same time while I am on this spiritual journey, I was on a gender transition, a physical, bodily transition from a female to a male, from a woman to a man … that is congruent to myself, as well as to be recognized socially and by other people as a man in society … And I found God (with emphasis) in *this* body.

Religiosity and sexuality as mutually constitutive is apparent in Adam's testimony above where he elides the boundaries of spiritual/material, male/female and man/woman. It is with the congruence of 'body and spirit' that enabled Adam to find God which is synonymous in finding himself. As he adds, 'the incongruence made it a struggle, a daily struggle of self-acceptance. If you can't accept yourself, how can you accept God?' His yearning for legitimacy is two-pronged: self-recognition and societal recognition of himself as a man. His piety is evident as he recounts his first *solat* (ritual prayer):

> I just felt an energy running through my body you know. I was vibrating. And I felt like I've come home. So I embraced Islam in a very physical way.

The physicality of his experience of God that so energizes his body that it vibrated contrasts with the somewhat more feminized experiences of peace that other interviewees speak of in articulating what it means to live out the congruity of becoming queer and religious. He was so overwhelmed that he 'cried first time' when he performed this ritual prayer. Adam goes on to recount his 'first experience of fasting'. At the *azan* (call to prayer) to signal the breaking of a whole day's fast (during the thirty-day *Ramadan* period which he likens to a Buddhist retreat), when the mango juice 'touched [his] tongue', he exclaimed, 'What perfection!...the perfection of creation, the perfection of fulfilling your needs...of being alive, the gift, the blessings'. This sense of God literalized as sweetness on the tongue blurs the boundaries of material and spiritual hungers. Adam's sensuous rapture of God, the gratitude in being alive, the humility in becoming a man, coalesced in that instant of his giving thanks to God, *Al-Rahman*, who is All Loving.

The rapture of embodying the congruity or 'balance' of spirituality and intersexuality is thus articulated by Jagadiswari:

> My being intersex, I can do anything (e.g. rituals). It's about the equality of the energies, whether Shiva and Shakti are in connection, whether the male and female energies are in balance. I'm in a very particular situation that I don't need to have that. The moment I enter the arena being intersex, it's acknowledged that I embody both of them and I can carry on my duties alone.

She reiterates that the 'Hindu faith' is one that 'doesn't care about gender or sexuality' and neither does her present Guru. Supported by such a non-dualistic spiritual framework and mentor, Jagadiswari's intersexuality renders her the perfect vehicle for the performance of her religious duties to her deities as within her one being, there lies two sacred energies and the equal balance of these energies, 'Shiva and Shakti'. Where Adam transgresses the sex/gender boundary, Jagadiswari embraces both male and female, masculine and feminine identities, gender expressions as well as sex characteristic (e.g. she is chromosomally XXY, has ovaries and as an infant, a fused scrotum which was subsequently operated upon). The realization of how abundantly she is loved and cherished by her deities 'smacked me' as she puts it, when a friend remarked that, 'how much must they love you, Mother and Father, that they gave their body to you'. Is there greater affirmation? To mark her affinity with her deities, her faith, Jagadiswari was initiated as a priest a few years ago (having received the requisite permission from at least three male priests). She now wears the *poonal* (thread) that enables her to perform rituals hitherto reserved only for male priests (e.g. fire pujas).

Both Adam and Jagadiswari enact 'gender performativity' (Butler 1990: 151) in 'proliferating gender configurations' and, in doing so, open up previously unimagined possibilities of becoming:

> That gender reality is created through sustained social performances means that the very notions of an essential sex and a true or abiding masculinity or femininity are also constituted as part of the strategy that conceals gender's performative character and the performative possibilities for proliferating

gender configurations outside the restricting frames of masculinist domination
and compulsory heterosexuality. (1990: 141)

For Adam, becoming a Muslim and transgender is to be cognizant of the
value of being labelled 'gender dysphoric' – where (according to the American
Psychiatric Association) one's gender identity and gender expression are
incongruent with one's sex – as that would mean accessibility to treatment for
those thus diagnosed (this is especially salient for the young trans men whom he
mentors) (ARJ 2014). From an Islamic standpoint, he debunks the immorality
and illegality of being a Muslim transgender in an article that he had written
in the local press anonymously, 'knowing how cruel some people can become
about things they do not understand, things they fear ... [he does] not want
[his] mother to suffer because of how people will treat her son' (ARJ 2014).
Although the (Malaysian) National Fatwa Committee issued a religious edict
(fatwa) in 1982 to prohibit sex change operations for transgender persons but
not hermaphrodites, transgender activists met the *mufti* (religious leader) in
the hope of promoting understanding and ending discrimination against them
based on non-discriminatory readings of the Qur'an and Hadith (Fadli 2018).

For Jagadiswari, she has sustained a vision for the future of going back to
India with her partner 'to build a school that teaches boys and girls equally ... so
that they become priests and they become community leaders'. In the present,
she has to play out her 'human role' in being her father's primary care giver as he
has dementia. She adds that, she desires in particular 'to teach and bring more
women up ... [as] a lot of people leave their queerness because they don't know
they don't have to'. This articulation synthesizes so simply and elegantly not only
what it means to bring about congruence between becoming queer and religious
but also how to do that. Jagadiswari knows and shows through doing how
'performative possibilities for proliferating gender configurations outside the
restricting frames of masculinist domination and compulsory heterosexuality'
can someday be realized.

9

Finding reconciliation and affirmation

Becoming persons shows how being sexual and being religious are commensurable within the same body, not only those belonging to GLBTIQ persons but also those who are heterosexual, asexual, celibate and do not embody or embrace procreative sexuality. To 'love the sin' also exposes the limits of unconditional love (itself a contradiction in terms) which is tolerance as practised by most churches who 'love the sinner but hate the sin'. The book *Love the Sin: Sexual Regulation and the Limits of Religious Tolerance,* although set in the context of the United States, is highly instructive in this regard. Its authors Janet R. Jakobsen and Ann Pellegrini propose 'to make religion the ground of sexual freedom, rather than the *justification* for sexual regulation' by concurrently arguing for not only sexual freedom but also religious freedom (beyond Christianity as the *de facto* State religion), in order to imagine future democratic possibilities and moral alternatives that are more inclusive and socially just for its plural society (2004: 16–17).

By extension, the contiguity of sexuality rights and religion finds expression in the shared affirmation of the inherent worth of a human person. 'All human beings are born free and equal in dignity and rights' underscores the Yogyakarta Principles (ICJ 2007: 10), as sexuality rights as human rights are inalienable or inseparable from our humanness. And 'The Statement on Homosexuality' issued by the National Council of Churches of Singapore acknowledges that as 'every person is loved by God ... [h]omosexuals should be regarded and treated no less as persons of worth and dignity' (2004: 128). The common ground of bodily integrity and human dignity offers possibilities for queering space by and for GLBTIQ persons.

In this final research findings chapter, narratives of GLBTIQ persons who have in some way reconciled their sexuality and religion or spirituality are highlighted and discussed. Such reconciliation finds expression in the various coping strategies manifest collectively. They are: affirming gay sexuality and spirituality, with a special section on affirming gay sexuality and spirituality within the Free Community Church (FCC) and concomitant programmes such as LUSH (Lesbians United for Self-Help) and PLUSH (post-LUSH), and essentially, reconciling sexuality and spirituality.

Affirming gay sexuality *and* spirituality

The yearning and significance of yearning to seek affirmation from one's religion as a GLBTIQ person, that 'It's actually OK' as Adam puts it, cannot be overestimated. It is the premise on which this research project was conceptualized and evolved: to study the ways in which GLBTIQ persons negotiate processes of becoming religious or spiritual *and* queer. The narratives highlighted in this section show how for those who have found affirmation from their religions or spiritualities that 'religion [can become] the ground of sexual freedom, rather than the *justification* for sexual regulation (becoming straight or celibate as narrated by interviewees like Dave, AY and Janic)' (Jakobsen and Pellegrini 2004: 16).

Among those who identify as Christian, most, at the outset of their journey in realizing their selves and sexualities, experience their religion to be the inverse. Peter mentions an e-group that he 'occasionally participated' in when he was working in the United States, called 'Queer Asian Fellowship ... which was for gay Asian people who are related with Christianity'. He observes that this group is unique as ordinarily, 'people who are in the sexuality issues shun things in the religious aspect. They are like ... different worlds' [1:36 (447:459)]. Within this virtual safe space, Peter upon coming out to himself in his forties found external support from a group that does not compartmentalize sexuality and spirituality. On explaining what he takes away from his concurrent participation in a 'gay married men's' support group, he adds that:

> I think first you have to know that you're not alone. I think that's important. The ... experience which ... you have, you can share similarities with a lot of people I think and that helps you, helped me to think of what to do in my life because at that time, because when you first come out, or want to come out, then you don't know what, like how your next day will [be], so you live like one day at a time. So at least the other people are there, so you know ... the gay married men's group, that's where you actually meet the other people and that's where they actually talk about their lives more. [1:63 (744:756)]

The day after that follows the ending of one phase and the beginning of another, when 'you first come out, or want to come out', is, by Peter's testimony, fluid like an open book, as: 'you don't know what, like how your next day will [be], so you live like one day at a time'. The uncertainty of his day-to-day existence even survival post-coming out was alleviated by his bonding with the 'gay married men's group' as a 'gay married [man]' himself. Whilst Peter was somewhat 'alone' in his marriage that for him and his wife was unfulfilling, he is, having come out to himself and others, 'not alone' anymore. The collective narratives where, in this instance, 'you know' from gay married men's 'talk about their lives' become a knowledge that circulates among those who know because they do: they go about the everyday business of living with their decision to come out as gay and married and in Peter's case, gay and married and Catholic.

The hope for change, new ways of being and becoming when one's sexuality and religiosity or spirituality are mutually affirmed is articulated by Ling Jackie. Her hope finds expression in knowing that there are 'different kinds of Christian [*laughs*] perspective for us to study the Bible' [18:16 (208:226)], since coming across Ou Yang Wen Feng's publications (Ngeo 2013) on queer hermeneutics and interviews in the media as one who is touted as Malaysia's 'first openly gay pastor' (Yuan 2011). Taking the road less travelled, in diverging from the mainstream, revolutionized by an 'openly gay pastor', supports Ling Jackie in her journey towards self-acceptance as she initially sought psychiatric and spiritual counselling to alleviate her confusion and depression. In following through this divergent path, she was then part of a weekly Bible Studies 'gay-friendly group' [18:61 (733:749)] that is based in Kuala Lumpur and maintains the right to privacy of the group even secrecy, as she says that: 'most of my friends in that group, they don't want to let the public know about the existence of our group' [18:49 (582:591)]. She affirms the value of being part of this group by the same token that she is affirmed by the group, as she adds that: 'I feel quite comfortable. Because I know that all of us, we [belong] to gay and lesbians. No need to ... hide our sexuality during a session. So when we have any prayer request, we can share ... it without being [hesitant] ... regarding our relationship [*laughs*]' [18:52 (619:632)].

Ling Jackie desires to 'get married in a church ... [because] as a Christian, you should get married [*laughs*] in the church' and by inference, not be deprived of the right to do so. She cites the ideal and relatively accessible church to get married in, the FCC in Singapore as it is a 'gay-friendly church'. And she adds that: 'some of my gay friends, although they are in Malaysia but they are quite close with the gay people and gay organization in Singapore' [18:61 (733:749)], thereby attesting to the cross-border and virtual safe spaces and networking among GLBTIQ persons. Singapore is also held up to be an 'alternative for gay people in Malaysia to consider living there', says Ling Jackie. The exodus in search of an affirming *and* sacred space is articulated by others like J who facilitates the FCC Women's Ministry but who anticipates emigrating from Singapore when she and her then partner have the means to raise a family. As J says:

> And I always felt that it was very important that eventually in the future, whoever I was with, and I mean, from quite a while ago, I already wanted to have kids with a girl, I mean to set up family together. But I knew that God had to be in my life somewhere, somehow. So it was easier having, finding a partner that had the same values as me and eventually easier to bring kids up ... So we did talk about it. And because it's not possible here, so we're both working towards eventually migrating somewhere ... where you know, it's recognized. And the law is on your side. [23:65 (858:868)]

J calls on exercising the breadth of sexuality rights that ought to be inalienable (a birth right by virtue of her being a human person) and indivisible (civil and political liberties equally valued as economic, social and cultural rights) to her. Sexuality rights, among others, include for J: the right to sexual (and reproductive) self-determination and the right to self-realization, as she says that: 'I always felt that it was very important that eventually in the future, whoever I was with ... I already wanted to have kids with a girl, I mean to set up family together'. The impetus to 'eventually [migrate] somewhere' stems from the right to freely choose one's sexual partners and the right to publicly recognized sexual relationships (Richardson 2000) where in Singapore, 'it's not possible ... [as] the law is [not] on your side'.

She lays equal emphasis on sacred and secular law as supporting these sexuality rights where by virtue of FCC's vision and mission, the former is realized, as she is affirmed by the FCC but not the latter. Elsewhere, she refers to the movement to repeal Section 377a of the Penal Code of Singapore that 'provides for a jail sentence for up to two years should a man be found to have committed an act of "gross indecency" with another man'. Singaporean society, as she has resigned herself to, is 'not ready to accept it (gay unions) ... But ... I realised that the church has a very strong say in this issue, in the mainstream church' [23:66 (869:876)]. She exposes the complicity of sacred (tenets of faith) and secular law in negating gay unions: the former ('mainstream church' or 'straight church' as she labels it elsewhere) demonizes it (with the sanction of eternal damnation) whilst the latter criminalizes it (a two-year jail sentence). This brings home the point that whilst the FCC provides a 'Safe Haven' (eponymous for the gay and lesbian ministry outreach of the FCC) that affirms one's sexuality and she, in turn, affirms the FCC as a safe space to be, the reality is that GLBTIQ persons inhabit other spaces that are often not only unsafe but also threatening.

Affirming gay sexuality *and* spirituality within the Free Community Church

It is precisely because the FCC is ensconced in a city-state that is at best, tolerant of GLBTIQ persons (Offord 2003), that the FCC remains by and large a 'Safe Haven' for those like J, Joe and Dave where their sexuality is affirmed by their church, as the following narratives show. Joe, on the one hand, de-romanticizes the aesthetics of getting married at the FCC as he 'really [doesn't] want to hold [his] wedding in a parking lot … [or] industrial building' as the FCC is 'really a factory' (architecturally) that is converted as a church [27:69 (776:791)]. On the other hand, he knows that his then partner 'likes the whole idea of marriage more than me … as in like doing it in church know, like the church blessing and all' [27:70 (792:806)]. So whilst he says that: 'the last thing I want is to let people think that you have to get married in a heteronormative or in a heterosexual-type ritual' [27:70 (792:806)], he concedes that: 'it's nice to do it for other people I think. For them to see this celebrated in church' [27:69 (776:791)]. For Joe, there is the happier option of '[being] married out' [27:70 (792:806)] as a compromise. He points to having the choice to opt for a 'heterosexual-type ritual' within the FCC or not: to resist compliance with the heterosexual standard. In doing so, he is able to claim not only the right to publicly recognized sexual relationships (through the church wedding) but also his right to self-realization (through an alternative kind of commitment ceremony), as he conveys his aspiration: 'At some stage you want to celebrate that part of our relationship but it's [with emphasis] bigger than that'.

For J, the affirmation of her sexuality by the FCC leads to a realization of her personhood and maturity as a Christian, as she transitions from 'mainstream churches' where there is 'a very, like black and white thing' and 'a certain hierarchy' to the FCC where she has 'learned to accept that it's OK to not have structure' [23:29 (297:314)]. The binaries that she inadvertently draws are: 'mainstream churches'/the FCC, structure/structure-less, hierarchical/non-hierarchical and rigid ('black and white')/'liberal'. Her maturation as a woman of faith is evident with a mindset change wherein she says that: 'there must be a balance-lah; you cannot be too liberal as well'. Being a part of the FCC facilitates that degree of self-reflexivity that is empowering as J comes to the realization that: 'you have to make a decision for yourself … it's your own calling. And you find your own balance 'cause it's your responsibility, with your own walk with God'. Where previously she had experienced clerical paternalism as 'it's always like the church that makes the decision for [her]', she now unlearns that, supported as she is by the FCC and becomes accountable for her own faith journey, her 'walk with God'. In doing so, she enables her transitioning from being infantilized (in having decisions made for you) to personhood (in answering 'your own calling').

The FCC represents a space that is invested with multiple meanings in dealing with the complexities of negotiating the tension between sexuality and religiosity or spirituality. Firstly, it is church and according to J who has observed that: self-identified GLBTIQ persons may choose to not go back to the FCC to worship as 'they feel that they can be a Christian … [but] they don't have to go to church to be a Christian'. She explains that their withdrawal from church in itself is largely due to past negative experiences with their 'mainstream churches' [23:48 (623:639)]. An extension of this phenomenon of some withdrawing from a safe and scared space is, as J notes, a gender demarcation among the FCC congregation as she questions why is it that: 'gay men continue to come back to church … and the lesbian women don't' [23:99 (1213:1232)]?

Secondly, it is a space that is committed to facilitating the integration of sexuality and spirituality in providing a reconciliation group for lesbians between sexuality and their faith, e.g. LUSH, a weekly outreach support programme of the FCC that runs for six months, with posters that read, 'Gay but not happy'. It is a space, according to Dave, that 'allowed me to reconcile some parts of my faith with my sexuality … because of what they actually preach over there' where prior to his exposure with the FCC, he was taught that: 'as a Christian, homosexuality is a sin. And there's no two ways about it' [29:78 (872:880)].

And the process of integrating one's sexuality and spirituality is an iterative and neither linear nor instantaneous one, as J emphasizes: 'And I mean, it ("[studying] the six passages in the Bible that condemns homosexuality") wasn't exactly like life-changing or anything. In fact … I was more rebellious than anything … I felt that you know, what they were teaching was still wrong cause, for 20 over years of like doctrines in your head, you just can't like change it' [23:23 (236:244)]. J, quite conflicted still, went 'for the second round of LUSH' to continue her unlearning of twenty-year-old 'doctrines in [her] head'. She adds that: 'LUSH 2 was good … not just [because] of the dynamics of the group [where] we really learned a lot more [as] people were more open to share. But this time round, I felt that my heart was more open towards receiving' [23:24 (245:256)]. In letting go of her resistance to alternative ways of being and becoming Christian and lesbian through listening to the narratives of others, J goes on to participate in the third run of LUSH (LUSH 3) and, at the time of the interview, was preparing to co-lead LUSH 4. J's testimony is that: 'I feel that I've come quite a long way in terms of my spiritual walk with God-lah'. She not only reclaims agency through questioning that leads to a mindset change (as discussed elsewhere in this chapter) but also takes responsibility for her own 'spiritual walk with God'. And she has come to shed the self-expectation that 'we need to have an answer to everything' [23:27 (281:287)] and numbing comfort of 'being told (by pastors in her mainstream church) what to do, being told that everything is in black and white'.

Thirdly, the FCC thus represents a resistant space that nurtures the reconciliation of sexuality and spirituality by embracing those who occupy socially marginal positions. In recollecting one of the highlights of participating in LUSH, J adds that: 'they had this...lesbian couple [who] were pastors of a church...somewhere in L. A. (Los Angeles) I think...[and] they came and they shared with us. And it's like, it's amazing because you have this role model in front of you finally' [23:30 (315:328)]. J experiences an 'epistemological jolt' (Dyer 1997: 264) as she is 'finally' presented with the naturalization of not only a 'lesbian couple' but women who are 'pastors' who embody what it means to fully come out as Christian and lesbian by witnessing their faith in God and love for each other.

The FCC becomes not a safe space for heterosexism as it challenges the normalization and dominance of heterosexuality. This is effected through strategies of resistance (Offord 2003) such as setting up LUSH and sustaining it through the mentoring of its facilitators. As one of the facilitators of LUSH, J explains that it is structured in two phases: firstly, the study of the 'six passages of the Bible' [23:38 (434:439)] and, secondly, a discussion of issues that are 'very real and important to the group' such as 'coming out, or loving yourself, relationship issues or dating a straight woman ... so that people don't feel lonely' [23:39 (440:453)]. The facilitators, as J explains, are tasked with:

[Not] only bringing across what's ... to be learned but also constantly creating the dynamics of the group such that people are willing to share. And also ... showing concern for the group members because sometimes it can be a very mentally and emotionally draining process because you're constantly at war with yourself in a way. [23:36 (399:418)]

J's own faith journey testifies to being 'constantly at war with [herself]' in her struggle to reconcile her sexuality with her spirituality, as a participant of LUSH 1. She adds that:

> [That's how] we can get new people to lead. Every time one session ends, people from that session will be willing and feel ready to lead. So that's how we go about it. There's no like test … Just the heart. Like how much do you want to help others in that sense. Because the facilitators would also need support … because of the so-called burden of responsibility that you have … You got hard questions to answer sometimes. [23:60 (784:806)]

New facilitators come from graduating members who are mentored by existing facilitators (who sit in as participants) in the hope 'that it becomes this cyclical thing', as J elaborates on how they mutually empower each other to take on leadership of LUSH [23:59 (772:783)]. The willingness of 'new people' to 'help others' that comes from 'the heart' is the only criterion of acceptance, as J puts it. And these new facilitators who cope with not only reconciling their own sexuality and faith but also bearing the 'burden of responsibility' in journeying with others are richly supported by, among others, the late Reverend Yap Kim Hao who was Pastoral Advisor to the FCC. Graduating members of LUSH, already connected via e-support networks (e.g. yahoogroups), have the option of continuing with PLUSH (a post-LUSH women's cell group) which was set up by J's ex to continue journeying with those who, as J explains, 'actually have their own mainstream churches to go back to … [but are] still [trying to] figure out whether they want to continue (with FCC or not)' [23:42 (513:540)]. The six-month LUSH runs twice a year during weekday evenings and it is little wonder that J concedes that: being a LUSH facilitator is 'a bit hard and it's quite exhausting'. But they persevere as they recognize that 'there's a need … [for those who are] really going through a very tough period, being conflicted and all that … [as LUSH] might help them' [23:44 (553:569)].

Fourth, it is a space that enables you to gain a bigger perspective of not only sexuality but other things in faith to understanding the message of redemption with more clarity: that it is less about doing deeds to earn your salvation but rather that 'you are already saved when you believe' (not just in God but oneself). In facilitating the reconciliation of sexuality and spirituality, the FCC reminds its congregation of Christ's redemptive suffering that liberates all who believe.

Fifth, the FCC offers a safe space for youths to explore hence the setting up of a youth group to redress the generational gap: For J who has gone on to set up a Sunday School of kids within the FCC [23:49 (640:662)], the FCC represents a home away from home. It affirms her talents where she is obliged to 'lie to [her parents]' [23:53 (695:710)] because she is not serving 'in a straight church [and she is certain that from their perspective] everything that I do will be wrong', whereas 'if it was in a straight church, they'll be very proud of me'. Essentially, the meaning of the FCC is over-determined as it remains, as declared on its homepage:

> a congregation of diverse individuals and families gathering to worship and grow as a Christian community... [that] affirms that all individuals, including lesbian, gay, bisexual and transgender persons, are individuals of sacred worth created in God's image. Our church affirms that same-sex and transgender relationships, when lived out in accord with the love commandments of Jesus, are consistent with Christian faith and teachings. Indeed, we find discrimination based on negative judgment of others, fear of difference, and homophobia inconsistent with Christian teachings.

Sixth, the FCC for Dave is a space that is infused with ambivalence, as he says:

> But I was stubborn. And I told them like you know, I'm going to move on with every aspect of my life except for the relationship part because I, by hook or by crook [*laughs*], I still want him back... And basically the whole cell group or rather the whole church kind of like knows what's been happening... 'cause he's like one of the chairpersons for this organization called Safe Haven. It's like the gay and lesbian ministry outreach for the church. And so, like he's quite popular in church-lah. And like, I'm quite popular [*laughs*] because I'm his boyfriend. I was his boyfriend then-lah. And so like the whole church will know what's been happening. And they will ask like you know, 'Hey, how [is] everything? How are you?' Stuff like that. Yeah. [29:111 (1223:1237)]

By Dave's admission, he remained 'stubborn' in not taking their advice that 'it's time to move on' [29:110 (1215:1222)] when his then partner ended their relationship. Rather than effect closure, Dave remains adamant about 'still [wanting] him back' [29:111 (1223:1237)]. On the one hand, the FCC remains a 'Safe Haven' for him as whilst 'telling them (his cell group within the FCC) my story and how I felt... made me feel better-*lah*, having someone else to talk to', says Dave. On the other hand, the FCC can become less of a 'Safe Haven' or nurturing space, as for Dave, 'the whole cell group or rather the whole church kind of like knows what's been happening' on account of his partner's high-profile visibility as 'one of the chairpersons' of Safe Haven, the 'the gay and lesbian ministry outreach' of the FCC. The intrusiveness into his privacy is suggested by their incessant questioning of 'Hey, how [is] everything? How are you?' notwithstanding good intentions.

The FCC, as a God-centred GLBTIQ-loving space, in applying Ahmed's theorizing on 'queer phenomenology' 'becomes a field, a space that gives ground to, or even grounds, [homosexual] action through the renunciation of what it is not (heterosexual), and also by the production of what it is (homosexual)' (Ahmed 2006a: 558). In the case of Dave, the FCC 'becomes a field, a space' that had not only led him to his then partner but also away from his partner in considering the advice given to him by his cell group to 'move on'. Among like-minded GLBTIQs, the FCC continues to become for Dave: 'a field, a space that gives ground to, or even grounds, [homosexual] action through the renunciation of what it is not (passing as straight), and also by the production of what it is (identifying as a Christian gay man)'.

Ultimately, the FCC as a radical space resonates strongly with Joe's expression of faith:

> But I think other struggles I have, have come full cycle in that they're the same struggles I had when I thought I was straight. They're the same struggles I have whether you're queer, you're straight, you're bi. I think these are the struggles of faith. In FCC, I co-lead Living Water which is this reconciliation thing… you read the six scriptures and try to make sense of it. I'm always the devil's advocate. What if Sodom and Gomorrah really happened because it was gay sex [*laughs*]? … So I was sharing with a group something that to me is very real. And I think that in the whole faith journey, if people think that being gay or not or coming out or not, if that's the ultimate touchstone for them, then they really got it wrong. Because if your life is all about being gay, now that's really very, I think, unhealthy and obsessive. [27:52 (561:575)]

For Joe who co-leads Living Water, which aims to facilitate 'this reconciliation thing (between one's sexuality and spirituality)', the FCC provides not only a 'Safe Haven' but also a radical space. The first challenge of drinking from the metaphorical font of Living Water is to 'read the six scriptures and try to make sense of it'. A self-awakening is effected when you have '[made] sense' of the 'six scriptures' and come to the revelation that where you were once sinful, shameful or sick as a GLBTIQ person, you are now saved. One's fidelity to a faith that loves one unconditionally becomes easy to nourish. The ensuing challenge would be to question one's fidelity to a faith that does not condone homosexuality, which is instigated by Joe playing 'the devil's advocate' by suggesting that, 'Sodom and Gomorrah really happened because it was gay sex'. How then does one manage 'this reconciliation thing'? The third challenge put forth by Joe in '[having] come full cycle' is the realization that one's personhood may well be made up of 'being gay or not or coming out or not' but more importantly, it transcends that too. In drawing from his sexuality journey and 'whole faith journey' that are paralleled, he attests to FCC's standpoint where it '[does] not believe in easy answers to life's challenging questions'. He exhorts those whom he leads to move away from unhealthily obsessing 'about being gay' to focus instead on one's 'struggles of faith' which are 'the same ... whether you're queer, you're straight, you're bi'. In doing so, he de-essentializes the FCC by flattening out differences of becoming straight/GLBTIQ.

Reconciling sexuality and spirituality

This chapter concludes with expressions from those who recognize that on their own terms, they have reconciled their sexuality and spirituality. The narratives of the following are here discussed: Andy, Ling Jackie, J, Janic, Joe and Dave.

The first criterion noted lies in the dissipation or absence of guilt. Andy says: 'When it comes to guilt, I think I have dealt with my guilt. The guilt is still there ... it's already a part of who I am ... It really, really is no longer a problem' [2:44 (555:563)]. In Andy's case, the residual guilt that lingers, that has become 'a part of who [she is]', is guilt at having fallen in love with her then girlfriend where she ought to have been there to support her (who was in a rocky relationship with her boyfriend then) as a friend instead. As she adds: 'To make out was more the guilt. It wasn't a religious guilt' [2:45 (563:577)]. She had 'dealt with [her religious] guilt' [2:44 (555:563)] by taking on queer interpretations of the Bible (as discussed earlier in this chapter). Dave does not 'feel conflict' anymore where he used to before reconciling his sexuality and his spirituality. As he says: 'I don't feel guilty about who I am anymore whereas compared in the past ... after having some encounter with a guy ... I will like try and ask for forgiveness from God. But now I kind of like don't do that. I don't view that as a sin anymore' [29:79 (881:893)]. Like Andy, Dave has also been exposed to queer hermeneutics through the FCC. In loving himself, the 'sinner' and the 'sin', he shows that 'religion [can become] the ground of sexual freedom, rather than the *justification* for sexual regulation (becoming straight in a five-year relationship with a woman to please his parents)' (Jakobsen and Pellegrini 2004: 16).

Self-acceptance is paramount to overcoming guilt. Ling Jackie is able to identify that she had accepted herself in 2005. When asked how she knows, she thus replies: 'When I ... knew more and more friends like me I can see that, actually gay and lesbians or bisexual people, they are just like [the] norm, I mean normal, straight people. They also contribute a lot to our society and to the world' [18:29 (338:347)]. Her incremental self-acceptance comes about from dismantling the binary normal/deviant that is aligned with heterosexuality/homosexuality by flattening out the differences between 'gay and lesbians or bisexual people [as] they are just like ... normal, straight people'. In doing so, she reinvests worth back to 'gay and lesbians or bisexual people' who are 'friends like [her]' in the like manner that 'normal, straight people' are invested with inherent worth. She sees and reclaims her intrinsic worth that lies beyond the utilitarian value of '[contributing] a lot to our society and to the world'.

Where Ling Jackie emphasizes (equality as) sameness with 'normal, straight people', others emphasize (equality as) difference from 'normal, straight people', as GLBTIQ persons are a minority within a minority. As such, the FCC represents that safe and sacred space for such a minority within the minority, i.e. GLBTIQ and Christian. Notwithstanding its peripheral status in Singapore, the FCC is a beacon of hope and faith for those who invert the double marginalization of being GLBTIQ *and* Christian in Singapore by proudly reclaiming this hyphenated status. The FCC, with its vision 'to be an inclusive community that celebrates diversity in living out God's love and promise of abundant life for all', stands apart from a conservative even oppressive socio-political climate that merely tolerates the non-normative queer community in Singapore. The FCC's mission to 'create sacred space and give voice to the lives and experiences of minority communities' affords a safe space for Christian GLBTIQ-identifying persons in the secular state of Singapore. FCC's vision and mission well manifest the strength in being a minority that is, in turn, embodied through individual self-acceptance and collective identity.

And knowing who you are leads to self-acceptance. J explains how she deals with many who patronize her by asking her: 'You're so young. Are you sure?' [23:64 (847:857)]. She replies that: 'I experienced this whole lesbian identity of mine from a very young age and I feel really old actually [interviewer laughs] in terms of that'. Having come out to herself at a young age, J has come to a deeper appreciation of her then partner 'who's gay and who's very comfortable being gay and being so strong, having such a strong relationship with God'. In continuing to fully live out being lesbian and Christian as facilitators of LUSH and PLUSH of the FCC, they are both 'not at that exploring stage anymore [as they] pretty much know what [they] want'. Their individual and shared lives bear a marked contrast to the spectre of middle-aged others who are still closeted. Their partnership in faith and love is thus paralleled by the American lesbian couple who are pastors that J encountered during a LUSH 1 session, as she adds:

So seeing that they are so strong together gives you a lot of hope. And gives you a lot of possibility that how can these two women feel so right if so wrong you know, unless they're like totally nuts [interviewer laughs]. And that made me realize that maybe it's the way I approach the whole issue ... maybe it's possible that God made me the way I am which was their ... main point that they brought across to us. [23:32 (341:347)]

J bears witness to firstly knowing that she is a child of God and therefore believes that she is created in God's image and likeness and secondly committing her relationship to God. Rather than an aberration of creation, J has come to realize that 'God made me the way I am' and this, in turn, gives rise to 'a lot of possibility' in living out her sexuality in faith. She embodies this 'hope' not only in her own 'Christian walk with God' [23:26 (270:280)] but also in her faith-based relationship with her then partner who has 'such a strong relationship with God' herself [23:64 (847:857)]. And 'it's amazing ... [having] this role model in front of you finally' [23:30 (315:328)], as J exclaims elsewhere, referring to the illuminating encounter with the Christian lesbian pastors, as they not only embody but also authenticate the reconciliation of sexuality and spirituality.

The living out of one's sexuality and spirituality for Janic lies in the integration of her spirituality as her life's vocation: she was then a Christian missionary serving in Africa and later a 'personal assistant to the (Tibetan Buddhist) Lama in our centre' [7:97 (1259:1272)], having given up a coveted job in the electronics industry. Her chosen vocation is to 'do everything I can to spread the teachings, meaning you know, whatever ideas the Lama has to carry out the work, my job would be to amplify it. To make sure that it's carried out'. Her dedication is channelled not only to the 'highly reincarnate Lama' but also to personal 'spiritual capacity' which is harnessed in the daily 'learning' and 'practice' that has become her job. Her process of reconciling her sexuality and spirituality from '[putting] a side of me on hold ... being attracted to same-sex people' [7:105 (1369:1384)] subsequently found full expression in loving Stephanie and co-parenting Stephanie's son. Their mutually supportive relationship was spiritually based on living out the 'Dharma principles' of Tibetan Buddhism.

To conclude, reconciling one's sexuality and spirituality does not signify the end of the journey and this is best articulated by irrepressible Joe who says:

Even today, I think ... for a person who wants to be truly open, I have to be open to the possibility that I got it wrong somewhere ... read the map wrongly [interviewer laughs]. You know like [smiles], I think that I've reconciled but maybe I haven't reconciled. I think that it is right. Maybe I'm wrong, like it's still wrong nonetheless, no matter how I answer it … it's a true intellectual honesty you must have that you might be wrong. But at least right now, I think I'm right. I'm on the right track, at least that's what I think right now. [27:29 (316:331)]

In the quotation above that is littered with travel imagery, Joe's fidelity to 'a true intellectual honesty you must have that you might be wrong' is apparent. In his journey to reconcile his sexuality and spirituality, he remains 'open to the possibility' that he took a 'wrong' detour in having 'read the (figurative) map wrongly'. Where he elsewhere plays 'the devil's advocate' to those he leads in Living Water by suggesting that, 'Sodom and Gomorrah really happened because it was gay sex' [27:52 (561:575)], he likewise plays 'the devil's advocate' to himself. He genuinely questions the implications of being 'wrong … no matter how I answer it', alluding to the theological training that has empowered him to lead the discursive space of Living Water on queer hermeneutics. On the one hand, the fuzzy articulations of 'I've reconciled but maybe I haven't reconciled', 'Maybe I'm wrong', 'I think I'm right' are seeming vacillations between certainty and doubt. On the other hand, they belie a moral imperative 'to be truly open' to self-reflexivity. As shown in earlier discussions the effect of rigorous questioning is to change mindsets, demystify misconceptions on sexuality and challenge biased religious interpretation. As such, the breakdown of systemic structures of inequalities and inequities, beginning with personal biases, potentially leads to a transformative breakthrough. This finds fullest expression in the reconciliation of one's sexuality and spirituality, as Joe puts it, in being 'on the right track' in the integrity of claiming and living out a life of abundance.

10

Conclusion: Becoming and belonging

The narratives of becoming of two postcolonial Southeast Asian nation-states, from the prism of how gender and sexual diversity is imagined and managed, are exercises in 'maintaining the fiction of unity' (Bailey 2007: 83): wherein the body of the citizenry is constructed as a heterosexual thus stable subject. Belonging is contingent on being heteronormative as the hegemonic ideal and majority practice for the common good. 'Maintaining the fiction of unity' requires work, a kind of 'ignorance' which 'is a form of not knowing (seeing wrongly), resulting from the habit of erasing, dismissing, distorting, and forgetting about the lives, cultures, and histories of peoples [*heterosexual fundamentalists*] have colonized' (Bailey 2007: 83, 85). Consonant with such 'ignorance' which is not the absence of knowledge but rather the bracketing off whose knowledge counts and whose do not are national discourses that are premised on secular and religious heterosexism. The family as a microcosm of the nation becomes the site of production of these state-sponsored 'Asian values' of exclusivity, with gender and sexual minorities 'rightfully' discriminated against. As the heterosexualization of desire works for the common good, progress of the nation, even fidelity to God or adherence to spiritual precepts, gender and sexual minorities cannot fully belong.

The narratives of becoming of the sixteen GLBTIQ persons interviewed who chose to remain with this study, interpreted qualitatively, serve as counter-narratives in two ways: making this macrocosmic 'ignorant' work visible and responding with *strategic ignorance* and *strategic ambivalence*. The qualifier 'strategic' to these neologisms denotes how ignorance and ambivalence are purposefully performed by GLBTIQ persons who encounter interpersonal or institutional (family, the state and religious or spiritual communities) discrimination, criminalization and demonization of the integrity of their genders and sexualities. Performing ignorance lies in becoming straight (in willing the heterosexualization of one's desire), passing as straight, doing celibacy or playing along with the hegemony of heteronormativity. Performing ambivalence, which is a corollary strategy, lies in managing sexual, religious, familial, interpersonal guilt. It also lies in opting to come out or not, on one's terms (i.e. for the sake of family 'face', for the sake of peace) and in one's own time in navigating the spatiality of the closet and beyond. Individuated 'Asian values' are here re-imagined as binaries of collective/personal good are eschewed to pave the way for valuing both collective (familial being paramount) and personal well-being sometimes whilst privileging one over the other at other times.

The GLBTIQ persons interviewed in this study reclaim the right to belong to one's family, religious or spiritual community and nation, as part of the body of citizenry by living out the costs of not belonging. Their embodied practices of 'intimate citizenship' that signifies a 'multiplicity of new worlds... [and] a language of recognition, rights, responsibilities and care' (Plummer 2001: 251) expose the containment of gender and sexual diversity that '[maintains the] fiction of unity' of an immutable, monolithic, heterosexual subject. Through becoming religiously or spiritually sexual and sexually religious or spiritual, they also expose the ontological, ideological, political and experiential limits of incommensurability, incompatibility and false claims of ascendency between universalism and particularism with regard to religious and sexuality discourses and practices. They challenge: secular and religious heterosexism through their narratives of becoming that embody both incommensurability and commensurability (in reconciling one's religiosity or spirituality and sexuality); incompatibility and compatibility (in recognizing the rights-based and faith-based affirmation of the human person); and exclusivity and mutuality of universalism-particularism (narratives of becoming of a nation and GLBTIQ persons as mutually constitutive informed by the integrity of rights and religious discourses and practices at global and local levels), along with the multiple transitioning between these categories.

They expand the temporality of becoming a nation. Within postcoloniality, a linear historicity of precolonial, colonial and postcolonial seems imminent in charting the progress of a nation. This trajectory that privileges the colonized centre is problematic and renders the 'post' in postcoloniality illusory (Ahmed 2000: 11). With regard to gender and sexual minorities, neocolonization takes the form of competing claims of ascendency between religious fundamentalism and the fundamentalism of sexuality rights with no common ground tolerated. As subjects whose genders and sexualities remain somewhat to largely colonized, regulated by state-legal-religious apparatuses, these narratives of becoming embody *time as process* in its individuated, interpersonal and inter-generational forms. The trope of a journey in being and becoming gay, lesbian, bisexual, transgender, intersex and queer and/or questioning is predominant. Time is experienced as linear (where then/now marks the transitioning from unknowing to knowing, suicidal to healing, self-disgust to self-acceptance), cyclical (where processes of learning and unlearning are iterative), paralytic (where the stasis of putting aside either one's sexuality or religiosity seems impenetrable), fragmented (where the liminality of in-betweenness is its own end, e.g. lying and not lying to the self) and epiphanic (where the mindset change of loving the sinner and the sin becomes a lived reality). Halberstam's 'queer temporality' (Dinshaw et al. 2007: 182) finds resonance but does not adequately contain these practices of time as process as they evince not only a 'perverse turn away from the narrative coherence' but also a '[turning towards] the narrative coherence' of heteronormativity paradoxically in becoming GLBTIQ persons.

They also expand the spatiality of belonging. They do so by recasting disgust and shame that are levelled at them by the tyranny of the heterosexualized majority in working to maintain the 'fiction of the "normal"' (Nussbaum 2004: 336). 'In the case of disgust', as Nussbaum explains, 'properties pertinent to the subject's own fear of animality and mortality are projected onto a less powerful group, and that group then becomes a vehicle for the dominant group's anxiety about itself.' 'In the case of shame', she adds, 'a more general anxiety about helplessness and lack of control inspires the pursuit of invulnerability.' These resonate with Kristeva's 'abjection' (1982) and Douglas's 'dirt as matter out of place' (2002: 44): the heterosexual subject (matter) is made stable through dis-identifying with gender and sexual minorities (analogous to 'dirt' and the 'abject').

Yet these limits are subverted. Through desiring to adopt and parent as a gay man and bisexual woman, with the attendant legal barriers and stigmatization of a father-father and mother-mother reconfiguration of the family, the gendered script of *doing family* beyond the natural family is rewritten. Where maternal shame and filial shame converge in the failure to inculcate and imbibe 'straight' values that are juxtaposed with parental love that is (un)conditional, doing family is manifest too (Bong 2011b). In doing so, they show the hollowness, the fiction of nation-building discourses that only legitimate the natural family. In transitioning from private to public spaces, secular and in particular, faith-based social networks like the FCC that abound proliferate and sacralize spaces of belonging (which includes cyberspace). Spaces inhabited by the organic body of the citizenry become sites where the universalism of rights and religious discourses are practised on the bodies and sexualities of GLBTIQ persons within the particularisms of their social, cultural and political realities.

In these ways that narratives of becoming of GLBTIQ persons expand the temporality of becoming a nation and expand the spatiality of belonging by according legitimacy to their lived realities, they embody the subversion of limits. They queer time and space as bodies and sexualities that can and do exist: through the insistence that their narratives matter as 'dirt'! Yet, there are limits of subversion, as Butler intuits: whilst '*gender* is not a noun, but neither is it a set of free-floating attributes' (1990: 24). Where it matters to belong and not always on their own terms, queer theorizing with its anti-identity stance does not fully resonate with these aspirations. Becoming is not the inverse of *being* GLBTIQ: all sixteen interviewees in this study speak of knowing they are different at various intervals of their lives, mostly as a child. Becoming is but not limited to the plethora of strategies used in negotiating the tensions in the spectrum of conflict, ambiguity and reconciliation. Becoming is to desire an abundant life that is graced with peace, as a full citizen and invested with the full potential in achieving transcendence.

It is thus fitting to conclude with Adam as his narrative of becoming is emblematic of the rupture and rapture of 'breaking down boundaries and borders' in effecting a paradoxical breakthrough, that is the symbolic heart of this study:

> So I just felt like my journey was one of discovering myself and others and breaking down boundaries and borders. Even though in the first place, I asked for people to break down their boxes, step out of their box and look at me as a human being but I was setting up ... boundaries also. But in my journey, I was breaking down my own boundaries of what is good, what is bad, what is right, what is wrong which I don't consciously know ... But I know that I've gone through quite a bit, opening up and exploring my transsexual part, my bisexual part and to be a full human being. I think that's a good journey to walk to you know, to be a full human being and not to be closed up. [22:81 (905:914)]

Notes

Chapter 1

1   At the Human Capital Summit held last month (the comment was posted on 10 November 2008, 3.40 p.m.), the Minister Mentor is reported to have said: 'You marry a non-graduate, then you are going to worry if your son or daughter is going to make it to the university.' This 'personal philosophy' has been touted since 1967 and has resulted in part in his then political party's (People's Action Party) 'neglect of the poor' (Poh 2008).

2   The use of 'womyn' rather than 'women' is purposeful to eschew the ontological de-privileging of women as subordinate, merely tagged on to men.

3   See the testimonies of women who have completed the run of LUSH, available at http://fcc-lush.blogspot.com/.

4   The '"Kindom" of God' serves to de-masculinize the more traditional usage of 'Kingdom' and, in doing so, is more inclusive from a queer and feminist standpoint.

5   PAS, the Islamic party of Malaysia, banned the *mak yong* when it took control of the state of Kelantan in 1991. There have been calls for PAS to reconsider banning what is held to be 'one of the oldest traditions' of dance-drama in Kelantan, now 'recognised as a world heritage by UNESCO' (Bernama 2010).

6   Unnatural offences covering Sections 377, 377 A, 377B, 377C, 377D and 377E read as follows (Commissioner of Law Revision, Malaysia 2015: 201–2):

Unnatural Offences

Buggery with an animal

> 377. Whoever voluntarily has carnal intercourse with an animal shall be punished with imprisonment for a term which may extend to twenty years, and shall also be liable to fine or to whipping. Explanation – Penetration is sufficient to constitute the carnal intercourse necessary to the offence described in this section.

Carnal intercourse against the order of nature

> 377A. Any person who has sexual connection with another person by the introduction of the penis into the anus or mouth of the other person is said to commit carnal intercourse against the order of nature.
>
> Explanation – Penetration is sufficient to constitute the sexual connection necessary to the offence described in this section.

Punishment for committing carnal intercourse against the order of nature

377B. Whoever voluntarily commits carnal intercourse against the order of nature shall be punished with imprisonment for a term which may extend to twenty years, and shall also be liable to whipping.

Committing carnal intercourse against the order of nature without consent, etc.

377C. Whoever voluntarily commits carnal intercourse against the order of nature on another person without the consent, or against the will, of the other person, or by putting the other person in fear of death or hurt to the person or any other person, shall be punished with imprisonment for a term of not less than five years and not more than twenty years, and shall also be liable to whipping.

Outrages on decency

377D. Any person who, in public or private, commits, or abets the commission of, or procures or attempts to procure the commission by any person of, any act of gross indecency with another person, shall be punished with imprisonment for a term which may extend to two years.

Inciting a child to an act of gross indecency

377E. Any person who incites a child under the age of fourteen years to any act of gross indecency with him or another person shall be punished with imprisonment for a term which may extend to five years, and shall also be liable to whipping.

7   Under Sexual Offences, Section 377A provides:

Any male person who, in public or private, commits, or abets the commission of, or procures or attempts to procure the commission by any male person of, any act of gross indecency with another male person, shall be punished with imprisonment for a term which may extend to 2 years.

See also 377B on 'sexual penetration with living animal' or bestiality, 377C (c) (ii) where 'a person who has undergone a sex reassignment procedure shall be identified as being of the sex to which that person has been reassigned' and 377D 'Mistake as to age' (Singapore Statutes Online 2018).

8   Modified from the 'man standard' which women are measured against in the context of institutional sexism (Cudd and Jones 2005: 75).

9   Article 12(1) of the *Constitution of the Republic of Singapore* on 'Equal protection' reads as follows: 'All persons are equal before the law and entitled to the equal protection of the law' (Singapore Statutes Online 1965).

10 Article 12(2) reads as follows: 'Except as expressly authorised by this Constitution, there shall be no discrimination against citizens of Singapore on the ground only of religion, race, descent or place of birth in any law or in the appointment to any

office or employment under a public authority or in the administration of any law relating to the acquisition, holding or disposition of property or the establishing or carrying on of any trade, business, profession, vocation or employment' (Singapore Statutes 1965).

11 And neither has Malaysia ratified the ICCPR. Both Malaysia and Singapore have not ratified the complementary International Covenant on Economic, Social and Cultural Rights too (United Nations, n.d.).

12 Chua cites the father of liberty, J. S. Mill, where the Liberalism discourse is essentially a Millian one, wherein 'the only purpose for which power can be rightfully exercised over any member of a civilized community, against his will, *is to prevent harm to others*... In the part which merely concerns himself, his independence is, of right, absolute. Over himself, over his own body and mind, the individual is sovereign' (2003: 229).

13 Stivens uses an apt neologism, 'westoxification' (Mir-Hosseini 1996 cited in Stivens 2006: 356).

14 Chua notes parliamentary debates where Singapore's political elites pay homage to Confucian thinking, saying: 'The foundation of the nation lies in the family, and the foundation of family lies in the individual self' (Chua 2003: 249).

15 tan beng hui (she prefers the use of lowercase for her name) makes a similar point on the subtext of the Women and Girls' Protection Legislation in Colonial Malaya (c. 1960–1940s): that it was legislated to protect British troops from defilement from venereal diseases by native prostitutes rather than to protect the prostitutes from the health hazards of prostitution (1999).

16 There is existing scholarship on GLBTIQ persons, mostly gays and lesbians in Malaysia and Singapore, that considers the religious dimension, if at all, tangentially. In the context of Singapore, Chua (2014) provides a critical review of the trajectory of the mobilization of the gay movement from the early 1990s to 2005 within a legal and human rights framework and the intersection of religion and sexuality is nominally dealt with as many activists self-identify as religious; Au (2003) on sexual values between gay and straight men; Chua (2008) on the management of gays and elderly; Goh (2008) on HIV as weapons against homosexuality; Heng (2001) on the visibility of the gay community; Laurent (2005: 196–9) on the legal situation of LGBTs; Lim (2002) on attitudes towards homosexuality; Lim (2004) on silencing the gay community; Lim (2005) on performing gay; Ng (1999) on the internet and gay community; Ng (2006) profiling of queers in the twenty-first century; Tan and Lee (2007) on imagining the gay community; Tan (2011) on challenging the impetus to come out and posits 'going home' instead; Tang (2017) on postcolonial lesbian identities in Singapore in conversation with global sexualities; Tsoi (1990) on the development profile of male and female transsexuals; and Yue (2007) on the pragmatic resistance and mobilization of sexuality rights in Singapore.

In the context of Malaysia, research that privileges the intersection of gender, sexuality and religion includes Bong (2018) on transgenderism and theology; Bong (2009b, 2011b) on the intersection of same-sex partnerships and religiosity; Bong (2011a) on bisexuality and religion; and Goh (2018, 2017a, b, 2016, 2014) on theologizing on the narratives of non-heteronormative men in Malaysia and Singapore; and Shah (2018) on the making of gay Muslims in the contexts of Malaysia and Britain. Research that tangentially works on this intersection includes Baba (2001) on gay and lesbian couples; Laurent (2005: 193–6) on the legal situation of LGBTs; Lee (2011) on policing sexuality; and Shamsudin and Ghazali (2011) on a discursive construction of homosexual males; Tan (1999) on cross-dressing and Asian values; and Wong (2012) on the marginalization of *pengkids* (masculine-identified woman) and their girlfriends.

17 For more details on the challenges faced by indigenous peoples of Malaysia although Malaysia has adopted the UN Declaration on the Rights of Indigenous Peoples, refer to the webpage of the International World Group for Indigenous Affairs, a global human rights organization based in Copenhagen, Denmark, that is dedicated to fighting for indigenous rights at https://www.iwgia.org/en/malaysia.

18 The Yogyakarta Principles as such encompass twenty-nine principles that are 'interdependent, indivisible and interrelated' of equal import and among them are the right to the universal enjoyment of human rights, the right to life, the right to privacy, the right to a fair trial, the right to work, the right to an adequate standard of living, the right to education, protection from medical abuses, the right to freedom of movement, the right to found a family and the right to participate in public life (ICJ 2007).

19 The argument is expanded elsewhere (Bong 2006).

20 And to a lesser extent, Sexual and Reproductive Health and Rights (SRHR) have a similar focus following five-year, ten-year and fifteen-year reviews of the 1994 International Conference on Population and Development.

21 These 'texts of terror' that are commonly used to vilify same-sex acts on the ground of Biblical law are from the Old Testament, Genesis 19.5, Leviticus 18.22 and 20.13; and from the New Testament, Romans 1.24–25, 1 Corinthians 6.9 and 1 Timothy 1.10 (Cheng 2010: 106).

22 Goh's queer theologizing is richly informed by Robert Goss and the late Marcella Althaus-Reid.

23 Formerly SCERH (Standing Committee on Research Involving Humans) and the project number assigned is MUHREC CF07/3596 (previously, 2006/646 with SCERH). See Bong (2009a) for a detailed audit trail of the project.

24 A Constructivist Grounded Theory Methodology differs from an Objectivist Grounded Theory Methodology (GTM). The former 'places priority on the phenomena of study and sees both the data and analysis as created from shared

experiences and relationships with participants'. The latter is more aligned with the positivist tradition that 'attends to data as real in and of themselves and does not attend to the processes of their production'. It is in that sense far less contextualized than the former (Charmaz 2006: 130). The relationship between researcher, interview respondents (as sources of data) and the data itself is highly interactive with a constructivist approach.

Chapter 2

1 Quotations from interviews use citations from ATLAS.ti (version 4.2) which is a Computer-Assisted Qualitative Data Analysis Software to facilitate code-and-retrieve functions. For example, Juuk's quotation cited as [9:12 (124:137)] means: Primary Document or interview 9, quotation number 12, lines 124 to 137.
2 'I have come so that they may have life and have it to the full' (John 10.10).

Chapter 3

1 The position of the National Council of Churches of Singapore is in fact the inverse; i.e. it deems homosexuality as a lifestyle from Biblical, medial, sociological, theological and pastoral perspectives (2004).
2 See also her expanded thesis on queer phenomenology (Ahmed 2006b).
3 See Dalmiya (2000) on a feminist reclamation of the Goddess Kali.

Chapter 6

1 See Numrich (2009: 71).

References

Abbott, E. (2000), *A History of Celibacy*, Cambridge, MA: Da Capo Press.

Abraham, C. (2004), *The Naked Social Order: The Roots of Racial Polarisation in Malaysia*, Subang Jaya, Malaysia: Pelanduk Publication.

AFP (2011), 'Malaysian Court Rejects Transsexual's Name Change', *Inquirer.Net*, 18 July. Available online: http://newsinfo.inquirer.net/25479/malaysian-court-rejects-transsexuals-name-change (accessed 2 January 2018).

Ahmed, S. (2000), *Strange Encounters: Embodied Others in Post-coloniality*, London and New York: Routledge.

Ahmad, S. (2005), 'Islam in Malaysia: Constitutional and Human Rights Perspectives', *Muslim World Journal of Human Rights*, 2 (1): 1–32.

Ahmed, S. (2006a), 'Orientations: Toward a Queer Phenomenology', *GLQ*, 12 (4): 543–74.

Ahmed, S. (2006b), *Queer Phenomenology: Orientations, Objects, Others*, Durham, NC and London: Duke University Press.

Al Arabiya News (2010), 'Pastor Defends Malaysia's First Gay Church', *Al Arabiya News*, 4 September. Available online: http://www.alarabiya.net/articles/2010/09/04/118431.html (accessed 2 January 2018).

Altman, D. (1996), 'Rupture or Continuity? The Internationalization of Gay Identities', *Social Text*, 48: 77–94.

Amnesty International (2012), 'Malaysia: Anwar Case Shows Why Sodomy Law Must Be Scrapped', Amnesty International, 9 January. Available online: http://www.amnesty.org/en/news/malaysia-anwar-case-shows-why-sodomy-law-must-be-scrapped-2012-01-09 (accessed 2 January 2018).

Anand, R. (2017), 'Could Sexual Minorities Join the Armed Forces One Day? "LGBT Not Suited to Our Culture," says DPM', *Malay Mail Online*, 24 October. Available online: http://www.themalaymailonline.com/malaysia/article/could-sexual-minorities-join-armed-forces-one-day-lgbt-not-suited-to-our-cu#XUEmbZ0RHptJVCwD.97 (accessed 2 January 2018).

Andaya, B. W., and L. Y. Andaya (2001), *A History of Malaysia*, 2nd edn, Basingstoke, Hampshire: Palgrave.

Ar, Z. (2013), 'Seksualiti Merdeka Organisers Hope to Outlast "Prejudicial" Law', *Malay Mail Online*, 13 August. Available online: http://www.themalaymailonline.com/malaysia/article/seksualiti-merdeka-organisers-hope-to-outlast-prejudicial-law#mQQQ08UQPyZe1pmd.97 (accessed 2 January 2018).

ARJ (2014), 'Being a Muslim and Transgender', *The Malay Mail*, 21 November. Available online: https://www.malaymail.com/news/what-you-think/2014/11/21/being-a-muslim-and-transgender-arj/787381 (accessed 2 January 2018).

Arnold, W. (2003), 'Quietly, Singapore Lifts Its Ban on Hiring Gays', *The New York Times*, 5 July. Available online: http://www.nytimes.com/2003/07/05/news/quietly-singapore-lifts-its-ban-on-hiring-gays.html (accessed 2 January 2018).

Au, W. (2003), 'The Challenge to Decency: Differences in Sexual Values between Gay Males and Straights', in J. Lo and H. Gonqin (eds), *People Like Us: Sexual Minorities in Singapore*, 52–7, Singapore: Select Publishing.

Au-Yong, R. (2019), 'Workers' Party Will Not Call for Repeal of Section 377A, as There Is No Consensus among Its Leaders: Pritam', *Straits Times*, 5 April. Available online: https://www.straitstimes.com/singapore/workers-party-will-not-call-for-repeal-of-section-377a-as-there-is-no-consensus-among-its (accessed 5 May 2019).

Aw, M. (2012), 'Should Singapore Repeal Section 377A?' *Yahoo! News*, 17 May. Available online: https://sg.news.yahoo.com/should-singapore%E2%80%99s-repeal-section-377a-.html (accessed 2 January 2018).

Aziz, Z. A. (2008), 'Mechanisms to Promote Gender Equality in Malaysia: The Need for Legislation', *WLUML*, Dossier 29 (July): 79–94. Available online: http://www.wluml.org/sites/wluml.org/files/import/english/pubs/pdf/dossier29/dossier29-en.pdf (accessed 2 January 2010).

Azizan, H. (2016), 'From Religion to Science', *The Star Online*, 17 April. Available online: https://www.thestar.com.my/news/nation/2016/04/17/from-religion-to-science/ (accessed 2 January 2018).

Baba, I. (2001), 'Gay and Lesbian Couples in Malaysia', *Journal of Homosexuality*, 40 (3–4): 143–63.

Bailey, A. (2007), 'Strategic Ignorance', in S. Sullivan and N. Tuana (eds), *Race and Epistemologies of Ignorance*, 77–94, Albany: State University of New York Press.

Barr, M. D. (2002), *Cultural Politics and Asian Values: The Tepid War*, London and New York: Routledge.

BBC (2011), '"Effeminate" Boys in Malaysia Sent to "Anti-gay" Camp', *BBC*, 19 April. Available online: http://www.bbc.co.uk/news/world-asia-pacific-13133589 (accessed 2 January 2018).

BBC (2017), 'Singapore LGBT Rally Says "No Choice" but to Bar Outsiders', *BBC*, 15 May. Available online: http://www.bbc.com/news/world-asia-39916201 (accessed 2 January 2018).

Bernama (2010), 'Review Ban on *Mak Yong*, Kelantan Govt Urged', *The Star Online*, 6 June. Available online: https://www.thestar.com.my/news/nation/2010/06/06/review-ban-on-mak-yong-kelantan-govt-urged/ (accessed 2 January 2018).

Blackwood, E. (1998), '*Tombois* in West Sumatra: Constructing Masculinity and Erotic Desire', *Cultural Anthropology*, 13 (4): 512–21.

Blackwood, E. (2005), 'Gender Transgression in Colonial and Postcolonial Indonesia', *The Journal of Asian Studies*, 64 (4): 849–79.

Blackwood, E. (2007a), 'Regulation of Sexuality in Indonesian Discourse: Normative Gender, Criminal Law and Shifting Strategies of Control', *Culture, Health and Sexuality*, 9 (3): 293–307.

Blackwood, E. (2007b), 'Transnational Sexualities in One Place: Indonesian Readings',
    in S. E. Wieringa, E. Blackwood and A. Bhaiya (eds), *Women's Sexualities and
    Masculinities in a Globalising Asia*, 181–99, New York and Basingstoke: Palgrave
    Macmillan.

Blackwood, E. (2008), 'Transnational Discourses and Circuits of Queer Knowledge in
    Indonesia', *GLQ: A Journal of Lesbian and Gay Studies*, 14 (4): 481–507.

Boellstorff, T. (2004), 'The Emergence of Political Homophobia in Indonesia:
    Masculinity and National Belonging', *Ethnos: Journal of Anthropology*, 69 (4): 465–86.

Boellstorff, T. (2005a), 'Between Religion and Desire: Being Muslim and *Gay* in
    Indonesia', *American Anthropologist*, 107 (4): 575–85.

Boellstorff, T. (2005b), *The Gay Archipelago: Sexuality and Nation in Indonesia*,
    Princeton, NJ and Oxford: Princeton University Press.

Bong, S. A. (2006), *The Tension between Women's Rights and Religions: The Case of
    Malaysia*, Lewiston and New York: Edwin Mellen Press.

Bong, S. A. (2009a), 'The Sexuality-spirituality Project', in L. Richards (ed), *Handling
    Qualitative Data: Companion Website*, 2nd edn. Available online: https://study.
    sagepub.com/richards3e/student-resources/methods-in-practice/the-sexuality-
    spirituality-project.

Bong, S. A. (2009b), 'Not "For the Sake of Peace": Towards an Epistemology of the
    Sacred Body', *Asian Christian Review*, 3 (1): 50–68.

Bong, S. A. (2011a), 'Beyond Queer: An Epistemology of Bi Choice', *Journal of
    Bisexuality*, 11 (1): 39–63.

Bong, S. A. (2011b), 'Negotiating Resistance/Resilience through the Nexus of
    Spirituality-sexuality of Same-sex Partnerships in Malaysia and Singapore', *Marriage
    and Family Review*, 47 (8): 648–65.

Bong, S. A. (2018), 'Transgender', in L. Isherwood and D. von der Horst (eds),
    Contemporary Theological Approaches to Sexuality, 40–52, London and New York:
    Routledge.

Butler, J. (1990), *Gender Trouble: Feminism and the Subversion of Identity*, New York and
    London: Routledge.

Charmaz, K. (2000), 'Grounded Theory: Objectivist and Constructivist Methods', in N.
    K. Denzin and Y. S. Lincoln (eds), *Handbook of Qualitative Research*, 2nd edn, 509–
    35, Thousand Oaks; London and New Delhi: Sage.

Charmaz, K. (2006), *Constructing Grounded Theory: A Practical Guide through
    Qualitative Analysis*, London; Thousand Oaks and New Delhi: Sage.

Chase, C. (2003), 'Hermaphrodites with Attitude: Mapping the Emergence of
    Intersex Political Activism', in R. J. Corber and S. Valocchi (eds), *Queer Studies: An
    Interdisciplinary Reader*, 31–45, Oxford: Blackwell.

Cheah, B. K. (2002), *Malaysia: The Making of a Nation*, Singapore: ISEAS.

Cheng, P. S. (2010), Rethinking Sin and Grace for LGBT People Today', in M.
    M. Ellison and K. B. Douglas (eds), *Sexuality and the Sacred: Sources for Theological
    Reflection*, 2nd edn, 105–18, Louisville, Kentucky: Westminster John Knox Press.

Chou, W.-S. (2001), 'Homosexuality and the Cultural Politics of *Tongzhi* in Chinese Societies', *Journal of Homosexuality*, 40 (3–4): 27–46.

Chua, B. H. (2008), 'Singapore in 2007: High Wage Ministers and the Management of Gays and Elderly', *Asian Survey*, 48 (1): 55–61.

Chua, L. J. (2003), 'Saying No: Sections 377 and 377A of the Penal Code', *Singapore Journal of Legal Studies*, July: 209–61.

Chua, L. J. (2014), *Mobilizing Gay Singapore: Rights and Resistance in an Authoritarian State*, Philadelphia: Temple University Press.

Clammer, J. (2002), *Diaspora and Identity: The Sociology of Culture in Southeast Asia*, Subang Jaya, Malaysia: Pelanduk Publications.

Commissioner of Law Revision, Malaysia (2010), *Federal Constitution of Malaysia*. Available online: http://www.agc.gov.my/agcportal/uploads/files/Publications/FC/ Federal%20Consti%20(BI%20text).pdf (accessed 2 January 2018).

Commissioner of Law Revision, Malaysia (2015), *Laws of Malaysia: Act 574 Penal Code*. Available online: http://www.agc.gov.my/agcportal/uploads/files/Publications/LOM/ EN/Penal%20Code%20%5BAct%20574%5D2.pdf (accessed 2 January 2018).

Cruz, G. T. (2011), 'Interrupting Normal Ways of Thinking: Resistance and Asian Women's Struggle for Peace and Liberation', in J. A. Gallares, RC and A. Lobo-Gajiwala (eds), *Feminist Theology of Liberation Asian Perspectives: Practicing Peace*, 101–19, Quezon City, Philippines: Claretian Publications.

Cudd, A. E., and L. E. Jones (2005), 'Sexism', in A. E. Cudd and R. O. Andreasen (eds), *Feminist Theory: A Philosophical Anthology*, 73–83, Malden, MA: Blackwell.

Dalmiya, V. (2000), 'Loving Paradoxes: A Feminist Reclamation of the Goddess Kali', *Hypatia*, 15 (1): 125–50.

Davies, S. G. (2010), *Gender Diversity in Indonesia: Sexuality, Islam and Queer Selves*, London and New York: Routledge.

De Beauvoir, S. (1989), *The Second Sex*, New York: Vintage Books.

Department of Statistics, Malaysia (2011), 'Population Distribution and Basic Demographic Characteristic Report 2010'. Available online: https://www.dosm.gov. my/v1/index.php?r=column/cthemeByCat&cat=117&bul_id=MDMxdHZjWTk1S jFzTzNkRXYzcVZjdz09&menu_id=L0pheU43NWJwRWVSZklWdzQ4TlhUUT09 (accessed 2 January 2018).

Dinshaw, C., L. Edelman, R. A. Ferguson, C. Freccero, E. Freeman, J. Halberstam, A. Jagose, C. Nealon and T. H. Nguyen (2007), 'Theorising Queer Temporalities: A Roundtable Discussion', *GLQ*, 13 (2–3): 177–95.

Douglas, M. ([1996] 2002), *Purity and Danger: An Analysis of Concept of Pollution and Taboo*, London and New York: Routledge.

Dyer, R. (1997), 'Heterosexuality', in A. Medhurst and S. R. Munt (eds), *Lesbian and Gay Studies: A Critical Introduction*, 261–73, London and Washington: Cassell.

Esterberg, K. G. (2002), 'The Bisexual Menace: Or, Will the Real Bisexual Please Stand Up?', in D. Richardson and S. Seidman (eds), *Handbook of Lesbian and Gay Studies*, 215–27, London; Thousand Oaks and New Delhi: Sage.

Fadli, M. (2018), 'Transgenders Meet Mufti to End Discrimination against Them', *FMT News*, 15 February. Available online: https://www.freemalaysiatoday.com/category/nation/2018/02/15/transgenders-meet-mufti-to-end-discrimination-against-them/ (accessed 15 March 2018).

Falk, M. L. (2007), *Making Fields of Merit: Buddhist Female Ascetics and Gendered Orders in Thailand*, Copenhagen: NIAS Press.

Faucette, J. A. (2010), 'Human Rights in Context: The Lessons of Section 377 Challenges for Western Gay Rights Legal Reformers in the Developing World', *The Journal of Gender, Race and Justice*, 13: 413–39.

Flentje, A., N. C. Heck and B. N. Cochran (2014), 'Experiences of Ex-ex-gay Individuals in Sexual Reorientation Therapy: Reasons for Seeking Treatment, Perceived Helpfulness and Harmfulness of Treatment, and Post-treatment Identification', *Journal of Homosexuality*, 61 (9): 1242–68.

Foucault, M. (1977), *Discipline and Punish: The Birth of the Prison*, trans. A. Sheridan, London: Penguin Books.

Foucault, M. (1978), *The History of Sexuality, Vol. 1: An Introduction*, e-book.

Frisk, S. (2009), *Submitting to God: Women and Islam in Urban Malaysia*, Copenhagen: NIAS.

Gamson, J. (2000), 'Sexualities, Queer Theory, and Qualitative Research', in N. K. Denzin and Y. S. Lincoln (eds), *Handbook of Qualitative Research*, 2nd edn, 347–65, Thousand Oaks; London and New Delhi: Sage.

Garber, M. (2000), *Bisexuality and the Eroticism of Everyday Life*, New York: Routledge.

Gellner, E. (1992), *Postmodernism, Reason and Religion*, London and New York: Routledge.

Gjorgievska, A. (2012), 'NUS Professor Addresses Gay Rights', *Yale Daily News*, 1 November. Available online: http://yaledailynews.com/blog/2012/11/01/nus-professor-addresses-gay-rights/ (accessed 2 January 2018).

Goh, B. L. (2002), 'Rethinking Modernity: State, Ethnicity, and Class in the Forging of a Modern Urban Malaysia', in C. J. W.-L. Wee (ed), *Local Cultures and the 'New Asia': The State, Culture, and Capitalism in Southeast Asia*, 184–216, Singapore: ISEAS.

Goh, D. (2008), 'It's the Gays' Fault: News and HIV as Weapons against Homosexuality in Singapore', *Journal of Communication Inquiry*, 32 (4): 383–99.

Goh, J. N. (2012a), '*Mak Nyah* Bodies as Sacred Sites: Uncovering the Queer Body-sacramentality of Malaysian Male-to-female Transsexuals', *Crosscurrents*, 62 (4): 512–21.

Goh, J. N. (2012b), 'The Word Was *Not* Made Flesh: Theological Reflections on the Banning of *Seksualiti Merdeka*', *Dialog: A Journal of Theology*, 51 (2): 145–54.

Goh, J. N. (2014), 'Fracturing Interwoven Heteronormativities in Malaysian Malay-Muslim Masculinity: A Research Note', *Sexualities*, 17 (5–6): 600–17.

Goh, J. N. (2016), 'Imaginative Assemblages of Transcendent/Desire: Non-heteronormative Malaysian Men Speak up and Talk Back', *Critical Research on Religion*, 4 (2): 125–40.

Goh, J. N. (2017a), 'Bridging Benedictions, Enlightening Embodiment: Interpretations of Spirit through Desire among Gay and Bisexual Malaysian Men', *Journal for the Study of Spirituality*, 7 (2): 128–41.

Goh, J. N. (2017b), 'From Polluted to Prophetic Bodies: Theo-pastoral Lessons from the Lived Experiences of Gay, HIV-positive Christian Men in Singapore', *Practical Theology*, 10 (2): 133–46.

Goh, J. N. (2018), *Living Out Sexuality and Faith: Body Admissions of Malaysian Gay and Bisexual Men*, London and New York: Routledge.

Halberstam, J. (1998), *Female Masculinity*, Durham, NC: Duke University Press.

Halberstam, J. (2005), *In a Queer Time and Space: Transgender Bodies, Subcultural Lives*, New York: New York University Press.

Hamzić, V. (2011), 'The Case of 'Queer Muslims': Sexual Orientation and Gender Identity in International Human Rights Law and Muslim Legal and Social Ethos', *Human Rights Law Review*, 11 (2): 237–74.

Heng, R. H. K. (2001), 'Tiptoe Out of the Closet: The before and after of the Increasingly Visible Gay Community in Singapore', *Journal of Homosexuality* 40 (3–4): 81–96.

Ho, K. L. (2003), 'Imagined Communion, Irreconcilable Differences? Perceptions and Responses of the Malaysian Chinese towards Malay Political Hegemony', in Ding C. M., and Ooi K. B. (eds), *Chinese Studies of the Malay World: A Comparative Approach*, 239–62, Singapore: Eastern Universities Press.

Huang, S., and D. C. Brouwer (2018), 'Coming out, Coming Home, Coming with: Models of Queer Sexuality in Contemporary China', *Journal of International and Intercultural Communication*, 11 (2): 97–116.

Husso, M., and H. Hirvonen (2009), 'Feminism, Embodied Experience and Recognition: An Interview with Lois McNay', *NORA – Nordic Journal of Feminist and Gender Research*, 17 (1): 48–55.

Inglis, T. (2002), 'Sexual Transgression and Scapegoats: A Case Study from Modern Ireland', *Sexualities*, 5 (1): 5–24.

International Commission of Jurists (ICJ) (2007), *Yogyakarta Principles: Principles on the Application of International Human Rights Law in Relation to Sexual Orientation and Gender Identity*. Available online: http://www.unhcr.org/refworld/docid/48244e602.html (accessed 2 January 2018).

Isherwood, L. (2000), 'Erotic Celibacy: Claiming Empowered Space', in L. Isherwood (ed), *The Good News of the Body: Sexual Theology and Feminism*, 149–63, Sheffield: Sheffield University Press.

Jagose, A. (1996), *Queer Theory: An Introduction*, New York: New York University Press.

Jakobsen, J. R., and A. Pellegrini (2004), *Love the Sin: Sexual Regulation and the Limits of Religious Tolerance*, Boston, MA: Beacon Press.

James, C. (1996), 'Denying Complexity: The Dismissal and Appropriation of Bisexuality in Queer, Lesbian and Gay Theory', in B. Beemyn and M. Eliason (eds), *Queer Studies: A Lesbian, Gay, Bisexual and Transgender Anthology*, 217–40, New York and London: New York University Press.

Kala, S. (2008), 'Fatwa on *Pengkid* Should Not Be Questioned: Nik Aziz', *The Nutgraph*, 17 November. Available online: http://thenutgraph.com/fatwa-pengkid-not-questioned-nik-aziz (accessed 2 January 2018).

Kessler, C. (2008), '"A Shared Nation": Constitutionalism, the "Social Contract" and Mutuality in the "Negotiation of Belonging"', in N. Othman and M. C. Puthucheary (eds), *Sharing the Nation: Faith, Difference, Power and the State 50 Years after Merdeka*, 81–90, Petaling Jaya, Malaysia: SIRD.

Klesse, C. (2006), 'Polyamory and Its "Others": Contesting the Terms of Non-monogamy', *Sexualities*, 9 (5): 565–83.

Kok, X. (2018), 'Singapore Allows Gay Couple to Adopt Their Surrogate Son in Landmark Ruling', *South China Morning Post*, 17 December. Available online: https://www.scmp.com/news/asia/southeast-asia/article/2178279/singapore-allows-same-sex-fathers-adopt-their-surrogate-son (accessed 2 January 2019).

Kristeva, J. (1982), *Powers of Horror: An Essay on Abjection*, trans. L. S. Roudiez, New York: Columbia University Press.

Kuah, K. E. (2018), *Social Cultural Engineering and the Singaporean State*, e-book, Springer.

Kugle, S. a.-H. (2003), 'Sexuality, Diversity, and Ethics in the Agenda of Progressive Muslims', in O. Safi (ed), *Progressive Muslims: On Justice, Gender and Pluralism*, 190–234, London: Oneworld Publications.

Lara, M. P. (2003), 'In and Out of Terror: The Vertigo of Secularization', *Hypatia*, 18 (1): 183–96.

Laurent, E. (2005), 'Sexuality and Human Rights: An Asian Perspective', *Journal of Homosexuality*, 48 (3–4): 163–225.

Leach, A. (2012), 'Ministers Says Malaysians Should Protest Same-sex Marriages', *Gay Star News*, 8 August. Available online: http://www.gaystarnews.com/article/minister-says-malaysians-should-protest-same-sex-marriages080812 (accessed 2 January 2018).

Lee, J. C. H. (2011), *Policing Sexuality: Sex, Society, and the State*, Petaling Jaya: SIRD; London and New York: Zed Books.

Lee, Y. C. L. (2008), '"Don't Ever Take a Fence Down until You Know the Reason It Was Put Up" – Singapore Communitarianism and the Case for Conserving 377A', *Singapore Journal of Legal Studies*, December: 347–94.

Leyl, S. (2009), 'Singapore Gays in First Public Rally', *BBC*, 17 May. Available online: http://news.bbc.co.uk/2/hi/asia-pacific/8054402.stm (accessed 2 January 2018).

Lim, E.-B. (2005), 'Glocalqueering in New Asia: The Polities of Performing Gay in Singapore', *Theatre Journal*, 57 (3): 383–405.

Lim, K. F. (2004), 'Where Love Dares (Not) Speak Its Name: The Expression of Homosexuality in Singapore', *Urban Studies*, 41 (9): 1759–88.

Lim, V. K. G. (2002), 'Gender Differences and Attitudes towards Homosexuality', *Journal of Homosexuality*, 43 (1): 85–97.

Lim, Y. (2012), 'Colourful Send-off for "Asha Amma"', *The Star Online*, 9 August. Available online: https://www.thestar.com.my/news/nation/2012/08/09/colourful-sendoff-for-asha-amma/ (accessed 2 January 2018).

Loong, L. H. L. (2012), 'Deconstructing the Silences: Gay Social Memory', *Journal of Homosexuality*, 59 (5): 675–88.

Lorber, J. (1994), *Paradoxes of Gender*, e-book, Yale University Press.

MAC (2017), 'Protecting Dignity of LGBT and Other HIV-impacted Communities Critical in Ending AIDS', Malaysian AIDS Council, 4 June. Available online: http://www.mac.org.my/v3/protecting-dignity-of-lgbt-and-other-hiv-impacted-communities-critical-in-ending-aids/ (accessed 2 January 2018).

Mah, W. K. (2001), 'Amendment to Article 8(2) of the Federal Constitution', The Malaysian Bar, 26 July. Available online: http://www.malaysianbar.org.my/press_statements/amendment_to_article_82_of_the_federal_constitution.html (accessed 2 January 2018).

Mandal, S. K. (2004), 'Transethnic Solidarities, Racialisation and Social Equality', in E. T. Gomez (ed), *The State of Malaysia: Ethnicity, Equity and Reform*, 49–78, London and New York: Routledge.

Matsuoka, E. (2007), 'The Issue of Particulars and Universals in Bioethics: Some Ideas from Cultural Anthropology', *Journal of Philosophy and Ethics in Health Care and Medicine*, 2: 44–65.

Miller, W. R., and C. E. Thoresen (2003), 'Spirituality, Religion and Health: An Emerging Research Field', *American Psychologist*, 58 (1): 24–35.

Mir-Hosseini, Z. (1996), 'Women and Politics in Post-Khomeini Iran: Divorce, Veiling and Emerging Feminist Voices', in H. Afshar (ed), *Women and Politics in the Third World*, 145–73, London and New York: Routledge.

Mohamad, M. (2002), 'The Politics of Gender, Ethnicity, and Democratization in Malaysia: Shifting Interests and Identities', in M. Molyneux and S. Razavi (eds), *Gender Justice, Development, and Rights*, 347–83, Oxford: Oxford University Press.

Mosbergen, D. (2012), '"Guidelines for Gay and Lesbian Symptoms" Endorsed by Malaysia Education Ministry Spark Outrage', *Huffington Post*, 13 September. Available online: http://www.huffingtonpost.com/2012/09/13/guidelines-for-gay-and-lesbian-symptoms-malaysia-education-ministry_n_1881863.html (accessed 2 January 2018).

Mosbergen, D. (2015), 'How One of the World's Richest Countries Is Limiting Basic Human Rights', *Huffington Post*, 13 October. Available online: https://www.huffingtonpost.com/entry/lgbtsingapore_us_561633d5e4b0e66ad4c67fe7 (accessed 2 January 2018).

Mosher, D. L., and Cross, H. J. (1971), 'Sex Guilt and Premarital Sexual Experiences of College Students', *Journal of Consulting and Clinical Psychology*, 36 (1): 27–32.

MT Webmaster (2011), 'A Queer Case of UMNO Wrath', *Malaysia Today*, 4 November. Available online: https://www.malaysia-today.net/2011/11/04/a-queer-case-of-umno-wrath/ (accessed 7 October 2019).

Murray, K. M., J. W. Ciarrocchi and N. A. Murray-Swank (2007), 'Spirituality, Religiosity, Shame and Guilt as Predictors of Sexual Attitudes and Experiences', *Journal of Psychology and Theology*, 35 (3): 222–34.

Muthiah, W. (2012), 'New Leader for Transgenders', *The Star Online*, 18 September. Available online: https://www.thestar.com.my/news/nation/2012/09/18/new-leader-for-transgenders/ (accessed 2 January 2018).

Nambiah, P. (2018), 'LGBT Activists' Portraits Removed after Complaints, Says State Secretary', *Free Malaysia Today*, 8 August. Available online: https://www.freemalaysiatoday.com/category/nation/2018/08/08/lgbt-activists-portraits-removed-after-complaints-says-state-secretary/ (accessed 2 January 2019).

National Council of Churches of Singapore (2004), *A Christian Response to Homosexuality*, Singapore: Genesis Books.

New Straits Times (2014), 'Landmark Ruling for Transgender Muslims', *New Straits Times*, 8 November. Available online: http://www.nst.com.my/news/2015/09/landmark-ruling-transgender-muslims (accessed 2 January 2018).

Newman, P. A., S. Fantus, M. R. Woodford and M. -J. Rwigema (2018), '"Pray That God Will Change You": The Religious Social Ecology of Bias-based Bullying Targeting Sexual and Gender Minority Youth – A Qualitative Study of Service Providers and Educators', *Journal of Adolescent Research*, 33 (5): 523–48.

News Editor (2012a), 'Singapore's First-ever Night Pink Dot 2012 to Be Held Jun 30', Fridae, 9 April. Available online: http://www.fridae.asia/newsfeatures/2012/04/09/11642.singapores-first-ever-night-pink-dot-2012-to-be-held-jun-30 (accessed 2 January 2018).

News Editor (2012b), 'Singapore's 8th IndigNation Festival to Focus on LGBT Heritage, Aug 3–25', Fridae, 30 July. Available online: http://www.fridae.asia/newsfeatures/2012/07/30/11824.singapores-8th-indignation-festival-to-focus-on-lgbt-heritage-aug-3-25 (accessed 2 January 2018).

Ng, K. K. (1999), *The Rainbow Connection: The Internet and the Singapore Gay Community*, Singapore: KangCuBine Publication.

Ng, Y.-S. (2006), *SQ 21: Singapore Queers in the 21st Century*, Singapore: Oogachaga Counseling and Support.

Ngeo, B. L. (2013), *Gay Is OK! A Christian Perspective*, Petaling Jaya, Malaysia: Gerakbudaya Enterprise.

Numrich, P. D. (2009), 'The Problem with Sex According to Buddhism', *Dialog: A Journal of Theology*, 48 (1): 62–73.

Nussbaum, M. C. (2004), *Hiding from Humanity: Disgust, Shame and the Law*, Princeton, NJ, and Oxford: Princeton University Press.

Offord, B. (2003), 'Singaporean Queering of the Internet: Toward a New Form of Cultural Transmission of Rights Discourse', in C. Berry, F. Martin and A. Yue (eds), *Mobile Cultures: New Media in Queer Asia*, 133–57, Durham, NC and London: Duke University Press.

Oswald, R. F. (2002), 'Resilience within the Family Networks of Lesbians and Gay Men: Intentionality and Redefinition', *Journal of Marriage and the Family*, 64 (2): 374–83.

Palansamy, Y. (2018), 'Terengganu Duo Publicly Caned Six Times over Lesbian Sex Attempt', *Malay Mail*, 3 September. Available online: https://www.malaymail.

com/s/1668766/terengganu-duo-publicly-caned-six-times-over-lesbian-sex-attempt (accessed 2 January 2019).

Pang, K. T. (2019), 'How Selective Liberal Outrage against Brunei Is Missing the Point', *Queer Lapis*. Available online: https://www.queerlapis.com/how-selective-liberal-outrage-against-brunei-is-missing-the-point/ (accessed 2 April 2019).

Peletz, M. G. (2007), *Gender, Sexuality and Body Politics in Modern Asia*, Ann Arbor, MI: Association for Asian Studies.

Peletz, M. G. (2011), 'Gender Pluralism: Muslim Southeast Asia since Early Modern Times', *Social Research*, 78 (2): 659–86.

Piechowiak, M. (1999), 'What Are Human Rights? The Concept of Human Rights and Their Extra-legal Justification', in R. Hanski and M. Suksi (eds), *An Introduction to the International Protection of Human Rights*, 3–14, Turko/ Abo, Finland: Institute for Human Rights, Abo Akademi University.

Plummer, K. (2001), 'The Square of Intimate Citizenship: Some Preliminary Proposals', *Citizenship Studies*, 5 (3): 237–53.

Poh, A. P. (2008), 'The Ideas of Lee Kuan Yew: Eugenics in Singapore', *SG Forums*, 10 November. Available online: http://sgforums.com/forums/10/topics/336662 (accessed 2 January 2019).

Rajeswari, I. (2017), *Same but Different; A Legal Guidebook for LGBT Couples and Families in Singapore*, Singapore: Give Asia.

Reid, A. (1993), *Southeast Asia in the Age of Commerce 1450–1680. Vol. II: Expansion and Crisis*, New Haven and London: Yale University Press.

Renzetti, C. M., and R. M. Lee, eds (1993), *Researching Sensitive Topics*, Newbury Park; London and New Delhi: Sage.

Reuters (2019), 'Uproar in Malaysia over LGBT Groups at Women's Day March', *The New Straits Times*, 10 March. Available online: https://www.nst.com.my/news/nation/2019/03/467792/uproar-malaysia-over-lgbt-groups-womens-day-march (accessed 2 April 2019).

Rich, A. (1980), 'Compulsory Heterosexuality and Lesbian Existence', *Signs*, 5 (4): 631–60.

Rich, A. (2004), 'Reflections on "Compulsory Heterosexuality"', *Journal of Women's History*, 16 (1): 9–11.

Richardson, D. (2000), *Rethinking Sexuality*, London; Thousand Oaks and New Delhi: Sage.

Richardon, D. (2017), 'Rethinking Sexual Citizenship', *Sociology*, 51 (2): 208–24.

Roberts, R. (2017), 'Malaysian Government Openly Endorses Gay Conversion Therapy', *Independent*, 14 February. Available online: http://www.independent.co.uk/news/world/malaysia-gay-conversion-therapy-endorses-lgbt-rights-islam-a7578666.html (accessed 2 January 2019).

Rooke, A. (2010), 'Queer in the Field: On Emotions, Temporality and Performativity in Ethnography', in K. Browne and C. J. Nash (eds), *Queer Methods and Methodologies: Intersecting Queer Theories and Social Science Research*, 25–39, Farnham, Surrey and Burlington: Ashgate.

Rosario II, V. A. (1996), 'Trans (Homo) Sexuality? Double Inversion, Psychiatric Confusion and Hetero-hegemony', in B. Beemyn and M. Eliason (eds), *Queer Studies: A Lesbian, Gay, Bisexual and Transgender Anthology*, 35–51, New York and London: New York University Press.

Schippert, C. (2011), 'Implications of Queer Theory for the Study of Religion and Gender: Entering the Third Decade', *Religion and Gender*, 1 (1): 66–84.

Sedgwick, E. K. (1990), *Epistemology of the Closet*, Berkeley: University of California Press.

Seidman, S., C. Meeks and F. Traschen (1999), 'Beyond the Closet? The Changing Social Meaning of Homosexuality in the United States', *Sexualities*, 2 (1): 9–34.

Shah, S. (2009), 'Sodomy Laws: A British Import', *The Nutgraph*, 21 August. Available online: http://www.thenutgraph.com/sodomy-laws-a-british-import/ (accessed 2 January 2019).

Shah, S. (2018), *The Making of a Gay Muslim: Religion, Sexuality and Identity in Malaysia and Britain*, e-book, Palgrave Macmillan.

Shamsudin, Z., and K. Ghazali (2011), 'A Discursive Construction of Homosexual Males in a Muslim-dominant Community', *Multilingua*, 30: 279–304.

Shamsul, A. B. (1996), 'Nations-of-intent in Malaysia', in S. Tonnesson and H. Antlov (eds), *Asian Forms of the Nation*, 323–47, London: Curzon Press.

Shamsul, A. B. (1997), 'The Making of a "Plural" Malaysia: A Brief Survey', in D. Y. H. Wu, H. McQueen and Y. Yasushi (eds), *Emerging Pluralism in Asia and the Pacific*, 67–83, Hong Kong: The Chinese University Press of Hong Kong.

Shamsul, A. B. (1998), 'Debating about Identity in Malaysia: A Discourse Analysis', in I. Zawawi (ed), *Cultural Contestations: Mediating Identities in a Changing Malaysian Society*, 17–50, London: ASEAN Academic Press.

Shen, R. (2014), 'Wear White to Protest Singapore Pink Gay Rally, Religious Groups Say', *Reuters*, 23 June. Available online: https://www.reuters.com/article/us-singapore-protests/wear-white-to-protest-singapore-pink-gay-rally-religious-groups-say-idUSKBN0EY0SB20140623 (accessed 2 January 2019).

Shurentheran, V. (2017a), 'Netizens Fume over Shameera's Murder as She's Laid to Rest on Birthday', *The Malaysian Times*, 24 February. Available online: http://www.themalaysiantimes.com.my/netizens-fume-over-sameeras-murder-as-laid-to-rest-on-birthday/ (accessed 2 January 2019).

Shurentheran, V. (2017b), 'LGBT: Siti Kasim Warns of Consequences if Extremists Not Checked', *FMT News*, 3 June. Available online: http://www.freemalaysiatoday.com/category/nation/2017/06/03/lgbt-siti-kasim-warns-of-consequences-if-extremists-not-checked/ (accessed 2 January 2019).

Singapore Department of Statistics (2011), Census of Population 2010: Demographic Characteristics, Education, Language and Religion. Available online: https://www.singstat.gov.sg/-/media/files/publications/cop2010/census_2010_release1/cop2010sr1.pdf (accessed 3 October 2019).

Singapore Statutes Online (1965), 'Constitution of the Republic of Singapore'. Available online: https://sso.agc.gov.sg/Act/CONS1963 (accessed 2 January 2018).

Singapore Statutes Online (2018), *Singapore Penal Code.* Available online: https://sso. agc.gov.sg/Act/PC1871, https://statutes.agc.gov.sg/Act/PC1871?ProvIds=pr377A- .&ViewType=Advance&Exact=377A&WiAl=1#pr377A- (accessed 2 January 2019).

Sinnott, M. J. (2004), *Toms and Dees: Transgender Identity and Female Same-sex Relationships in Thailand,* Honolulu: University of Hawaii Press.

Sinnott, M. J. (2008), 'The Romance of the Queer: The Sexual and Gender Norms of *Tom* and *Dee* in Thailand', in F. Martin, P. A. Jackson, M. McLelland and A. Yue (eds), *AsiaPacificQueer: Rethinking Genders and Sexualities,* 131–48, Urbana and Chicago: University of Illinois Press.

Sreenevasan, A., and J.-A. Ding (2018), 'Terengganu Caning: Was It Constitutional?', *Malay Mail,* 18 September. Available online: https://www.malaymail.com/ news/malaysia/2018/09/18/terengganu-caning-was-it-constitutional/1673738 (accessed 2 January 2019).

Stivens, M. (2006), '"Family Values" and Islamic Revival: Gender, Rights and State Moral Projects in Malaysia', *Women's Studies International Forum,* 29 (4): 354–67.

SUARAM (2018), *SUARAM's Human Rights Overview Report on Malaysia 2018.* Available online: https://www.suaram.net/wp-content/uploads/2018/12/HR-Overview-2018-28-Nov.pdf (accessed 2 January 2019).

Sullivan, N. (2006), 'Transmogrification: (Un)Becoming Other(s)', in S. Stryker and S. Whittle (eds), *The Transgender Studies Reader,* 552–64, New York and London: Routledge.

Tan, b. h. (1999), 'Women's Sexuality and the Discourse on Asian Values: Cross-dressing in Malaysia', in E. Blackwood and S. E. Wieringa (eds), *Female Desires: Same-sex Relations and Transgender Practices across Cultures,* 281–307, New York: Columbia University Press.

Tan, C. K. K. (2011), 'Go Home, Gay Boy! Or, Why Do Singaporean Gay Men Prefer to "Go Home" and Not "Come Out"?', *Journal of Homosexuality,* 58 (6–7): 865–82.

Tan, E. K. B. (2002), 'Reconceptualising Chinese Identity: The Politics of Chineseness in Singapore', in L. Suryadinata (ed), *Ethnic Chinese in Singapore and Malaysia: A Dialogue Between Tradition and Modernity,* 109–36, Singapore: Times Academic Press.

Tan, K. P. (2008), 'Religious Reasons in a Secular Public Sphere: Debates in the Media about Homosexuality', in Lai A. E. (ed), *Religious Diversity in Singapore,* 413–33, Singapore: Institute of Southeast Asian Studies.

Tan, K. P., and G. J. J. Lee (2007), 'Imagining the Gay Community in Singapore', *Critical Asian Studies,* 39 (2): 179–204.

Tang, S. (2017). *Postcolonial Lesbian Identities in Singapore: Re-thinking Global Sexualities,* e-book, Routledge.

Tay, T. Y. (2011), 'Blessing Instead of Approval', *Sin Chew Daily,* trans. Soong Phui Jee, 1 August. Available online: http://www.mysinchew.com/node/61525 (accessed 2 January 2019).

Teh, Y. K. (2002), *The Mak Nyahs: Malaysian Male to Female Transsexuals,* Singapore: Eastern Universities Press.

Tergel, A. (1998), *Human Rights in Cultural and Religious Traditions*, Uppsala, Sweden: Acta Universitatis Upsaliensis.

The Star Online (2018a), 'LGBT or Same-sex Marriage Not for Malaysia, Says Dr M', *The Star Online*, 22 September. Available online: https://www.thestar.com.my/news/nation/2018/09/22/lgbt-or-samesex-marriage-not-for-malaysia-says-dr-m/ (accessed 2 January 2019).

The Star Online (2018b), 'Four Charged with Murder of Transgender', *The Star Online*, 25 December. Available online: https://www.thestar.com.my/news/nation/2018/12/25/four-charged-with-murder-of-transgender/ (accessed 2 January 2019).

The Straits Times (2019), 'Gays? No Such Thing in Our Country, Says Malaysian Tourism Minister', *The Straits Times*, 6 March. Available online: https://www.straitstimes.com/asia/se-asia/gays-no-such-thing-in-our-country-says-malaysiantourism-minister (accessed 2 April 2019).

TOI-Online (2018), 'What Is Section 377 of IPC?', *The Times of India*, 31 December. Available online: https://timesofindia.indiatimes.com/india/what-is-section-377/articleshow/66067994.cms (accessed 2 January 2019).

Trocki, C. A. (2006), *Singapore: Wealth, Power and the Culture of Control*, London and New York: Routledge.

Tsoi, W. F. (1990), 'Developmental Profile of 200 Male and 100 Female Transsexuals in Singapore', *Archives of Sexual Behavior*, 19 (6): 595–605.

United Nations (n.d.), 'Treaty Collection'. Available online: http://treaties.un.org/Pages/ViewDetails.aspx?src=TREATY&mtdsg_no=IV-4&chapter=4&lang=en (accessed 2 January 2019).

Vanita, R. (2004), '"Wedding of Two Souls": Same-sex Marriage and Hindu Traditions', *Journal of Feminist Studies*, 20 (2): 119–35.

Vanita, R. (2005), *Love's Rite: Same-sex Marriage in India and the West*, New York and Basingstoke, Hampshire: Palgrave Macmillan.

Westcott, B. (2019), 'Will Brunei's Anti-LGBT Sharia Law Spread across Southeast Asia?', *CNN*, 8 April. Available online: https://edition.cnn.com/2019/04/08/asia/brunei-indonesia-malaysia-islam-intl/index.html (accessed 9 April 2019).

WHO (2019), 'Sexual and Reproductive Health'. Available online: https://www.who.int/reproductivehealth/topics/sexual_health/sh_definitions/en/ (accessed 2 January 2019).

Wong, Y. (2012), 'Islam, Sexuality, and the Marginal Positioning of *Pengkids* and Their Girlfriends in Malaysia', *Journal of Lesbian Studies*, 16 (4): 435–48.

Yip, A. K. T. (2005), 'Queering Religious Texts: An Exploration of British Non-heterosexual Christians' and Muslims' Strategy of Constructing Sexuality-affirming Hermeneutics', *Sociology*, 39 (1): 47–65.

YP+10 (2017), *The Yogyakarta Principles Plus 10*. Available online: http://yogyakartaprinciples.org/wp-content/uploads/2017/11/A5_yogyakartaWEB-2.pdf (accessed 4 January 2018).

Yuan, E. (2011), 'Malaysia's First Openly Gay Pastor to Marry', *CNN*, 31 August. Available online: http://edition.cnn.com/2011/US/08/31/malaysian.pastor.gay.wedding/index.html (accessed 2 January 2019).

Yue, A. (2007), 'Creative Queer Singapore: The Illiberal Pragmatics of Cultural Production', *Gay and Lesbian Issues and Psychology Review*, 3 (3): 149–60.

Zakaria, F., and Lee K. Y. (1994), 'Culture Is Destiny: A Conversation with Lee Kuan Yew', *Foreign Affairs*, 73 (2): 109–26.

Zawawi, I. (1998), 'The Making of a Subaltern Discourse in the Malaysian Nation-state: New Subjectivities and the Poetics of *Orang Asli* Dispossession and Identity', in I. Zawawi (ed), *Cultural Contestations: Mediating Identities in a Changing Malaysian Society*, 145–94, London: ASEAN Academic Press.

Zhuo, T. (2019), 'Millennial Activism: Daryl Yang Fights for LGBT Issues and More', *The Straits Times*, 14 April. Available online: https://www.straitstimes.com/lifestyle/millennial-activism-daryl-yang-fights-for-lgbt-issues-and-more (accessed 15 April 2019).

Zolkepli, F., and N. Ramli (2011), 'Sex-change Man Dies', *The Star Online*, 31 July. Available online: https://www.thestar.com.my/news/nation/2011/07/31/sexchange-man-dies/ (accessed 2 January 2019).

Index